D1596680

Polarized Families, Polarized Parties

American Governance: Politics, Policy, and Public Law

Series Editors: Richard Valelly, Pamela Brandwein,
Marie Gottschalk, Christopher Howard

A complete list of books in the series is available from the publisher.

Polarized Families, Polarized Parties

Contesting Values and Economics in American Politics

Gwendoline M. Alphonso

PENN

UNIVERSITY OF PENNSYLVANIA PRESS

PHILADELPHIA

Published by
University of Pennsylvania Press
Philadelphia, Pennsylvania 19104-4112
www.upenn.edu/pennpress

Printed in the United States of America
on acid-free paper

10 9 8 7 6 5 4 3 2 1

Library of Congress Cataloging-in-Publication Control Number: 2017058297
ISBN 978-0-8122-5033-6

To Ted, Nate, Pius, and June

Contents

Introduction

> We must first discuss household management, for every city-state is
> constituted from households.
>
> —Aristotle

Struggles to define the soul of America roil through American politics. Reproductive rights and abortion, immigration, and gay, lesbian, and transgender equality are some of the controversies that serve as rallying points for significant electoral groups. Undoubtedly, the American family lies at the core of these strident cultural battles. However, the alignment of family with social or cultural issues is only a partial picture, a manifestation of the New Right's late twentieth-century success in elevating "family values" as the focus of family policy. This portrayal obscures divisions over family economics, which intertwine with and shape the so-called culture wars over family.[1]

Polarized Families, Polarized Parties documents and analyzes the extraordinary rise of family in twentieth-century party politics in the United States, revealing the political parties' rightward turn in the later decades toward family values and its enduring tussle with family economics, two frames that have long organized policy debates. By situating late twentieth-century family wars within a broad historical arc that extends back to the start of the past century, the book suggests that the political salience of family values beginning in the 1970s is part of a long-term dynamic of competition in American politics between sectional family ideals, termed Hearth and Soul. Hearth and Soul are two central ideational frameworks through which political actors have viewed family; its normative relationship to the state, economy, and society; and its policy significance. The Soul family approach is southern and champions values, morality, and religiosity in policy, and the Hearth family approach is demonstrated as northern and more materialist, targeting economic conditions facing families. Both are also shown to contain distinct ideologies of state, society, and economy, including ideals of race and gender relations.

The chapters tell the story of politicized Hearth and Soul family ideals and attendant policy approaches, their intertwining developmental trajectories, and their evolving impact on the substantive policy agendas of the Republican and Democratic Parties through the twentieth century. The central argument is that the shifting allegiance of parties to these family ideals and their policy frameworks reflects changes in the family lives of their constituent bases as well as manipulation by political elites, as the parties court and respond to changing cores of supporters.

The book demonstrates that the late twentieth-century ascendance of family values onto the national political stage is neither a new nor unprecedented political development; it is an old song but sung more loudly and with modified lyrics. In particular, it reflects the growing southern influence in American politics in the century's last three decades and the Republican Party's successful revival of a Soul family values approach to appeal to a southern electorate, facilitating both parties' turn to family values since. Family economic assistance, once the salient fault line between the two parties, came to be articulated in valuational terms, such that family values emerged as a crucial axis of partisan divisions, obscuring (but not replacing) policy differences over economic assistance to families. This complex empirical story is told in the context of two previous periods in American history: the Progressive Era and the post–World War II period, in which similar political contestations over family ideals occurred in conjunction with widespread demographic family changes, decisively shaping partisan policy debates then and their legacies thereafter.

In telling this story, the book makes a larger theoretical claim regarding family and the history of party competition. It suggests that family is a valuable thematic tapestry on which to study American political development.[2] Much like race, gender, or constitutional orders, family is a major organizing feature of American experience through time, whose evolving political relevance hinges on its recurrent capacity to serve as a vital site on which political actors assemble and combine ideologies of state, economy, and society, often in response to large-scale social and demographic changes.

In the narrative, although Hearth and Soul family frameworks each pivot on a unique family political ideal (i.e., family as instilling values or family as providing material/economic resources), each trades off politically against multiple values/ideals that Americans widely share, thus leaving substantial room for exchange and manipulation of their components by the two parties. Thus, for instance, the chapters reveal how the parties have differentially deployed the Soul family values approach at different periods of time to invoke a positive and negative state, to deploy more or less of a market-based rationality, or to emphasize family values that are at times more moralistic or racial and at others more neoliberal or patriotic; all are mutable and capable of change depending on the actors and contingencies of each historical period. A key motivation behind charting family political development is thus to assemble the shifting compositional elements of politicized family frameworks (their ideals of state, society, and economy) and to simultaneously trace the partisan dynamics of these elements through time—how the parties borrow from, build upon, and/or reverse each other's elaborations from one period to the next.

This longitudinal investigation into family, as an evolving and composite partisan institution, reveals its three developmental stages across the past century. In the earliest, most amorphous, stage of the Progressive Era, the significance of family to party competition is shown as muted by prevailing constitutional boundaries between national and state legislative powers. However, even then the book demonstrates how family served to tie contrasting sectional visions of American state, economy, and society in policy, albeit in a loose, less cohesive way. In the second stage, in the midcentury post–World War II period, the investigation finds that family began to assert its presence more visibly within partisan debate, emerging for the first time as a significant *national* policy issue, central to the well-being of the nation. At this time, sectional differences, even more than partisanship, are found to have shaped family's political relevance, insofar as southern Democrats constituted a powerful third bloc, separate from nonsouthern Democrats and Republicans, in advocating their ideals of family. In the final, late twentieth-century period, extending from the late 1970s and arguably into our own, the book demonstrates family as crystallized into a central polarizing issue between the two parties, acting as a vital force to guide and shape Republican and Democratic divisions over policy and electoral constituencies.

In an observable sense, family has thus progressively increased its impact on American party politics, ultimately emerging as a lightning rod between the two political parties. However, insofar as family binds together ideals of state, society, and economy, and these ideals have varied across geographical regions and often parties, it is more useful to envision the political relevance of family in a far more durable way. This is best understood by way of a loose chemistry analogy: at a visceral level, water appears progressively "weighty" when transformed from a gaseous, to a liquid, and then to a solid state, yet its compositional elements (hydrogen and oxygen) remain in all three states. Similarly, although the form (nebulous then forming and finally crystallized) by which family has impacted party development has altered considerably and progressively, its ideational components (and political function) have remained the same. Through the three periods of analysis, the book reveals that family has served as the means by which political groups have reproduced ideologies of state, society, and economy as also race and gender. In this sense, regardless of its historically contingent electoral or policy salience, family remains integral and indispensable to the study of American political development.

The book thus makes two primary theoretical claims regarding the importance of families to American politics: the first asserts that family shapes party competition in important and overlooked ways, necessitating a fresh look at the conceptual understanding of party ideology and providing an alternative explanation for the late twentieth-century conservative ascendance; the second elevates family as central to the study of American political development (APD) and, in so doing, speaks more broadly to the significance of ideational political change. The following sections discuss each of the two claims in turn and how each contributes and/or modifies existing literature.

Family and Party Competition in American Politics

There is now a burgeoning literature that emphasizes the importance of family to American politics.[3] Several works demonstrate the significance of family as a political institution, underlying and driving debates over morality, culture, and society.[4] Political scientists also document the impact of family and parenthood on voting behavior, political beliefs, and public opinion,[5] and recent works suggest motherhood, in particular, as an important frame for organizing political participation and influencing political attitudes.[6] In the field of public policy, Patricia Strach demonstrates three ways by which family directly shapes policy: as a criterion of eligibility for goods and services, as an administrator that distributes goods and services to its members, and as a normative ideal to gain support for a policy position. She asserts the political significance of family *ideals*, a central focus of this book, stating that policy makers "hold and incorporate into policy very real and concrete assumptions about what constitutes a family, what roles members of families may be expected to perform, and what families can expect from the state."[7]

The political significance of family political ideals or ideational frames is also central to works by historians Robert Self, Rebecca Edwards, and cognitive linguist George Lakoff. Collectively, the authors demonstrate that competing family ideals shape policy and political ideologies through a variety of mechanisms: (a) they serve as underlying assumptions or cognitive frames consciously or unconsciously invoked by parties and policy makers when crafting policy (Lakoff), (b) they act as rhetorical tools/justifications purposively used to gain support for policy positions (Edwards), or (c) they form "political projects" or policy objects actively pursued by dominant political coalitions (Self).[8]

Despite the growing prominence of family in public opinion and political behavior literature and, more recently, in APD work, family remains overlooked in American politics scholarship on parties. In parties' literature, partisanship is conceptualized and measured narrowly—as Democratic and Republican ideological and policy divergence over the economy,[9] such that American party competition is understood as operating along a liberal-conservative dimension,[10] where liberalism implies an ideology of an expansionist state, positively intervening into the economy for redistributive purposes, and conservatism a negative state philosophy, privileging free enterprise and market-based individualism. Typically, the two political parties, particularly at the level of elites (legislators), are thus viewed as falling on either side of the liberal-conservative divide, and the history of party competition is described in terms of their varying support for a liberal or conservative economic ideology. For instance, Larry Bartels, in demonstrating the continued class bias among voters contrary to accounts that privilege the importance of moral or cultural issues, claims, "Economic issues continue to be of paramount importance in contemporary American politics as they have been for most of the past 150 years."[11] Even among works on political parties that do demonstrate that American party politics also involve struggles over social, racial, and cultural ideologies,[12] there too, none analyze the significance of family, in particular, as shaping partisan alignments.

This book aims to do just that. It contributes to the American politics literature on political parties by connecting party development to family, demonstrating the impact of family on ideological divergence and political party competition. It argues that family has been at the root of partisan divisions over economics *and* culture and challenges the existing artificiality of the economics-culture dichotomy by uncovering deep interconnections between political ideologies of state, economy, *and* family.[13] In this way, it modifies the underlying framework or premise for charting the development of liberalism, conservatism, and their association with the two parties, particularly at the elite level but as nested in mass-level demographic and cultural change. For instance, Keith Poole and Howard Rosenthal's seminal D-NOMINATE and DW-NOMINATE models highlight economic ideological differences between liberals and conservatives in Congress, for and against economic redistribution, as the one enduring dimension that explains congressional roll call voting from 1789 to the end of the twentieth century. This book suggests that the focus on liberal and conservative economic ideologies obscures the important role of family ideological divergences, which shape that very economic division in the first place. Far from a separable "cultural" issue, distinct and subordinate to economics, whose presence may be validated only as an alternative dimension, family instead maps *onto* views for and against economic intervention, often serving as the very justification for or against redistribution. As others have argued, albeit from the perspective of race, "political science accounts stressing redistributive issues are not wrong, but they do not capture the range of goals and members in the modern (party) alliances."[14] By demonstrating the claim that family shapes party competition even on issues of redistribution, as also other issues, the book thus expands the range, scope, and content of partisan politics in political science.

The impact of family, how and in what ways it shapes legislators' economic preferences, is more observable through qualitative discourse analysis, not roll call analysis, that examines patterns in the content of how legislators talk about, illustrate, and justify their policy responses. By paying attention to family in legislative *discourse*, this examination unearths the latent layers that underpin the very differences in legislators' preferences of economy that are the current focus of prevailing political science literature. American party development is thus much more than a story of dueling ideals of state and its role in the economy; it is also, at its core, a competition between dual political ideals of family.[15]

Differing family ideals, that is, divergences over the nature, function, and purpose of family—what families are for and how they should raise their children—inextricably contain alternative worldviews of economy, society, and state, as captured by Figure 1.[16]

As depicted in Figure 1, conservative economic and social policy goals, such as maintaining an unregulated economy, lowering taxes, and sustaining

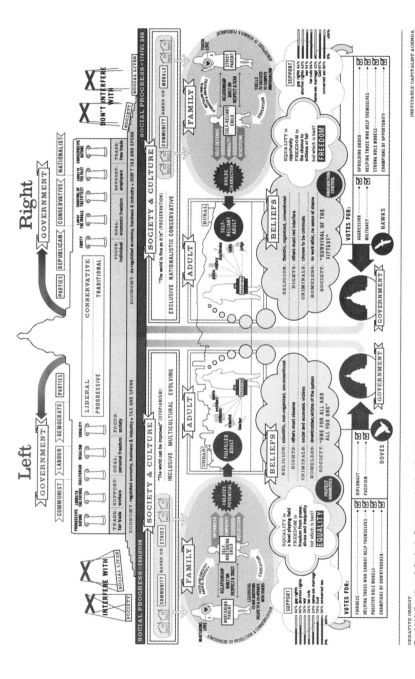

Figure 1. Political ideologies of family, state, and economy. Creative credit: David McCandless and Stefanie Posavec // v1.0//, October 2009.

CREATIVE CREDIT
David McCandless & Stefanie Posavec // v1.0 // v1.0 // Oct 09
InformationIsBeautiful.net / ItsBeenReal.co.uk

INEVITABLE CAPITALIST AGENDA
from the new infographic book of visual exploria
The Visual Miscellaneum

free enterprise and individual market-based freedoms, pivot on a conception of family as geared to produce *self-reliance* (self-reliant adults), all of which form intertwined parts of a conservative socioeconomic vision that seeks to conserve, not upend, existing social arrangements. The book reveals that these conservative goals have largely privileged a valuational political ideal of family (Soul ideal), unmoored from economic conditions, where values, not income, determine family strength. In contrast, the liberal expansive state ideal that underlies the set of liberal economic and social policy beliefs, such as faith in regulated economies, broader distribution of rights and burdens, and greater social equality, hinges on a liberal conception of family as rearing *self-nurturing* adults, which subordinates self-reliance to personal fulfillment; these ideals form imbricated parts of a more progressive socioeconomic vision that aims to improve existing social arrangements. As the following examination finds, these liberal policy goals highlight, more or less consistently, a Hearth family view that conceives of economic well-being as fundamental to family cohesion, nurturing, and strength, wherein family values are determined by economic condition and are not separable from it.

The two family-centered worldviews are found to be poles of a continuum upon which Democratic and Republican Party competition at the level of elites has long occurred. In their quest for electoral success, the parties at various times cluster toward one family framework over the other, upholding differing visions of state and its nexus with economy and society. Hearth and Soul political ideals, empirically assembled in this book, are summarized in Table 1.

Through the demonstration of this imbricated framework, the book also revises the conventional understanding of *what* constitutes party ideology. In contrast to conventional treatments, where party ideology is seen as a coherent constellation of ideas, rhetorical tools, or abstract principles devised for electoral gain and *unconnected* to material structures or to lived practice and cultural experience,[17] here, party ideology is shown as grounded in the family lives and the material and cultural realities of real-life Americans.[18] The book does this by focusing on real-life family stories recounted by congressional members during committee hearings to glean which family practices and experiences have and have not been politically valued and highlighted by legislators in their policy discussions as positive or negative family images.[19] By analyzing family and policy variables such as the socioeconomic characteristics of these families, the regional patterns of where

Table 1. Summary of Intertwining Ideals of Family, Society, and Economy in Hearth and Soul Frameworks

	Hearth Framework	Soul Framework
Political orientation	Liberal	Conservative
Family ideal	Materialist: economics essential to family well-being	Valuational: morality/values essential to family well-being
Society ideal	Existing social arrangements must be improved	Existing social arrangements must be conserved
Economy ideal	Redistributive: broader distribution of economic benefits	Anti-redistributive: opposed to redistribution of economic benefits

they reside, and the policies they are used to illustrate, legislators' partisanship and family (policy) ideals are found to be linked to distinct regional family patterns and characteristics, suggesting that a party's aggregate family ideology and its social policy agenda are grounded in (or crafted upon) the lived family experiences of dominant factions within their base. The book thus argues that party ideology is the product of not only top-down but also bottom-up forces, reflecting a party's internal dynamics as *nested* within the actual family lives, the materiality and culture of those they represent. In this way, it complements existing literature on party polarization that situates increased polarization in the late twentieth century within widespread social and economic changes. Much of polarization literature, however, relies heavily on statistical and quantitative macro-level data, which limits their ability to illuminate *how* partisan polarization among elites relates to polarization of masses. By highlighting family stories at the heart of partisan policy making, this book connects individualized narratives to coherent partisan positions, uniquely demonstrating ideas as the *discursive mechanisms* through which family has come to bind party competition among elites and citizens alike, in the wake of massive internal demographic change.[20]

Finally, the family-centered investigation evokes an alternative interpretation of a specific era in party development: the conservative ascendance in the late twentieth century. Similar to recent parties' literature on conservatism in APD, this investigation finds that conservatives played a more influential role in shaping partisan policy developments *across* the twentieth century, more than that which is often depicted in accounts that highlight only programmatic expansion.[21] This may be in part because family is the subject of examination here, as well because of how this book defines conservatives. Admittedly hard to define,[22] conservatives in the following pages are characterized first and foremost as "traditionalists" akin to Rogers Smith's proponents of the "ascriptive tradition" (i.e., defenders of prevailing social arrangements as opposed to upholders of the "liberal tradition" who seek to broaden political and economic rights). To this extent, conservatives are sometimes "constitutional traditionalists," advocating a traditionalist view of the Constitution, and at other times they may also include libertarians, defending liberty (of various stripes) above equality.[23] In every instance, however, conservatives here seek to *conserve* prevailing, often gendered and racial, social arrangements and oppose redistribution of political and economic rights (as summarized in Table 1), sometimes invoking a positive state and, at other times, opposing it. Given their close interest in preserving traditional social arrangements, conservatives are found to display a prominent interest in family for all periods of investigation, their interest often invoked by their perception of family as the very unit of social reproduction, seen as uniquely capable of upholding prevailing social orders or upending them. Family conservatives also enduringly turn to family values to highlight their policy positions, displaying a long-lasting affinity to the Soul family approach.

While conservatives most certainly have not always been Republican, and family did not become a Republican policy focus until the 1970s, family and conservatism have had a long and significant relationship, with conservatives playing a more formative role than merely obstructing policy development. Instead, conservatives are the yin to the yang of liberals in family policy development, both reflexive, historically contingent, codependent, dialectical coalitions—neither developing without the other, even when one eclipses the other in certain periods.

Despite their shifting partisan stripe, family conservatives have had an unfailing sectional home—the South. More than any other legislative delegation, southern legislators most consistently—across the Progressive, post–World War II, and late twentieth-century periods—are found to have advocated conservative family positions. Southern legislators have tended to use their own southern family examples, more frequently than legislators from other regions, to illustrate their policy positions, suggesting a distinctive localism to their process of policy ideology formulation and elaboration. The turn to family in late twentieth-century party politics, the increasing adoption of the Soul family values ideal by the Republican Party (and then, to a lesser extent, by the Democratic Party), and the salience of family values as a significant national policy frame are thus directly related to southern realignment, the increasing electoral significance of the South, and the Republican Party's pursuit of a southern strategy.

Instead of viewing the rightward "southernization" of the Republican Party and the subsequent conservative ascendance in American party politics as driven solely by race and civil rights issues[24] or even battles over sex and gender,[25] the book suggests that family ideals were at its core. Neoliberal views of economy and conservative views of society, historically separated by party, came to be melded into a common GOP "politics of family," facilitating the Republican southernization trajectory and the subsequent ascendance of conservatism in party politics. Conservative ascendance in this account is thus tied to the increased prominence of southern domestic ideals within the Republican Party and subsequently in national American politics. As the Republican Party moved south, it increasingly incorporated southern family ideals to craft a Soul family values policy agenda, with Democratic legislators continuing to rely on ideals from families in the Northeast to advocate for a materialist Hearth family approach.

The account also highlights the formative role of massive family demographic change since the 1970s, its disparate occurrence and reception in the South as opposed to elsewhere, and so complicates the picture of the Republican Southern Strategy further as not merely an elite-driven phenomenon formulated by conservative political strategists and evangelical leaders. The timing of family demographic change and the coincident rightward shift toward family values within the Republican Party agenda underscore the importance of the southern *cultural* context in which conservative family ideals had long been prevalent but were brought to the fore by the family transformations of the late twentieth century. The book argues that family political ideals are thus rooted in distinct demographic regional realities, and overlooking these material and cultural contexts misses the lived regionalism that underlies partisan (family) appeals and political strategies.

In sum, by focusing on family, this account contributes to the literature on political parties in the following ways: (1) it highlights family as a crucial, albeit overlooked, site of party ideological divisions over state and economy; (2) it reconceives political party ideology as more than abstract principles and instead shows the lived material and cultural realities on which it is founded; and (3) it presents an alternative account of the conservative ascendance and/or southernization of the Republican Party since the 1970s, demonstrating that southern family ideals, southern reaction to family demographic transformations, and the rising electoral salience of the South with its distinctive conservative (Soul) family ideal markedly shaped this phenomenon.

The next section situates the book in APD literature, highlighting its contribution in terms of the prevailing understanding of political change in general and the significance of ideas and conceptual narratives as facilitating this change.

Family and American Political Development

Polarized Families, Polarized Parties captures change in party ideology and policy debate from Hearth to more Soul family frameworks as part of the increasing southernization of American party politics from the early to the late twentieth century. In its focus on partisan ideology and policy preferences, as assembled from in committee hearings, bill sponsorships, and co-sponsorships, the narrative highlights the formative role of ideas in shaping political change. In so doing, the book joins other recent calls for expanding American political development to incorporate more fully ideational and not just institutional change.

Ideological change has now been largely accepted as significant in mapping party transitions, in no small part due to John Gerring's seminal work, *Party Ideologies in America*. Nevertheless, interpretive studies of political ideas and discursive narratives continue to play a limited role in charting or explaining political development within APD, a relatively recent subfield whose overarching methodology is characterized as "historical *institutionalism*."[26] Recent work in APD has challenged the original institutional bias, arguing for greater recognition of ideas and their role in shaping politics and political development.[27] This has led to a reconceptualization of "ideas" themselves and how and why ideational and discursive narratives matter to a story of political change. Political scientists Victoria Hattam and Joseph Lowndes, for example, note that discursive change often precedes formal shifts in governing authority and rightly assert, "To understand political change, we need to attend to discourse, since this is where political identifications and social cleavages are made and remade," whereby "the very words used, the political appeals made, and the identifications evoked" become "*the* ground of politics, *the* site of change."[28] Rogers Smith in his recent book, *Political Peoplehood*, also demonstrates "how different narrative structures and content themes shape policy making . . . and how, within the constraints and using the resources their contexts provide, leaders build support by knitting their personal stories and those of their constituents together within their communal narratives of collective identity and purpose."[29]

Hattam and Lowndes's discourse-centered "cultural analysis" and Smith's idea-centered framework of political development align closely with the model of partisan change developed in this book. Here too, (family) ideational development is used to organize and map partisan change in the twentieth century, highlighting how partisans weave together personal family stories and the ideational threads of state, economy, society, race, and gender into coherent political family ideologies that evolve and get repurposed through three periods in the twentieth century. The book then connects such historically contingent composite partisan family ideals to specific types of policy positions, identified as ascription, autonomy, welfare, and regulation, tying why and how parties have come to support certain kinds of policies to their prevailing family ideals (see Figure 2). For example, Democratic support of "ascriptive-based" policies in the Progressive Era is linked to their support of a variant of the Soul family ideology, in contrast to their support of a strong Hearth family ideal in the postwar period, which instead shaped their "welfare" policy positions at that later time. In other words, party *development*—coherent, discernible shifts in the parties' policy positions—is dependent on the kind of family ideologies the parties uphold, such that changing family ideals shape shifting partisan agendas.

The importance of ideas, especially simplified narratives, within the immediate process of policy making is also highlighted in Deborah Stone's classic work, *The Policy Paradox*.[30] Stone stresses the use of stories (or "narratives with heroes and villains") as a key mechanism by which political actors define policy problems, contextualize, and justify their preferred policy actions, thereby "trying to get others to see a situation as one thing rather than another" so as to facilitate reasoning by metaphor and analogy.[31] The essence of policy making is thus the struggle over ideas, often presented as binaries; as Stone writes, "Ideas are a medium of exchange and a mode of influence even more powerful than money and votes and guns. Shared meanings motivate people to action and meld individual striving into collective action. Policy making, in turn, is a constant struggle over the criteria for classification, the boundaries of categories, and the definition of ideas that guide the way people behave."[32] Hearth and Soul family ideals, as described in this book, are just such simplified ideational means or composite political narratives through

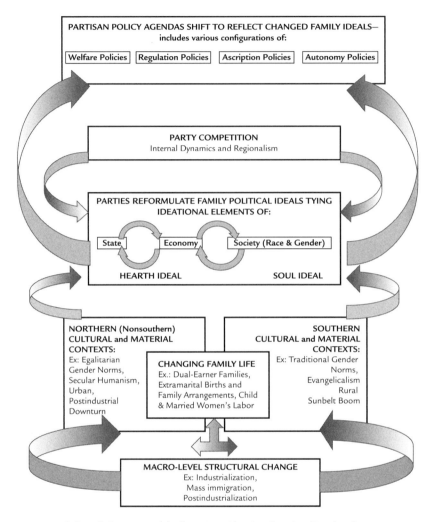

Figure 2. Cultural change model of partisan ideational and policy development.

which parties struggle to define family, combining elements of state, economy, society, race, and gender into what Hattam and Lowndes call "natural affinities" that suture "disparate elements into apparently coherent political positions."[33] Whereas the two family ideals are evolving, recombining various discursive elements through time, sometimes intertwining and sometimes separating, their enduring appeal is also most striking and affirms the persisting duality by which other scholars have theorized family political ideals at diverse periods in American history.[34]

As noted previously, ideas in the following narrative are not self-generated by parties and political elites but are demonstrated as grounded in the material and cultural contexts of their bases and electoral groups. Family ideals, as other political ideals, deploy positive and negative cultural images associated with established identities and policies, such as "working mothers" or "deadbeat dads," that resonate in similar ways among sets of elites and voters alike, signaling the symbiotic relationship between legislators' party ideology and that of their constituents. Coherent partisan family ideals are thus strongly nested in and woven from families' own demographic and "real" lives, their cultural and material contexts, changes in which both co-occur and are codependent. The book does not make deterministic or causal claims regarding the relationship between parties' policy agendas, their family ideals, and family demographic and cultural life. The emphasis instead is on the imbricated, interwoven nature of this multifaceted relationship, suggesting that shifts in parties' ideologies co-occur with demographic and cultural changes in the lives of their constituent families, with mass-level change acting as both constraints and opportunities for elite formulations of policy change, as seen in Figure 2.

Like overlaying circles in a spiral, there are three imbricated central layers to the cultural change model of party policy development followed in this book, as in Figure 2. The first captures the relationship between structural developments and family shifts, wherein macro-level changes, such as industrialization and mass immigration, engender changes to family life on individual and aggregate scales. Family changes are shaped by preexisting sectional contexts, both material and cultural, that impact distinctive patterns in how family practices both occur and are multiply interpreted in regionally specific ways. The second layer, the mainstay of the book, emphasizes the top-down and bottom-up formulation of sectional family political ideals by partisans in Congress. This process is shown as an interplay between evolving party dynamics such as intraparty strategies and regional coalitions, on one hand, and sectional family shifts, on the other, shaping competing ideational interpretations, articulations, and assemblies by legislators into coherent family political ideologies. Changes in party politics and in social behavior, such as transformations in family practices, emergence of new party activists such as the New Right and Left, and the opening of new issue contexts (e.g., abortion, busing, and school integration) in the late twentieth century, all contribute to the displacement of the parties' existing family ideals and their reformulation of the discursive links between their ideals of state, society, and economy into a revised family political ideal. The third layer connects parties' reformulated and repurposed family ideals to changes in partisan *policy* positions, as assembled from the parties' altered preferences in differing historical periods for one or the other kinds of family policy: welfare, regulation, ascription, and/or autonomy.

Patricia Strach offers a complementary model of policy development, revealing how large-scale changes in American families challenge family ideals embedded in public policies, creating "policy gaps" that form, she says, "when the social practice is at odds with values or assumptions of public policy."[35] In turn, she shows how these policy gaps allowed for policy change to occur, configured around newly emergent family ideals. This book adds to that model by expanding the historical arc to include changes across three historical eras, focusing more squarely on the formation and influence of partisan family *ideals* on parties' legislative agendas and empirically demonstrating the discursive links between preexisting regional family practices/norms, parties' family ideologies, and party policy preferences.

Institutions, such as congressional parties, find mention in the book's narrative, but institutions are more contextual and less central to this story of party policy development than the (family) ideals themselves. Ideas do not simply "cluster" with prevailing governing arrangements as some have implied they do;[36] ideas also structure and guide those very arrangements. For example, not only did the precise content of the New Deal Democratic Hearth family ideal, which advocated national government responsibility for family economic welfare, arise out of context of an uneasy alliance between southern Democratic legislators and their nonsouthern counterparts (and the institutional strength of senior southern committee chairs in Congress) but also, more crucially, the substance of this ideal also served as the ideational rallying point for the organization and mobilization of Republican opposition to the New Deal political order. This ideational opposition then grew and developed into a resurgent Soul family ideal pursued by the New Right in the late twentieth century, more actively structuring Republican policy ideology and strategy in that subsequent period. Seen in this way, party competition over ideals plays a vital role in shaping the parties' electoral and policy strategies from one period to the next. Ideational shifts, changes, and alignments are thus the very ground or site of political party development, even when those ideational changes do not immediately translate into tangible policy change.

Patterns in the very origination of ideas and their process of formulation and reformulation—*which* groups of legislators combine *which* narratives and forms of policy, highlighting *what* kinds of human experience and *how* those aggregate, if at all, into a more macro (party) agenda—are crucial to the study of political development and are an important goal of this research. Legislators offer real-life family cases in their remarks during committee hearings as illustrations of policy failures and/or success, embodiments of the kinds of family arrangements by which their ideals of society, economy, and state come together. In so doing, they draw upon positive and negative cultural imagery that is widely shared among Americans even while they reconstruct and/or reify some of that imagery. Every interaction of a member of Congress with a real family case by way of questions or comments, in which he or she raises a policy issue (coded as one event in the data set), provides a window through which to examine how legislators express their ideas and beliefs regarding family; its role in society, economy, and vis-à-vis the state; and the types of policy issues involving that family that are of interest to them, both positively and negatively. By coding these events across three historical periods covering almost sixty years' worth of congressional hearings, for characteristics of family mentioned by members of Congress, their party, state, and region, as well as the policy issues highlighted by them, specific legislators are demonstrated to invoke historically contingent and evolving patterns of family political ideals, also suggesting ideational aggregate patterns of legislators' family ideals across party and region.[37] Thus, empirical examinations of ideas, while first and foremost reliant on qualitative methods such as discourse and content analysis, can also deploy quantitative approaches, as also developed (in an alternative methodology) in Gerring's book on *Party Ideology*. Moreover, the revealed aggregate patterns in partisan and sectional family ideals over time enable one to see, in a tangible way, the process of formation and elaboration of policy ideas and to also discern how macro (and institutional) forces, such as political parties and demographic change, can and do enable the groupings of ideas into coherent policy ideologies.

At a macro level, in each of the three eras examined, Hearth and Soul family ideals emerge as two grand narratives that have durable political appeal and recurrent salience. At this scale, both operate much like ideational "orders" or "regimes," similar, for instance, to James Morone's depiction of "social gospel" and "neopuritan" approaches that have continually shaped responses to moral panics across American political history.[38] At a mesa policy level, however, these family ideologies engender variations in how they link ideas of race, gender, economy, and state into composite policy positions in different periods of time, manifesting in alterations in which policies most support that ideology, when, and how. In the Progressive Era, for example, Soul family values ideology largely supported ascriptive policies, whereas in other periods, such as the late twentieth century, it was harnessed to craft autonomy and even welfare policies.[39] Depicted in this way, family political development simultaneously illustrates the durability and dynamism of politics, best perceived in terms of the valuable insight of Adam Sheingate as differences in "speed" and "scale" of political developments, such that slower change at the macro level coexists with change occurring at a quicker tempo at the mesa and micro levels of analysis.[40]

Shifting the spotlight on ideas and discursive narrative formation continues to see important roles played by political actors. In the present account, although legislators (and party elite) operate within prevailing pre-structured (sectional) material and cultural contexts (northern and southern family conceptual frameworks, for instance), they can and sometimes do display significant agency in the imaginative ways they reformulate, revise, and modify these inherited conceptions from one time period to the next, applying them anew to altered policy positions.[41]

In sum, while Hearth and Soul family ideologies revise and switch between the two parties in the twentieth century and align with different kinds of policies in different eras, these partisan changes occur alongside a more enduring reliance on family economics (Hearth) or family values (Soul) as durable family political ideals. The two ideational frameworks continue to frame how legislators imagine and conceive of family and generate parties' policy agendas while simultaneously serving as opportunities and constraints on successive political actors looking to formulate new approaches to changing realities.

Overview of Chapters

The first chapter provides an overview of the shifting significance of family within party policy agendas. It uses party platforms from 1900 to 2012 and periodic bill sponsorship/cosponsorship data to demonstrate the growing salience of family in the two parties' political and policy ideologies, as well as the parties' increasing attention to family values starting in the 1970s. It assembles the two organizing family ideals, family economics (Hearth) and family values (Soul), demonstrating how they have reversed in the agendas of the Republican and Democratic Parties and periodically supported alternative visions of the state. The chapter identifies three critical periods in the family party development. These three periods (Progressive, post–World War II, and late century) are subsequently examined as in-depth case studies in the following chapters.

The first of three case studies, Chapter 2 focuses on the Progressive Era and assembles the ideational, partisan, and sectional roots of the Hearth and Soul family ideals, demonstrating their deeply gendered and racial character in that early period. It discusses the emergence into national attention of women and child-related family issues in the wake of massive industrialization in the early twentieth century and widespread family demographic changes, and it uses women's suffrage and intermarriage policy debates to reveal the emerging, ascriptive roots of party competition over Hearth and Soul family ideals.

Chapter 3 picks up after the constitutional reordering of the New Deal and highlights family party development in the postwar period. It describes the anxiety over family behavior in the decade following World War II, demonstrating the wartime origin of the parties' initial recognition of family as the keystone to national social order. The chapter examines shorter policy case studies of debates over housing policies and the extension of the May Act (to suppress prostitution and the spread of venereal disease), revealing the centrality of the parties' alternative state visions (for and against the welfare state) as guiding family policy development at this time. It also finds three, not two, partisan ideational coalitions, with southern Democrats displaying mixed allegiances to Hearth and Soul family ideals.

The final case study, in Chapter 4, links the demographic demise of the nuclear family and the coincident southern realignment under way in the late twentieth century, examining policy debates over poverty/welfare reform and education policy to highlight the southern-conservative and northern-liberal family ideals of the New Right and Left, respectively. It situates these policy battles in the distinct southern and northern differences in families' lives, following the social and economic reconstruction of the late twentieth century, and the New Right's increasing turn to southern family values to craft anew the Republican Party agenda.

The final chapter ties together the threads of family political development as suggested by the three period case studies to examine the future direction of family in American politics. It suggests that while the story of Hearth and Soul is ongoing, it is now being played out in new ways, with regional electoral conditions now institutionalizing this ideational battle and embedding it even more deeply in American party politics than ever before.

Chapter 1

The Partisan Turn to Family Values: An Overview

During a news conference in December 1959, President Dwight D. Eisenhower was asked a question on birth control, to which he responded, "I cannot imagine anything more emphatically a subject that is not a proper political or governmental activity or function or responsibility."[1] More than fifty years later, in 2011, Rick Santorum, a presidential candidate also from the GOP, avowed to "defend America" from those who "say we need a truce on social issues." Said Santorum, "At the heart of this country . . . America is a moral enterprise and we are sick at the heart of our country—when we see millions of children aborted and marriage not being defended." A "truce," Santorum thus asserted, would amount to "surrender."[2]

Eisenhower and Santorum illustrate the transformed role of family in American party politics over the twentieth century. Until the late 1960s, most Republicans and Democrats considered family—its sexuality, poverty, health, formation, and childrearing—a state or local issue, firmly within the purview of the internal police and economy of the respective states or else wholly private, under the domain of the (male) head of household. Historically, of course, contestations over family episodically roiled national party politics. The issue of polygamous marriage, for instance, engrossed national debate in the nineteenth century; miscegenation embroiled the two parties during the Reconstruction and Progressive Eras, invoking doomsday predictions of "race suicide" and declining national greatness,[3] and with the onset of industrialization, child labor, mothers' working conditions, infant and maternal health, and hygiene aroused national attention and enlisted partisan consideration. However, the late twentieth century stands apart in the fact that family came to play an unprecedentedly large and more durable role in structuring party polarization, with Republicans and Democrats assigning it greater than ever political value. Even when viewed narrowly, merely as part of a larger constellation of "cultural" or "social" concerns, family issues began to decisively shape nationwide and statewide electoral outcomes, also playing a steady, durable role in legislative politics.

The year 1980 was decisive to the increased prominence of family to party competition. In that year, the Republican Party launched a new ideology, a repudiation of the Democratic-led progressive agenda that had long dominated since the New Deal.[4] The revised Republican ideology, which continues to prevail today, pivoted on two central themes: first, "antistatism," through which the party highlighted local institutions and emphasized their "private-ness" in opposing the liberal state, and, second, "traditional values," by which the party began to stress what political scientist Byron Shafer has termed "valuational" concerns, highlighting proper behavioral norms within which social life should proceed.[5] Family emerged as the primary issue through which Republicans combined their longer-term antistatism, on one hand, with their newfound emphasis on traditional values, on the other.[6]

Democrats responded to the late twentieth-century Republican focus on families by similarly elevating family within their own policy discourse but rejecting Republicans' antistatism and traditional values emphasis. For Democrats, "putting families first" meant more effective material/distributional benefits to encourage family strength regardless of diverse family forms and an enhanced, not reduced, state-family partnership. They claimed that families now came "in all different shapes and sizes," yet "they all face[d] similar challenges,"[7] and that the emphasis on family values by Republicans was a smokescreen masking state inaction and neglect. In this way, the late twentieth-century Democratic conception of family retained its New Deal and post–World War II focus, continuing to stress the material circumstances of families, as well as their economic stagnation or mobility, while also explicating the values underlying their economics-centered approach.

For Democrats, the family values they thus came to claim were progressive, secular-humanist values, not traditional or moral ones; these included values such as equality and equal protection, fairness, and individual self-determination. At the 2012 National Convention, First Lady Michelle Obama, for example, told a classic Democratic tale of family values when she recounted the "unflinching sacrifice," "unconditional love," and hard work of her father, a pump operator at a city water plant, who suffered from multiple sclerosis and often "struggle[d] to make it out of bed" but never missed a day of work. Mrs. Obama described how her father steadfastly pursued the dream of giving his children the "chance to go places they had never imagined for themselves." "Dignity, decency, gratitude, humility, fairness and compassion," she said, are "who we are"; they are the "values Barack and I are trying to pass on to our children."[8] On the face of it, the content of these values is not dissimilar from values often claimed and championed by Republicans, yet for Democrats alone, these values remained firmly imbricated within family economic conditions and state-regulated markets, and familiar arguments for state programmatic assistance based on family economic need were recast as programs that ensured fairness, inclusivity, and equality.

The two partisan approaches to family and their disparate alignments of values and economics align alternatively with a burgeoning "vulnerability" scholarship, most notably developed by feminist legal scholar Martha Fineman. Fineman points to five types of resources or assets that could mitigate human (including family) vulnerability and enhance resilience; these assets are identified as physical, human, social, ecological or environmental, and existential.[9] These posited resiliency resources, resources by which families may successfully resist hardships that come their way, can be broadly categorized into external/material assets, on one hand, and internal/valuational or psychological assets, on the other. The two political parties have similarly largely divided over family in policy, diverging over which of the two kinds of assets are central to policy and thus to projected family success. They either focus on the external, economic resources of families, such as their income, wages, jobs, and taxes, promising to improve them in some way, or highlight the internal—valuational or behavioral—assets of a family, such as a family's discipline, self-reliance, and responsibility. Family policy agendas thus either primarily aim at supporting the material character of families, bolstering their material resources (their Hearth), or have a more internal focus, directed at a family's Soul, purporting instead to enhance its values resources—its self-reliance, personal responsibility, commitment to marriage, and so on.

At the core of Hearth policies is thus a Hearth family ideal that assumes that a family's economics, its income, wages, material access to housing, health care, and such, is central to its flourishing and its values secondary, even if very important. And Soul policies assume a Soul family ideal that imagines family as essentially a valuational unit, loosely connected—if at all—to its economic circumstances. The two are poles, or central tendencies, within partisan policy framing of family, overlapping but also certainly distinctive.

This chapter analyzes party platforms and bill sponsorships to present an overview of family political development from 1900 to 2012, revealing the twists and turns of Hearth and Soul family ideals within party dialectics and demonstrating how, since the late twentieth century, there is a stronger than ever political assertion of a distinctive Soul family ideal.[10] In so doing, three significant periods of family partisan development are identified: (a) the Progressive Era (1900–1920), (b) the post–World War II period (1945–1955), and (c) the late twentieth-century period to the present (1980–2012). The current chapter demonstrates that through the three periods, family steadily grew in political importance while the parties reversed their family ideologies and began to increasingly polarize over Hearth and Soul, in contrast to earlier periods such as the postwar era, when the two family ideals were more overlapping and shared across the two parties. The three identified periods are then analyzed separately, as case studies, in the chapters to follow that unpack the precise interaction of family and party in each historical phase and analyze the historically contingent conditions that shaped how the parties treated family as they did, simultaneously revealing how family, in turn, shaped party developments in each of the three eras.

The Family in Party Platforms, 1900–2012

The parties have increasingly addressed the family in their platforms. Controlling for the total number of paragraphs in each platform, three distinct periods stand out in the parties' address of family (Figure 3): an initial period of low salience in the first two decades of the twentieth century, when both parties made reference to family in only 2 percent of their platforms on average; a second period following the Depression through post–World War II (1930s–1964), when the parties occasionally increased their attention to family, with family paragraphs forming 3 to 8 percent of their platforms; and a final period of a durable, sharp increase, starting from 1968 and extending into the twenty-first century, when the parties tripled their attention to family.

Later platforms are also distinctive insofar as more pledges were directed at family as a *unit* rather than targeting individuals or other collective groups. For example, the parties' pledges on taxes moved away from solely addressing individual citizens or corporations to also focusing on families; tax pledges shifted from their previous focus on "low-income Americans"

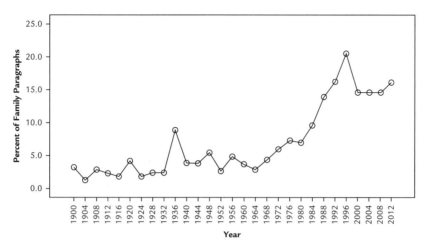

Figure 3. Family paragraphs in party platforms, as a percentage of total paragraphs, 1900–2012. N = 17,489 paragraphs. Data compiled by author.

and "workers," for example, to address "low-income families" and "working families." Since the start of the twentieth century, the percentage of tax pledges that invoked family first doubled and then tripled, from about 6 percent between the 1940s and 1960s to 15 percent in the 1970s, further increasing to upward of 20 percent in the twenty-first century (Figure 4).

Similarly, welfare and antipoverty promises, long directed only at children, the disabled, and the elderly with no reference to their families, have focused sharply on family units since the 1970s, invoking families as critical to the success or failure of antipoverty measures. From about 15 percent of all welfare paragraphs that invoked family from the 1940s to 1950s, this rose first to 25 percent in the 1970s and then to 43 percent of all welfare paragraphs in the twenty-first century (Figure 4).

Another central feature of family politics since the 1970s has been the increased prominence of the valuational, Soul family ideal. Whereas the parties increased both types of family references (economic and valuational) significantly from the late 1960s to 1970s, the upward trend is much more pronounced in the case of the Soul family approach, with pledges aimed at family values and character bursting onto the political stage, overtaking economic-based Hearth pledges, then falling but maintaining a heightened presence since (Figure 5). Compared to the 1950s and 1960s, party platforms

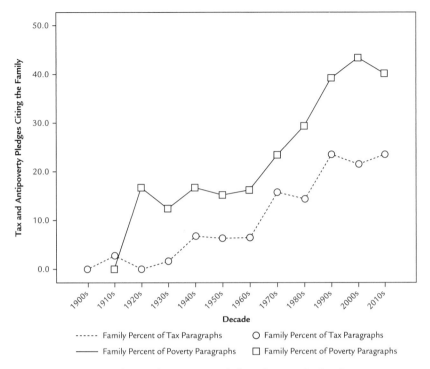

Figure 4. Percentage of tax and antipoverty pledges that cite the family in party platforms, 1900–2012.

of the 1970s doubled all references to economic family aspects, but they quadrupled the number of their references to family values and its nonmaterial character.

Figure 5 also reminds us that despite the current ubiquity of family values in party rhetoric, it was largely a subterranean feature of partisan policy discourse in earlier decades. The two parties previously invoked family more consistently in an economic sense, pledging to and primarily dividing over the distribution of economic welfare and benefits to families. Yet the Soul family values focus is not entirely new either. It persisted throughout the past century, with both parties alternatively emphasizing family values at differing points in history. In the early twentieth century (first two decades), the Democratic Party, for instance, stressed family morals and values in addition to family economics (see Figure 6), so distinguishing itself from the more progressive, exclusively economic-focused Republican Party. However,

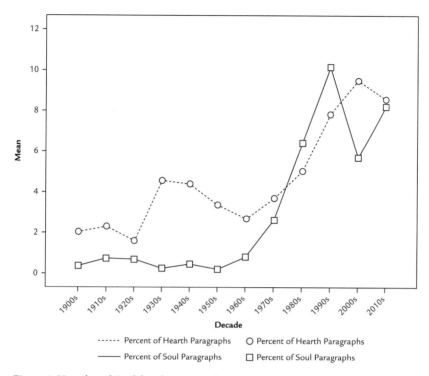

Figure 5. Hearth and Soul family paragraphs as a percentage of total paragraphs, party platforms, 1900–2012. $N=17,489$ paragraphs. Data compiled by author.

following the Great Depression and with the emergence of the New Deal, the Democratic Party altogether eschewed the Soul family valuational approach, emphatically addressing the family through its economics alone. In contrast, Republicans, in their opposition to the rising New Deal coalition, began to stress family values in the 1940s and 1950s even while accepting the dominant Hearth approach, only to strongly repudiate family economics in favor of family values in their concerted bid for electoral dominance in the 1970s. Since the 1980s, the Democratic Party also has incorporated a Soul family values approach, albeit in a more secular-humanist, not traditionalist, sense, while nevertheless continuing to assert its own economics-based Hearth family focus as well.

The ebb and flow of the political salience of an economic Hearth or valuational Soul family focus is thus part of a partisan dialectic. One is advanced by one party at any given time and used to repudiate the other, as the out

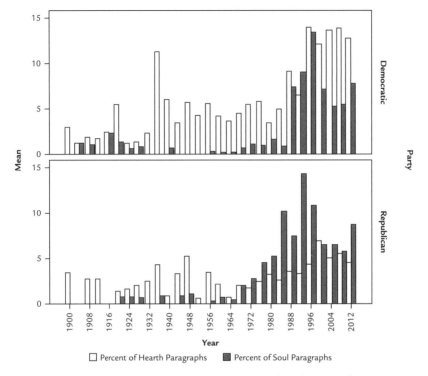

Figure 6. Hearth and Soul paragraphs as a percentage of total paragraphs, Democratic and Republican Party platforms, 1900–2012. *N* = 17,489 paragraphs. Data compiled by author.

party seeks to distinguish itself from the dominant party. The following section analyzes the specific issues and ways by which the two parties in different eras have utilized the Hearth and Soul family frames in their policy agendas, also demonstrating the ideals of state and, to a lesser extent, economy that have underpinned the shifting family conceptions.

Family in Partisan Agendas, the Early Years (1900–1932): Limited Salience, Marginal Polarization

During the Progressive Era (1900–1920), the social progressive reform movement focused much attention on the impoverished economic conditions of families. Social progressives advocated new public measures to improve working conditions, to economically assist families and children, and to ensure better products, services, and environmental conditions for consumers.[11] They targeted growing poverty as a product of rapid industrialization and urbanization, as well as unregulated markets and monopolies, invoking themes of nation building and tying the economic assistance of children and their families to the long-term success of the nation.

The social progressive project resonated with the state-centered ideology of national republicanism advocated by Republicans in this time.[12] Social progressives urged a variety of programs for children and their families, such as mothers' aid, children and women's labor regulation, compulsory public schooling, and maternal and infant health care programs. Much of this agenda was child (not family) centered and directed at state governments, as the constitutional boundaries circumscribing the national state were still rigid and social welfare matters fell predominantly within the purview of states. Even when the two political parties accommodated progressive policy planks in their national platforms, very rarely did they place them within a family context, invoking families in only about 2 percent of their pledges (see Figure 3). Nevertheless, in their few family-directed pledges, both parties typically addressed families' economic conditions, utilizing a Hearth family approach. The parties differed, however, in whether or not they used that family ideal to obligate the national state.

Of the two parties, Republicans were (then) more comfortable with the use of centralized state machinery and regulated markets for public welfare, including for child and family welfare. In 1908, they pledged support for child labor regulation in factories, provision of widows' pensions, and safety legislation for firefighters and railroad engineers, all of which they described as "wholesome and progressive . . . acts conserving the public welfare."[13] Also in pledges to veterans' families and their dependents, Republicans more than Democrats viewed that commitment to mean an expansion of national state obligations[14] by promising to harness federal state machinery to compensate veterans' families through promises of employment in the public service.[15]

Both political parties viewed veterans' families as legitimate subjects of national policy attention, acknowledging, for example, that the nation "owes [them] a debt of profound gratitude,"[16] and addressing veterans' families exclusively (in contrast to any other family) through pledges for pensions and other material support. However, in this case too, Democratic platforms were more hesitant to engage the federal state, for instance pledging support for widows' pensions only to "relieve the country of the necessity of a large standing army," rather than as a bona fide national public responsibility.[17]

In planks addressing homesteader families as well, Republicans approached the provision of public lands as an independent obligation of the national state,[18] pledging to it as a "constant policy of the Republican party to provide free homes on the public domain."[19] In contrast, Democrats framed their homestead policies only as part of a larger struggle against land monopolies,[20] also promising to free the homesteader from unnecessary state intrusion and regulatory constraints.[21]

However, in the late Progressive Era, as a harbinger of a tide soon to develop in the New Deal and perhaps in response to women winning the vote, Democratic platforms began to shift in their address of families, promising to obligate the national state more fully for family material support. In 1920, for example, Democrats pledged to support increased appropriations for the "Children's and Woman's Bureaus," vocational training in home economics, and "education in sex hygiene."[22] In pledges to limit the hours of work, they tied national security and safety to the "conservation of the strength of the workers and their families in the interest of sound-hearted and sound-headed men, women, and children" and proclaimed that labor laws "are just assertions of the national interest in the welfare of the people."[23] They now acknowledged the protection of children as "an important national duty."[24]

Despite the attention to economic family conditions in the early platforms, both parties in their policy agendas also used a moral tone, invoking values more generally. Keeping with their focus on nation, Republican platforms displayed strong nationalistic values, stressing common American patriotic ideals.[25] Although the early Republican platform referenced values unconnected to families, when Republicans did connect values to family (first in 1924), they did so again by referencing nation and common national ideals—for instance, they condemned "international traffic of women and children" as a "*universal* concern . . . affecting public health and morals"[26] and made reference to the national importance of preserving women's reproductive health.[27]

On the other hand, Democratic family values were organic and traditional, more focused on preserving and reproducing traditional families and values of white supremacy. For instance, Democrats vehemently opposed "amalgamation," the mixture of races, in repeated planks that stressed the problem with "Asiatic" immigration, arguing that "Asiatic immigrants . . . can not be amalgamated with our population, or whose presence among us would raise a race issue."[28] Democratic platforms also included planks demanding "the extermination of polygamy" and supporting legislation regulating the labor conditions of women, to maintain "the decency, comfort, and health" of "the mothers of our race."[29]

In sum, in the early twentieth century, family was mostly incidental to the agenda of the national parties and was invoked indirectly: primarily as the context for the well-being of children. Social progressives, also known as "child savers," were child focused, and family matters, family material, and cultural contexts were still within local or state authority. Republicans first and then Democrats began to see an increasing role for the national state on behalf of families, insofar as they considered it in the national interest to protect children as its future citizens. When the parties did address family in their platforms, they did so primarily through address of their economic conditions and less so through a focus on their values, although these were an important subtext.

However, the parties in this early period also engaged with family in distinctive ways. Republicans were more apt to embrace the Hearth family approach, consonant with their nationalistic state-building agenda. Democrats were instead more willing to use the national state to pursue a valuational family focus, particularly in regard to maintaining white family supremacy. Democratic platforms demonstrated more parochial values of white supremacy and social traditionalism in their family pledges, whereas Republican platforms referenced more macro, nationalistic, or patriotic values.

As the country moved into the Depression and the midcentury, the economic Hearth family approach increasingly gained leverage, engaging the two parties more and involving the national state still further. The family values Soul approach then underwent a fundamental transformation: cementing a new home within the Republican Party, utilized in opposition to the centralizing New Deal state and its unprecedented intervention into the economy.

Midcentury (1936–1964): Greater Convergence and Rising Salience of the Hearth Approach

The Great Depression was a transformative event. It directed the attention of the parties to the plight of impoverished lives and conditions as never before.[30] The widespread deprivation, hunger, and unemployment were front and center in the elections of the 1930s. As the economic collapse had occurred on the watch of Herbert Hoover's Republican administration, the Democratic Party was swept to victory in 1932. In that campaign, however,

Democrats did not pledge a bold new agenda but continued to embrace the constitutional traditionalism and parochialism of their previous platforms, supporting programs of unemployment and old-age insurance only under state laws and still promising "the removal of government from all fields of private enterprise except where necessary."[31] Preoccupied with lambasting Republican economic policies, the Democratic platform in 1932 made only a single reference to family, in the usual plank on veterans' family pensions.

By 1936, however, the party had fundamentally altered its ideology. Its platform now offered a new, expanded vision of the national state and its engagement with family. "Protection of family and home" became a central ideal of New Deal welfarist pledges and was elevated to top a list of three "inescapable obligations" of "a government in a modern civilization."[32] Several new economic assistance and contributory insurance programs such as savings and investment, old-age insurance and social security programs, consumer protection, family health programs, and housing assistance were promised by Democrats as part of their newfound national responsibility to the family.[33] Democrats went from devoting merely one pledge in 1932 to invoking family in 12.6 percent of their platform in 1936. They also vowed to seek constitutional amendments, if need be, to "clarify" the reconfigured nation-state's obligations and responsibilities, now berating the Republican platform for its narrow focus, which, they said, "propose[s] to meet many pressing *national* problems solely by action of the separate States."[34]

The increased Democratic attention to family also coincided with the New Deal coalition's emphasis on "*humanizing* the policies of the Federal Government."[35] Family material well-being, the Hearth family focus, was now front and center of New Deal Democratic ideology. Family was no longer seen in a piecemeal fashion, as a collective category of certain groups who were the real subject of their pledges, for example, pledges to families of laborers/workers or of veterans. Instead, Democratic programs were now more universally family centered, targeting family as a more universal context for experiencing human vulnerability and thus promising to boost *family* material assets and/or constructing family's "safety net."

The Republican response to the Great Depression reflected the party's new commitment to antistatism, begun before the economic collapse. Starting in 1928, the Republican Party had veered away from its previous statist, nation-centered ideology and began to embrace, then as now, an ideology of "neoliberalism" that focused on the individual and free-market capitalism and was hostile to the national state.[36] In their 1924 and 1928 platforms, Republicans thus asserted "private initiative" and "self-reliance" as cherished values, fundamental to the "prosperity of the American nation," and mandated limited (national) government intervention into the affairs of business and the states.[37]

Also, by the 1920s, Republicans shifted from their previous Gilded Age/Progressive Era focus on macro industry and big business to embrace more local, small business. In so doing, they combined capitalist, free enterprise values now with a localism, previously absent in their ideology. They promised to "stand against all attempts to put the government into business"[38] and "deplored" efforts by "the Federal Government [to] move into the field of state activities," claiming, "it weakens the sense of initiative and creates a feeling of dependence which is unhealthy and unfortunate for the whole body politic."[39] Within their new market-centered ideology, "private initiative" and "self-reliance" were individual values, central to both free markets and local government.

By placing their faith in the individual rather than government, Republicans in the Depression and midcentury eras soon began to assert (individualist) values and behavior as policy solutions rather than (nationalistic, government) material help or benefits. Despite persisting economic deprivation, the party steadfastly committed to the conviction that "the fate of the nation will depend, not so much on the wisdom and power of government, as on the character and virtue, self-reliance, industry and thrift of the people."[40]

Family did not play a significant role in the emerging Republican neoliberal values agenda of the midcentury. Whereas Democrats increased sixfold their pledges to families in 1936, Republican platforms through the 1930s and 1940s only marginally increased reference to families: from 2 percent to only about 4 to 5 percent of all their pledges. Nevertheless, Republican platforms through the 1950s also accepted the Hearth family approach to an extent, devoting some pledges to the provision of family economic security. In planks often entitled "Security," Republicans promised economic assistance to families in familial situations such as maternity and child health,[41] public assistance of dependent children,[42] and in the provision of low-cost and low-rent housing.[43] Both parties acknowledged the family's changing needs in light of wars (World War II, the Cold War) as creating further national state obligations.[44] Since 1936, Republican platforms also have promised their own safety net programs, cautiously admitting "society has an obligation to promote the security of the people, by affording some measure of involuntary unemployment and dependency in old age."[45] Republicans circumscribed that commitment to family economic security within their prevailing paradigm of individual self-initiative and free-market values, asserting that these programs would only "supplement . . . the productive ability of free American labor, industry, and agriculture."

Republicans also began to derive values from a special class of families—*farm families*—and asserted the achievement of these families' well-being as a "prime national purpose."[46] In the case of farm families, Republicans pledged much economic assistance and material benefits: farm subsidies, commodity loans, farm credit, crop research services, development of rural roads, and rural electrification services were promised in order, they said, to "make life more attractive on the family type farm."[47] When it came to farm families, seen as "traditional to American life" and as upholding cherished neoliberal values of self-sufficiency, self-regulation, and personal responsibility, Republican platforms thus incorporated the Hearth family approach, and the economic security of these select families was presented as a legitimate national state obligation. In a somewhat paradoxical fashion, they directed their programmatic promises at increasing the autonomy of farm families, strongly condemning Democratic production controls and "extensive . . . bureaucratic interference,"[48] which "limit[s] by coercive methods the farmer's control over his own farm."[49]

Thus, in the Depression and midcentury eras, the yeoman farm family was the first to be extolled by Republicans as a traditional, iconic, "American values" family inasmuch as it displayed free-market values of self-sufficiency and autonomy. In this way, economics-focused family pledges also began to promote neoliberal values, intertwining, for the first time, the Hearth and Soul family approaches within partisan (Republican) agenda and presaging a dynamic soon to come. On their part, Democratic platforms, much like the Republican ones in the Progressive Era, did not address family values but concentrated on addressing bare economic need, eschewing the Soul frame for the Hearth.[50] "Family need" was a prominent theme running through Democratic platforms of the 1950s, serving as the premise for multiple promises of state-provided material help, such as through the Food Lunch and Food Stamp programs[51] and numerous child welfare programs and services.[52] In this way, Democrats after the Depression and after World War II revived the earlier social-progressive creed that obligated the national state to achieving material family well-being, the Hearth ideal.

In sum, in the midcentury decades of the 1930s, 1940s, and 1950s, family came to slowly inform party competition and political development in new ways. Under the pall of the Great Depression and led by the New Deal Liberal-Labor Democrats, the economic security of families was elevated in the parties' agenda, now viewed as an "inescapable obligation" of the modern national state. Policy attention to family was no longer confined to "special" family categories, such as the families of veterans, workers' families, or immigrant families; instead, parties began to assert national state responsibility for a safety net for family as a more universal category. Democrats approached family as an economic distributional unit, a way to classify, direct, and target specific national programs to families based on their material need or income but also as the collective material context of the experience of human vulnerability.

Republicans at this time, more resembling Democrats of the earlier Progressive Era, were less committed to the economic family ideal as a lasting obligation on the national state. Instead, they circumscribed these pledges to their support of free markets and associated values such as private initiative and self-reliance, harnessing individualist market-based values to oppose the expansion of the national state. Although families remained incidental to Republicans' emerging neoliberal agenda, in pledges aimed at protecting the autonomy of the yeoman farm family, they began to construct neoliberal *family* values. The values of self-reliance and free enterprise were asserted as traditional American values, part of the "American method" to resolve all economic and social problems, and gained some traction with the onset of the Cold War and the battle against communism in the 1950s. In this way, family began to gain Republican attention as the potential locus of valuational, antistatist, market-based solutions to national and international problems.

The 1960s: Expansion of the Hearth Approach

Through the 1960s, Democrats continually promised to provide "a better life for all families," steadily pushing the bounds of national state obligations and its machinery to include more economic needs of families and individuals. In their 1956 platform, Democrats had made the first of many pledges to the elimination of poverty, avowing to increase all family incomes, especially of those earning the least.[53] In 1960, they went further, pledging to the "Economic Bill of Rights which Franklin Roosevelt wrote into our national conscience [in 1944]," many of which provided for family (not just individual) material welfare: promising "the right to earn a minimum wage sufficient for families basic needs (clothing, shelter, recreation)"; the right of a farmer to "give him and his family a decent living"; and "the right of every family to a decent home."[54]

Low-income families, in particular, received heightened attention, and the party pledged expanded programmatic assistance to them in the form of housing, city revitalization and slum clearance, public assistance benefits, community programs, and so on. To this end, Democrats called for further expansion of the national state, condemning "the present inequitable, under-financed hodgepodge [of] state (welfare) plans."[55] Republican platforms in the 1960s also addressed families' material well-being, particularly in the case of low-income families.[56] They pledged support for special education programs for poor preschool children,[57] help to low-income farm families,[58] and housing programs for low-income families.[59] Like Democrats, they too began to address poverty as a scourge capable of directed policy elimination, making references (albeit in a more subdued tone) to "our crusade against poverty" and to "conquering disease, poverty and grinding physical demands."[60]

Republicans, however, also continued to oppose the Democratic expansion of the national state on the grounds of free-market values and principles. In their pledges to address human needs and assist low-income families, they relied on monetary and fiscal policies and privatization, rather than only entitlement programs and bureaucracies. In the case of housing for lower-income families, they proposed a system of economic incentives to attract private industry to the low-cost housing market.[61] They condemned the Kennedy-Johnson administration for having "refused to take practical free enterprise measures to help the poor" and vehemently opposed the Democratic war on poverty insofar as it "would dangerously centralize Federal controls and bypass effective state, local and private programs."[62] Republican platforms thus did not elevate family economic need to the level of a *right* obligating the national state but addressed it more as a matter of compassion, repeatedly stating that "there are many things a free government cannot do for its people as they can do them [and] [t]here are some things no government should promise or attempt to do."[63] Despite these prevailing differences over the national state, in the long period from the New Deal through the Great Society, both parties increasingly converged in pursuing a Hearth family approach, focusing on a family's economic security as an important policy concern.

At the same time, Republican platforms—much more than Democratic ones—continued to also highlight market-based values. Initially, the Republican Party had embraced such values wholly as centered on the individual, and family was incidental to this focus. In the 1960s, this began to change. Republican platforms began their long turn toward a Soul *family* approach, now connecting "family" to free-market "values" first in planks on poor families and welfare reform. In planks on juvenile delinquency, the Republican Party began to call for federal programs to "strengthen family life."[64] The party also openly condemned Democratic welfare programs not only on the usual grounds that they created "debilitating dependence which erodes self-respect" but now also that the programs "discourag[ed] *family* unity and responsibility."[65] By 1968, the Republican Party was calling for revision of existing welfare programs to "encourage and protect strong family units."[66] It was on planks regarding welfare and the poor that the party first experimented with and developed what was to become a durable Soul family approach, crystallizing their broad valuational approach with a new focus on the family, connecting social traditionalist values such as family strength and stability to neoliberal, free enterprise values. The fact that the Republican Soul family approach was first politicized in welfare policy as a central ground to limit state involvement underscores the strongly uneven and punitive character of that approach that continued to apply to exclude certain categories of families from programs and benefits even while it created other programs to enhance the rights and autonomy of other kinds of families.

For its part, the Democratic Party too began to develop its own set of values in the 1960s, in this case incorporating values to extend material benefits to more families than ever before. Values of personal dignity, inclusion, and equity permeated its platforms and were increasingly applied to assert the inclusion of (economically) disadvantaged and vulnerable families. With the growing prosperity of the 1960s, the 1964 Democratic platform stressed the "common good" principle by entitling the platform "One Nation, One People." In that platform, Democrats asserted that the well-being of each American depends on the prosperity and (economic) well-being of all.[67] The party thus continued and expanded its focus on the poor and disadvantaged, condemning "the inequity and waste of poverty" and asserting that its national purpose was not only to "continue the expansion of the American economy" but also to "exten[d] the benefits of this growth and prosperity to those who have not fully shared in them."[68]

Equity, equal protection, and inclusion of marginalized families permeated Democratic platforms of the 1960s, where they asserted the ongoing necessity of federal programs in order "to assure that every American, of every race, in every region, truly shares in the benefits of economic progress."[69] The party thus opposed state eligibility restrictions, which denied assistance to children of unemployed parents or those that prohibited all assistance when the father was in the home; sought repeal of the "arbitrary limit" on the number of children who could receive assistance; and opposed the provision requiring mothers of young children to work in order for children to be eligible for aid.[70] The party also pledged a revamping of federal taxes "to make them more equitable as between rich and poor and as among people with the same income and family responsibilities."[71]

Thus, in the 1960s, both Republicans and Democrats began to increasingly invoke values in their pledges to American families. Democrats stressed secular-humanist values such as "inclusion" or "equal protection"/"equal access" and "personal dignity or fulfillment" in their promises for enhanced Hearth family policies. They did not formulate a valuational Soul family ideal distinct from material security but instead asserted the valuational structure underlying their economic approach. Republicans, on the other hand, were beginning to formulate a wholly noneconomic Soul family ideal: the "traditional family" as a fundamentally moral and valuational unit, assembling a valuational policy agenda that began to combine ideational elements of both a neoliberal and a social traditional cast. This approach would soon come to permeate and challenge the very essence of the long-dominant economic family approach, championed by New Deal Liberal-Labor Democrats.

Late Century to the Present, 1968–2012: Invigorated Soul Family Ideal and Enhanced Polarization

The year 1968 marked a decisive turn in partisan politics, with far-reaching effects on family political development. In the midst of the turbulent 1960s and 1970s, the tight grasp of the postwar Democratic Coalition over national politics began to loosen, making way for a shift in policy—away from economic security toward values and cultural battles.

Following riots at their National Convention in Chicago in 1968, Democrats adopted a series of changes to their nomination and convention rules, accommodating cultural progressives into their ranks and ensuring significant change to the party's ideology. In 1972, the Democratic platform avowed an agenda that was more attentive to values and postmaterial concerns than merely economic redistribution. The party described three things that "people want" as an interplay between secular-humanist values and material needs: "They want a personal life that makes us all feel that life is worth living," "a social environment whose institutions promote the good of all," and "an opportunity to achieve their aspirations and their dreams for themselves and their children."[72] This was a far cry from the agenda contained in the Economic Bill of Rights to which Democrats had long pledged, in which they had asserted hard economic rights, concerned only with a family's material life, such as "the right to earn a minimum wage," "the right of every famer . . . to earn a decent living," and the "right to a decent home."[73]

Through the 1970s and 1980s, Democratic platforms, however, continued to emphasize the postwar Hearth focus on family economics, attributing family change and "disintegrating families" not to changing cultural values or family norms but to disadvantageous economic conditions, such as poverty and unemployment. In their family pledges, they promised to hold families together by "provid[ing] the help a family needs to survive a crisis together."[74] Still concerned that "prosperity will not be evenly distributed among regions and communities," they pledged "special efforts to help families in economic transition who are faced with loss of homes, health benefits, and pensions."[75] In their family pledges, Democratic platforms expanded and made explicit their postwar commitment to values of equality, fairness, and inclusion underpinning their economic Hearth policy approach rather than develop anew their own valuational Soul family one.

Starting in 1976, the Republican Party on its part thoroughly revised its platform ideology and welded Judeo-Christian constructions of family values more centrally onto its neoliberal approach of free markets and private initiative.[76] In a large plank entitled "American Family," the Republican Party in that year asserted that "families must continue to be the foundation of our nation" and emphasized its role in preserving a traditional (social and economic) valuational order: "Families—not government programs—are the best way to make sure . . . our cultural and spiritual heritages are perpetuated, our laws are observed and our values are preserved."[77] As part of the pledge to create a "hospitable environment for family life," the Republican platform committed to several policy positions regarding taxation, economic policies, education, employment, reproductive rights, and welfare. The preservation of the nuclear (heterosexual) family emerged as a central organizing feature for many Republican social and economic policies.[78]

In 1980, the Republican platform used the rejuvenated Soul family ideal to launch its strongest repudiation yet of the postwar Democratic agenda. Family and its (independent social and economic) values were declared as "fundamental to the order and progress of our Republic."[79] The platform asserted that "all domestic policies, from child care and schooling to social security and the tax code, must be formulated with the family in mind."[80] In the immediate postwar period, free market–based Republican family values such as self-reliance, found in pledges on the family farm, were directed at *opposing* the liberal administrative state. However, starting in 1976, Republican platforms thereafter made the preservation of "the traditional family" and "traditional family values" a *positive* goal of public policy requiring not only the dismantling of existing Democratic programs but also the *creation* of new programs, to enhance and support traditional families in perpetuating traditional social-moral values.

Regardless of substantive differences in partisan family values, the difference over the relative role and *extent* of values (as major or minor) in defining the parties' late twentieth-century approach to families is evident from the extent to which both addressed values in their family pledges. Starting in 1976, Republicans far outpaced Democrats in their references to values in their platforms (Figure 7). Democratic platforms embraced values less and with greater inconsistency in their family pledges. Although Democrats invoked values more in family planks in 1972, under the influence of the New Left during the McGovern election, this did not result in a durable shift toward a Democratic (secular) valuational family approach. Instead, Democratic family pledges in the 1980s were much less preoccupied with values than their Republican counterparts. Values then began to feature more prominently in Democratic family pledges in the 1990s, falling in 2004, only to rebound during the elections of Barack Obama in 2008 and 2012.

In terms of substantive differences, each party turned to family to highlight its own social vision. Republican family pledges sought to restore a conservative social order, consistently invoking neoliberal-traditional values of *strong family life, faith/traditional moral values, family self-determination*, and *self-reliance* (Figure 8). On the other hand, the Democratic Party in its family pledges engendered a more progressive social order by repeatedly making reference to secular-humanist values of *diversity, equal protection, fairness*, the pursuit of *personal fulfillment*, and *individual self-determination*.[81]

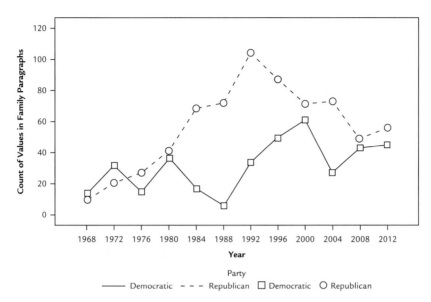

Figure 7. Sum of values invoked in family paragraphs, Democratic and Republican platforms, 1968–2012. Data compiled by author.

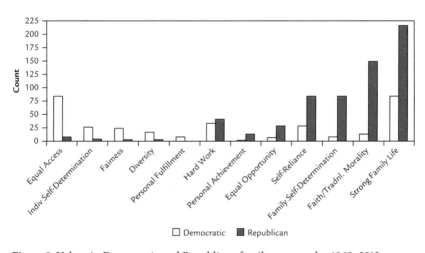

Figure 8. Values in Democratic and Republican family paragraphs, 1968–2012.

There were commonalties too, evidencing greater cross-party appeal of certain (Republican) values. First, the value of *hard work* was highlighted initially only in Republican planks on welfare reform but has since been embraced by the Democratic Party. Starting in 1992, Democratic platforms also began to tie eligibility for numerous social programs to work. Families "who work hard and play by the rules," they said, were entitled to the American Dream and to their share of the American pie.[82] As proxies embodying neoliberal qualities of hard work, self-reliance, and personal responsibility, "working" families now became the central focus of Democratic social policies, as opposed to poor families in a state of need. Democratic platforms embraced welfare reform, pledging "to make work and responsibility the law of the land."[83] The adoption of conservative neoliberal values, such as hard work, qualified but did not replace the Democratic focus on (national) state-provided family economic assistance. Their platforms continued to affirm the party's commitment to "match parents' responsibility to work with the real opportunity to do so, by making sure parents can get the health care, child care, and transportation they need."[84]

Moreover, Democratic family pledges in the 1990s also began to advocate the GOP's late twentieth-century value of parental responsibility (in addition to, but not instead of, state responsibility).[85] In its preamble, the 1992 Democratic platform called for a "Revolution of 1992," committing the party to a "new social contract . . . a way beyond the old approaches," which it described as putting "government back on the side of citizens who play by the rules" and "abandoning the something-for-nothing ethic of the last decade."[86] Democratic platforms through the 1990s and 2000s repeatedly directed redistributionist policies, such as increased minimum wage, child credit extensions, and earned income tax credits only to "parents who . . . take the responsibility to work full-time."[87] Like Republicans, Democrats characterized the failure of the AFDC welfare system as undermining values of "work, family, and personal responsibility," aiming assistance now to help only "[those] people who want to help themselves and their children."[88] Democrats in the 1990s thus, more than ever, embraced culturally conservative family values such as personal responsibility and strong family life (Figure 9).

In the twenty-first century, however, Democrats eschewed these conservative traditional family values and refocused their family pledges on underlying secular-humanist values: equity, fairness, self-determination, fulfillment, and choice. Democrats once again highlighted family "economic

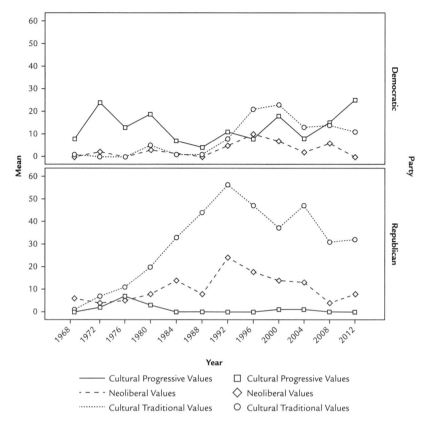

Figure 9. Types of values in family paragraphs, Democratic and Republican platforms, 1968–2012.

security" at the center of their agenda, now pledging to restore values of opportunity and fair and equal access "for everyone who works hard and plays by the rules."[89] By using a language of redistributionist values far more pervasively than in other eras, Democrats now continue to highlight the valuational structure of their own Hearth family approach while avoiding an approach that is centered on more independent, traditional, market-based values. Yet, as if to counter Republicans' "traditional family values," Democrats express the underlying (secular) values of their Hearth approach with greater alacrity and frequency than in previous eras (see Figure 7).

In the twenty-first century, Republicans, in contrast, continue to use family to stress their late twentieth-century Soul approach, focusing first on the values and nonmaterial qualities of families in their pledges. In its 2012 platform, the Republican Party extolled the private valuational function of the "American family" and reaffirmed its 1980 assertion that a family's "daily (values) lessons" such as "cooperation, patience, mutual respect, responsibility and self-reliance" are "fundamental to the order and progress of our Republic."[90] In many ways, the party, in its 2012 platform, reasserted its 1980 family approach, reasserting a free-market values initiative instead of its 1990s, Christian-dominated, traditional (religious) family values. Avowing to "Renew American Values" "to build healthy families, great schools, and neighborhoods," the platform reemphasized family values such as autonomy and self-reliance. In so doing, the Republican Party moved back to its market-based antistatist center of gravity, less concerned with religious moralism. In 2008 and 2012, the party invoked family and described "strong family life" in terms of free enterprise, not religious, values of "responsibility" and "self-reliance."[91] Yet for Republicans, family continues to be the repository of essentially *private* values, a means to oppose redistribution, such that preserving family values continues to frame much of their social policy agenda.

Family in Partisan Legislative Behavior: Progressive, Postwar, and Late-Century Eras

Developments in partisan family ideologies across the twentieth century were not reflected in the parties' national platforms alone but permeated down to the legislative behavior of members in Congress. An analysis of the kinds of family-related bills sponsored and/or cosponsored by members of Congress reveals the far-reaching impact of shifting family ideologies on individual partisans' legislative behavior and policy framing through time.

Bill sponsorship and cosponsorship are similar in important ways to party platforms. As political scientist Christina Wolbretcht writes, both "represent positions with which an individual or party wishes to be identified, even if in neither case does the member or party necessarily follow through by devoting energy or resources to making the bill or pledge a reality."[92] Unlike platforms, however, congressional data such as bills sponsored and/or cosponsored can be traced to individual members, allowing analysis of how much the ideological positions contained in national party platforms trickle down or are mirrored by individual members and their personal ideologies.[93] Moreover, as representations of ideological positions, sponsored and cosponsored bills have an advantage over other forms of legislative data such as roll call votes in that they are much more extensive. Numerous bills do not make it to the roll call stage, many are introduced but only a few are reported out to the floor by committees, and still others are killed through a variety of procedural maneuvers that may require unrecorded voice, not roll call, votes.[94]

For the three significant periods of family political development as identified through platform analysis in the previous section—Progressive (1899–1920), postwar (1946–1954), and late century (1989–2004)—2,004 family bills were identified and coded.[95] In all three periods, legislators introduced disproportionately more economics-centered Hearth bills than Soul ones, with this disparity being most apparent in the post–World War II era.

In the postwar period, almost all family bills (96.7 percent) had an economic Hearth focus, much more than the 86.4 percent or the 60.9 percent of family bills in the Progressive and late twentieth-century periods, respectively. A large proportion of family bills following World War II were concerned with the welfare of dependents of returning and fallen veterans and proposed expanded housing, educational, social security, insurance, and pension benefits for them. Postwar legislators also used an economics-focused Hearth approach in family bills to liberalize immigration and citizenship, provide for the admission and naturalization of war brides and families of war veterans, and, when addressing the growing phenomenon of women in the workforce, provide tax and social security changes to accommodate them and their families.

In contrast to the economics-dominated postwar period, in both the Progressive and late twentieth-century periods, congressional members also sponsored sizable proportions of bills that focused on family values (the Soul approach). In the Progressive Era, members sponsored several Soul-focused family bills in the 61st, 62nd, and 63rd Congresses (1909 to 1914; 39 percent, 20 percent, and 16 percent of all bills examined, respectively). Many of these bills were directed at preserving the sanctity, values, and morality of the white family structure, for instance, by condemning and criminalizing white slave traffic and intermarriage.[96] By the end of the first decade of the twentieth century, however, legislators began to introduce larger proportions of bills that had a Hearth focus: on average, seventeen Hearth-focused family bills were introduced for each Congress from 1899 to 1909, and this number rose to approximately thirty per Congress during the second Progressive decade, from 1910 to 1920. Members of Congress used the Hearth economic approach in veterans' pension bills—to provide relief to their widows, children, and dependents—also invoking family economics to call for regulation of marriage/divorce, care of abandoned children, provision of public lands/homesteads to families, and child support, many of which were not mentioned in party platforms at the time.

The late twentieth-century period stands apart in its unprecedented proportion of Soul family values bills, particularly during the 104th (1994–1995) and 105th (1996–1997) Congresses, even though economics-focused bills continued to otherwise prevail. During the Contract with America Congresses (104th and 105th Congresses), for the first time, legislators sponsored *more* Soul family bills, even exceeding the proportion of Hearth bills, a phenomenon that remained unmatched in any of the other congresses investigated.[97]

Moreover, in this more recent period, many more legislators clustered their support through cosponsorship around valuational Soul bills, evidencing the increased political salience of family values following the Republican takeover of the House in 1994. Of the 1,009 family bills examined in the period from 1989 to 2004, almost identical proportions of Hearth and Soul bills were cosponsored.[98] However, in the period following the 104th Congress, Soul bills began to attract *more* cosponsors (32.2 cosponsors per Soul bill) than Hearth ones (22.9 cosponsors).[99]

Thus, the late twentieth-century period is distinctive to family political development not only in terms of the increased proportion of Soul bills (despite the ongoing higher proportion of Hearth bills) but also because many more legislators began to attach their names, in larger numbers, to Soul family values bills rather than to Hearth ones. This development was put into play, beginning with the 104th Contract with America Congress in 1995 (Figure 10).

In terms of patterns of partisanship, the Progressive and late twentieth-century periods resemble each other in contrast to the postwar era. In these two periods, *party affiliation* of the legislator (as Democratic [coded as 0] or Republican [coded as 1]) was strongly correlated with the *kinds of family bills* he or she introduced (as Hearth [1] or Soul [0] (see Table 2).

Party attachment to *kind* of family bill also demonstrates a clear reversal in party family ideologies through the twentieth century. Whereas more Republicans sponsored Hearth bills in the Progressive Era, by the late twentieth-century period, more Republicans introduced bills with a Soul focus.[100] In the Progressive Era, the majority of Soul family bills (57.4 percent) introduced was sponsored by Democrats, while the majority of Hearth

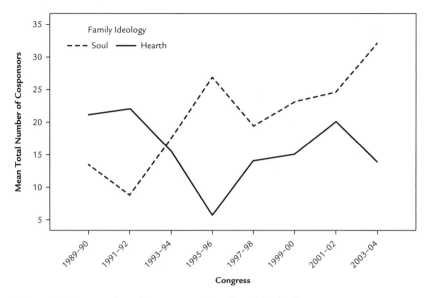

Figure 10. Mean number of cosponsors, Hearth and Soul bills, 1989–2004.

family bills (69.7 percent) was introduced by Republicans.[101] By the late twentieth century, however, Republicans introduced the vast majority of Soul bills (80.5 percent), and Democrats introduced many more Hearth ones (68.7 percent).

The increasing polarization in Hearth and Soul family ideologies is clearly evidenced in cosponsorship patterns as well. An average 17.1 percent of the congressional Republican delegation cosponsored a Soul family values bill in the late twentieth century compared to only 3.29 percent of the Democratic delegation.[102] In contrast, an average 12.8 percent of the congressional Democratic delegation cosponsored a Hearth family economics bill in contrast to 4.3 percent of the Republican contingent. For Republicans in Congress, cosponsorship percentage and Soul family bills bore a statistically significant relationship (at the .05 level) starting from the 104th Congress (1995–1996) through to the last Congress examined (the 108th [2003–2004]).[103] This was so for Democrats starting in the 105th Congress, when the size (percentage) of Democrats cosponsoring a bill and its Hearth ideology became statistically significant (at the .05 level). At this time, partisanship and the kind of family bill introduced (its ideology) thus became much more strongly correlated than ever before.

Table 2. Correlation Between Ideology of Family Bill and Party Membership
of Sponsor

Era	Pearson Correlation	Significance (Two-Tailed)	N
Progressive (1899–1920)	.197[a]	.000	583
Postwar (1945–1954)	−.072	.122	457
Contemporary (1989–2004)	−.495[a]	.000	723

[a] Correlation is significant at the .01 level, two-tailed.

In sum, whether in the kinds of family bills sponsored or the extent and
content of bills cosponsored, since the 104th Congress, party affiliation has
significantly divided Congress members in their family-related legislative
behavior. Republican victory in the election of 1994 was followed by a dramatic overall increase in the proportion of Soul family values bills introduced in Congress; this coincided with the sharp rise in the percentage of the
Republican delegation that began to cosponsor Soul bills. Among Democrats,
while the relationship between cosponsorship percentage and bills' family
ideology was *not* significant in the 104th Congress, since then—starting
from the 105th Congress—this relationship has become statistically significant, with significantly greater proportions of Democrats sponsoring Hearth
family economics bills. Legislative behavior on family-related bills thus
came to be strongly correlated with family ideology for both parties following the Republican takeover of the House in the mid-1990s.

Conclusion

There have been three historical periods marking partisan family development: the Progressive Era, in which Republicans embraced a Hearth family
economic ideology and Democrats were more aligned to the Soul family values approach; a midcentury, post–World War II period in which the Hearth
ideology emerged as clearly dominant across both parties; and finally, the
late twentieth-century period, when the Republican Party championed the
Soul family ideology as never before. The period since the 104th Congress is
especially significant because of the strong partisan character evidenced in
the introduction and cosponsorship of Hearth and Soul family bills since

then. Sponsorship and cosponsorship of Hearth bills were now much more strongly correlated with Democratic members of Congress, while bills espousing the Soul family values approach were much more correlated with Republicans. The polarization in family ideology, as evidenced in bill sponsor/cosponsorship data as well as party platforms, is thus both a recent phenomenon as well as one reminiscent of an earlier, albeit more muted, period at the start of the twentieth century.

This chapter's assembly of the historical development of the two parties' family ideologies over time is important for at least three reasons. First, unlike issues of race or gender, the parties' shifting (and reversed) position on the family has gone largely unnoticed in political science literature, and the description and classification of this empirical phenomenon are therefore necessary and worthwhile. Second, this assembly situates the more recent partisan focus on the American family within a larger historical frame, demonstrating that the two parties have long relied on family economics and values as discursive frameworks to address and approach family in policy. Third, the chapter also reveals specific dynamics that engender empirical puzzles: Why did family burst into political significance in the late twentieth century? Why did the Soul ideal gain unprecedented political traction in the late twentieth century despite being unable to gain a strong foothold previously? More generally, why have the parties framed and adopted their approaches to family differently in different eras?

The phenomenon of partisan family ideational development illustrates broad mechanisms in the dialectical nature of party ideologies themselves. The historical development of family party development is thus also important in that it begs investigation into the precise dynamics that shape the emergence of distinct party family ideologies—why the parties separate or converge on family. By so doing, it is possible to address the larger question of why parties adopt the ideologies and positions that they do and identify the conditions and contexts in which parties change and sometimes reverse their ideologies. The next three chapters do this. As in-depth case studies, they reveal the contexts and conditions under which Democrats and Republicans formed their family ideals in the Progressive, post–World War II, and late twentieth-century periods. Cumulatively, the chapters demonstrate the ongoing relation between state and society as the parties interact with demographic family change and shifts in lived families' experiences and attempt to translate them into coherent policy ideologies, to attract constituents and gain electoral traction and success.

Chapter 2

The Progressive Era: In the Path
of the Juggernaut

In 1893, ten-year-old Flossie Moore's life changed irrevocably. On the brink of insolvency, her family had been farming on rented land in the Piedmont countryside in North Carolina when her father died unexpectedly at the age of forty-three. Suddenly, her mother found herself in dire circumstances and responsible for eight children whose ages ranged from infancy to nineteen. After harvesting that year's crops and seeking the advice of kin, Mrs. Moore moved her family to the textile mill in Bynum; as Flossie remembered, "there were several of the men that come out and met first, trying to decide what to do. . . . They knew about Bynum, and it was a good little place to live. . . . And of course the cotton mill was running here then. And the ones that was old enough. . . . Well, I went to work at ten years old."[1] So began the Moores' new life as wage laborers in the mills, living in a company house in the mill village, with younger children earning alongside their widowed mother and older siblings. The Moore family experience was similar to that of millions of families in the Progressive Era (1890s to 1920s), caught in the midst of "the juggernaut," the turbulent tide of industrialization that was then engulfing the nation, with families experiencing upheavals and massive change in their struggle to survive and keep afloat.[2]

The structural transformation accompanying the move from a rural, agrarian-based economy to an urban, industrialized one had marked effects on *all* families, not merely those on the brink of destitution. Rising divorce rates, falling birthrates among the so-called better sort of people, the changing position of women, and a revolution in morals caused great alarm,[3] as did rising family poverty, child and adult mortality, and death and disease in urban families.[4] The economic and cultural dislocations accompanying the nation's industrialization were mirrored in the microcosm of family's shifting dynamics.

Family economy moved beyond the household, with several family members now employed in factories, canneries, and textile mills across the nation. Burgeoning labor markets as well as the transitory nature of several establishments meant low and sporadic wages for most working-class fathers. Mothers supplemented the family income either by home work (such as piecework, taking in laundry, boarders) or increasingly through wage labor outside the home, working as domestics and charwomen in private homes, office buildings, or railroad cars or in laundries or garment, textile, or cigar factories.[5] Children often worked—boys as messengers, newsboys, or factory hands and girls in department stores and textile factories. Dangerous and harsh industrial conditions, rising mortality and disability, and crowded urban and unsanitary living conditions all meant that most working-class families could expect to lose at least a few members, adding to the family's economic vulnerability.[6]

More affluent families also underwent transformations. Women began to move out of sheltered Victorian home life; they received higher education in growing numbers and challenged traditional gender roles by joining social clubs, engaging in voluntary and/or professional work, and becoming more politically active.[7] Children were no longer mini-adults; instead, through a variety of social movements—for compulsory schools, playground creation, and child labor regulation—childhood began to be viewed as a separate time of innocence, play, and leisure, distinct from the demands of adulthood.[8] Aided by technological advancements in transportation, fathers often traveled great distances to work and so spent many more hours outside of the home. With fathers now more rigidly associated with breadwinning, childrearing came to be firmly relegated to the sphere of mothers.[9]

Policy changes accompanying these family shifts were embedded within prevailing party politics, which was also in a state of embroilment.[10] The election of 1896 had marked the beginning of the Fourth Party System, in which Republicans were favored nationally but dominated in industrializing northeastern and midwestern states,[11] and Democrats were elected primarily from agrarian states in the South and West.[12] This emerging alignment marked a new era of Republican-dominated party competition, replacing the preceding "state of courts and parties" in which either party could equally hope for victories after every election.[13] As entities with distinct regional bases, political parties by and large channeled sectional interests. The Republican agenda was informed by the northern core's manufacturing interest, and the Democratic agenda was shaped by the southern and western periphery's agrarian interest. These commitments, however, were not rigid; instead, each party's ideology was more an amalgam of various positions, formed from a looser, more shifting coalition of interests than what came to be the norm later and into today.[14]

The political climate in the Progressive period was notably infused with the fervor of reform. Reformist groups decried the excesses and vagaries of the patronage-based political and laissez-faire economic systems and advocated instead widespread civil and social reform. Interest groups were active and attempted to press their agenda on the electorate, Congress, and state legislatures.[15] In a style of politics reminiscent of the late twentieth century, cultural and moral issues roiled a variety of social movements, such as temperance and women's suffrage, regulation of child labor, and prevention of white slavery, among others.[16] Other groups, such as Settlement House activists and the National Consumer League, railed against conditions of widespread economic deprivation—family poverty, low wages, failing health, and workplace casualties.

Social progressivism raised the economic Hearth approach as a viable solution to growing family problems, its appeal not confined to one party but somewhat dispersed across the two.[17] Other cross-party factions invoked Soul family values concerns, emphasizing values such as parental autonomy and the morality of white families, as threatened by increasing immigration and by a more active national state.[18] Despite some notable ideological overlaps across parties, this chapter reveals that even in this initial period of modern American politics, there were emerging partisan-sectional differences in how legislators approached family. More Republicans, from northern and midwestern regions, used the economic lens (the Hearth approach) to frame their family policy agenda, while southern (and some western) Democrats were more apt to use values and cultural qualities (the Soul approach) to craft their own policy visions.[19]

The prevailing strict constitutional division between national and states' powers significantly influenced the development of the two partisan family agendas at this time. It circumscribed the efforts of more liberal Hearth advocates, who attempted to deploy national state machinery in service of family material well-being. Nonetheless, these legislators laid the groundwork for a more full-blown Hearth position that came to define the New

Deal Democratic agenda. The existing constitutional strength of states also engendered a relatively strong Soul position, allowing Soul-leaning legislators to use parochial, localistic family values to resist the interventionism of economic Hearth policies more successfully in the Progressive Era than in later periods.

However, existing constitutional boundaries in the Progressive period did not deter Soul legislators from using family values to also call for *positive* engagement of the national state (much like in the late twentieth century), to preserve and protect certain values of so-called traditional white family structures. The Progressive Era thus not only reveals the antecedents and origins of late twentieth-century Hearth and Soul family policy ideals and approaches but also demonstrates their mutability and nascent flexibility as they came to be deployed by the two parties to further their own agendas.

The chapter examines the characteristics, contexts, and conditions of the emerging family party alignments in the Progressive Era, demonstrating the developing sectional polarities of northern Republican-Hearth and southern Democratic-Soul alignments at this time.[20] The first two sections primarily rely on congressional debates over woman suffrage and miscegenation to assemble legislators' differential conceptions of family, following which the chapter analyzes the policy configurations advanced to instantiate these family conceptions into legislation; the final section turns to the demographic conditions and characteristics of northern and southern families that underpinned the emerging Hearth and Soul family party coalitions, arguing that the partisan embrace of one or the other family frames was strongly tied to differences in the material lives and values of the parties' constituent bases.

Emerging Conceptions of Family, Gender, and State as Seen in Debates over Woman Suffrage

This section unpacks the conceptions of family and gender that were widely debated amid the era's social and political turbulence. How ideational divisions over family and gender interacted to uphold alternative state ideologies is most clearly seen in debates over "woman suffrage," a prominent policy concern of the time. These disagreements would come to be embedded in the emergent national state and serve as the latent ingredients for future partisan battles to follow.

For all members of Congress at the start of the twentieth century, family inhabited a domestic, private sphere that was in many ways distinct from the public one. The prevailing "separate-spheres ideology" divided public and private spheres by gender: women embodied moral qualities, purity, and nurturing abilities associated with the home, while men possessed physical qualities, aggressiveness, and firmness, seen as essential for the public spheres of work and politics.[21] A carryover from the nineteenth century, separate sphere ideals endured in the early twentieth century. However, the traditional separation of male and female gender roles and the exclusivity of their spheres were starting to be strongly challenged, dividing members of Congress accordingly. The more progressive faction applauded new developments in work and family that melded domestic and public spheres, and more conservative delegations opposed them. Underlying legislators' differences over the shifting boundaries between public and private were their strongly embedded ideas of family as foundationally economic and/or valuational.

Progressive members of Congress who supported women's suffrage attacked the traditional separateness of domestic and public spheres by using a predominantly economic family framework. They advocated an intertwined relationship between government, economy, and home, arguing that laws should actively intervene to improve primarily economic and, second, valuational conditions of home life. Senator Robert Owen (D-OK), for instance, approvingly recounted a long list of legislation enacted in Colorado when women were allowed to vote, citing "the most highly perfected school system that any State in the Union has," "laws taking care of defective children, laws punishing those who contributed to the delinquency of a child; laws taking care of the weaker elements of society, of the deaf and dumb, the blind, the insane, the poor; laws beautifying the cities and improving many other conditions of life," along with more values-laden laws, such as those "establishing the curfew to prevent children being exposed to temptation at night," also asserting that "women can not be persuaded to favor the liquor traffic, the white-slave traffic, gambling, or other evils of society."[22]

However, conservative legislators opposed to women's suffrage, distinctively many from the South, warned that the progressive conjoining of hitherto separate spheres would result in the degradation of the domestic sphere and debasing of traditional family values, such as the sanctity of marriage. For instance, Senator Nathan Bryan (D-FL) asserted the higher than average incidence of divorce in all the equal-suffrage states,[23] claiming, "Pretty soon after woman suffrage came, divorce would be as respectable as marriage."[24] These members opposed the political inclusion of women by extolling the virtues of the antisuffragette as "the woman who yet believes that the home and the child are her sphere and that politics and business are the sphere of the man."[25]

In their antisuffrage remarks, conservative southern legislators used a Soul approach to focus policy attention on preserving patriarchy as the dominant family form. The southern patriarchal family structure, they insisted, engendered a "chivalrous attitude" of men, such that women exercised far greater power *indirectly* through men than they would independently. Senator John Williams (D-MS) claimed to speak for "other Senators from the cotton States" when he asserted that "women have more influence with regard to public measures in Mississippi and those States to-day than they have in any suffrage State in this Union." When women "put themselves behind anything in the State of Mississippi," he said, "that thing the men vote for, and the politician who dares oppose it gets defeated by the other men. Let it be prohibition; let it be anything else; if the women of Mississippi say to the men of Mississippi in sufficient tones, so that the men can understand them, 'we want this thing,' the men give it to them."[26] Using racially charged language to impugn the virtue of suffragettes, suffrage opponents claimed that these women looked upon the "indissoluble Christian marriage" as a "slave union" and were seeking to upstage it;[27] this, they warned, would lead to a precipitous decline in male authority, "a state of society where man will not figure except as the father of her child."[28]

For prosuffrage legislators, the conservative emphasis on preserving patriarchal families and hierarchical gender values was an illegitimate, sectional concern, an innate southern "prejudice" against women that must be "overcome." Senator George Chamberlain (D-OR) offered his own personal story as an example of this, recounting how he was born and reared in "a Southern State" and went to the "western country" with "a feeling, which many southern men had of antagonism to the propriety of enfranchising women." Yet, he said, he was able to "overc[o]me the prejudice, which was inborn in me, and which still lurks in the bosom of nearly every southern man, I am sure," and became "an ardent supporter of the doctrine of equal suffrage."[29]

Illustrating the gender liberalism that would come to persist within the Hearth family approach, prosuffrage legislators instead emphasized the desirability of moving toward egalitarian gender ideals. They presented an

egalitarian family view, centered on companionship, nurturing, and affection, instead of on chivalry and hierarchy—a family ideal that could be best
realized, they said, if women were granted suffrage. Senator Everis Hayes (R-
CA), for example, celebrated "the ideal of a home where human nature can
develop to the full," saying, "you who have never enjoyed the privilege of
going to the polls, our most sacred shrine, in company with your mother and
your wife, as I have done, can not realize the supreme pleasure of sharing
with your nearest and dearest the highest of privileges, that of full American citizenship."[30]

Yet, their support for progressive gender relations and more active participation of women in politics did not stop those in favor of suffrage, like
their colleagues on the other side, to continue to view the domestic sphere
as feminine and women as first and foremost mothers. For them too, women's
moral capacities flowed from their *familial* roles, interests, and qualities,
as *mothers, wives, and daughters* and not as independent actors. Far from
being gender neutral, the Hearth family economics approach in the Progressive Era specifically targeted women as mothers and housewives. In
numerous policies for the encouragement of "American" dietary norms, food
and clothes consumption, and family health-related practices, mothers were
seen as central to family behavior, and Hearth policies devised to improve
material family practices were expressly directed at them. In so doing, legislators were echoing the prevailing ideologies of "maternalism" and "civic
housekeeping" advocated by prominent female reformers of the time. Jane
Addams, founder of the Hull House settlement in Chicago, popularized
"civic housekeeping," arguing that a city ought to be conceived as a household
needing continuous housekeeping, cleanliness, and caring to rectify social
problems, tasks for which women were especially suited.[31] Characterized as
"maternalists," female reformers used their position as mothers to seek social reform of primarily Hearth (but some Soul) problems such as increasing poverty, full female citizenship, labor unrest, runaway crime, high levels
of child mortality, and public health issues such as increasing workplace in-
juries and spread of epidemic diseases—all while seeking more egalitarian
gender relations and the political inclusion of women as bureaucrats, admin-
istrators, and voters.[32]

The Soul-aligned conservative faction in Congress, however, viewed such
modern women reformers as women who chose to abandon the hearth and
their domestic responsibilities. For instance, Representative Jerome Donovan had the following exchange with maternalist witness Lillian William-

son, from the National Federation of Women's Clubs, who was testifying before the Committee on Education in favor of Federal Aid for Home Economics. Doubting the need for federal government programs in home economics, Congressman Donovan (D-NY) asked, "How was it that the mothers whom you have so pictured . . . that were the ideal mothers and were the ideal home builders, how was it that they did not have the advantage of these things: and yet that they attained a great strength of attainment which they did as home builders and mothers?" To which Ms. Williamson replied by emphasizing the economic transformations in family lives, saying, "The mother that trained her children 200 years ago had different processes to deal with . . . there was no great number of things that engaged her outside of the home. All the household tasks were in the home." Congressman Donovan used Williamson's words to instead extoll traditional separate-sphere motherhood, saying, "In other words, her life and duties were concentrated upon her home, were they not? She attended to what was her business."[33]

In addition to gender, the debates over women's suffrage also reveal diverging, often sectional, ideologies of state, which were deeply imbricated with the gender and family ideals of the Hearth and Soul family approaches. Illustrating a more conservative ideal of state, conservative legislators opposed to women's suffrage condemned reformers' faith in government as a cure for social ills. One such example can be found in the words of southern Senator Nathan Bryan (D-FL), deriding the position of suffragist Senator Henry Ashurst (D-AZ) in this way: "[According to Ashurst] just so surely as at midnight there is a centrifugal force which in due time will whirl the world into the gladsome presence of the morning, just that surely in the fullness of time will poverty be abolished. Sweatshops, crowded slums, and starving children will be only a horrid memory . . . the extension of the ballot to women will be a helpful influence in assisting to solve this great problem in the future." "Politicians who promised the negroes of the South, immediately after the war, that they, each one, should have 40 acres and a mule," said Senator Bryan, "were pikers alongside the Senator from Arizona."[34] Opposing a redistributionist state, Bryan challenged the support given to the suffrage movement on the basis that such "people have actually believed that the Government will fix the wage they shall receive; that the independent, upstanding citizen, who has heretofore relied upon his own intelligence and brawn and muscle, and asked no favors of the Government or of anybody, will pass away, and, instead, the State will support everybody and will fix the wages by law."[35]

Antisuffrage opposition to government involvement in home involved upholding certain traditional and laissez-faire values over state assistance: parental independence and (male) individual autonomy above all else. In several committee hearings, particularly on regulatory issues such as vaccination and disease control, child labor regulation, compulsory schooling, and the establishment of juvenile courts and other state institutions, witnesses and members of Congress using a Soul family values framework used language reminiscent of late twentieth-century neoliberalism to argue that "no one has such vital interest and concern in the welfare of the child as the parents themselves."[36] Witnesses espousing parental autonomy and responsibility often testified in favor of business and industries. They even testified against federal censorship of the budding motion picture industry, chiding parents for shirking their responsibilities and placing an "impossible undertaking" on the federal government "by having it attempt to look after the proper upbringing of their own and everybody else's children and grandchildren." The federal government, they said, "would not only be required to keep the children from all contamination while the parents allowed them to wander about the community but it would have to come closer home and take up the matter of the wearing of Indian suits by children and the playing with toy pistols and pop guns."[37]

Progressive arguments for intertwined domestic and political spheres among suffrage supporters were part of the emerging social-progressive faith in an interventionist state. These legislators asserted a Hearth family framework insofar as they claimed that the national state had a legitimate responsibility in child (and therefore family) economic welfare, particularly when parents were incapacitated; they used the state's interest in child welfare to justify regulatory measures directed at employers and industry, as well as delinquent parents, and to provide assistance to dependent families, all of which sought to re-create the "ideal of home life" for vulnerable children.[38]

During congressional hearings, the Hearth family economics framework was thus referred to in many more examples of lower-income rather than higher-income families, a large proportion of the former also cited as single-mother families. Moreover, in 23 percent of family examples that focused on family economic conditions, legislators raised family health and living conditions as well as child labor regulation in 19 percent of these cases, women's equality in 10.5 percent of cases, and juvenile institutions such as work homes and orphanages in 9 percent of such Hearth family cases.[39]

Progressive legislators championed enhanced federal government involvement on grounds that unlike individual parents, local communities, and even state governments, the federal government alone could conduct large-scale investigations, gather data, coordinate policy efforts, and thereby stimulate state action on several issues, critical to the welfare of families.[40] Conservative legislators more concerned with family values, such as family self-regulation and parental autonomy, were openly critical of the reformist faith in centralized planning, redistribution, scientific inquiry, and universal standards and instead valued local knowledge and the right of communities to regulate themselves.[41] Illustrating a localism that would come to endure in the Soul family approach, these conservatives argued that local entities such as family, locality, and community played a more important role in real-world social behavior, not national-level policies that were based on artificially universal assumptions of human nature.[42] Twenty-two percent of family examples invoking the Soul family values frame promoted parental rights, 7 percent of these cases advocated for limited government, and 6 percent supported traditional gender protections.

However, when it came to issues of sex, sexuality, and biological reproduction, highlighted in 24 percent of all Soul family cases (the largest bloc of all Soul family examples), conservative legislators promoted *positive* state intervention to preserve traditional family practices. Family sexuality concerns were inextricably bound with anxieties over race. The next section reveals the extent to which the emerging Soul family values approach was preoccupied with questions of sex and race, prompting conservatives to call for *positive* engagement of the national state, a position that ran contrary to their otherwise antistatist and laissez-faire-ist ideology.

Sex and Race—Intermarriage and Other Sexual Questions: A Positive-State Soul Family Approach

For conservatives, family values, not economics or material services, was the rightful focus of policy. White supremacy was central to the traditional family values they sought to uphold and underpinned much of their Soul legislative focus. This was especially evident among legislators from the South. The nineteenth-century South had embraced an organic patriarchal family ideal that was substantively different from the northern, contractual view of domestic relations. The southern family ideal had roots that extended far back into slavery, infusing racial and sexual power dynamics onto the patriarchal authority of male slaveowners over members of their household, free and slave. As historian Peter Bardaglio writes, "The sexual access of slaveholders to their wives and (to their) bondswomen provided the undergirding of patriarchy as a [family] system that shaped both race and gender relations . . . important as the household was as a private institution in the Victorian South, it was even more important as a political institution in the broadest sense: it not only constituted the chief vehicle for the exercise of power in southern society but also served as the foundation of southern public beliefs and values."[43] The political southern family ideal then was an amalgam of southern racial and gender ideals, whose patriarchal values preserved southern (white male) power, a slave-based economy, and a hierarchical social order.

Yet patriarchal authority of the head of household was not considered absolute or universal in the antebellum South or impervious to state intervention. Instead, there existed a localized southern domestic ideology, wherein the authority of patriarchs over their households was subjected to a metaphorical "social peace," an overarching public order that permeated all southern private domestic relations.[44] Within this framework, the state was indispensable in regulating family behavior in defense of the traditional social order. Southern legal historians describe a "strong element of coercion that enforced inclusion in this system. Although everyone had a place, coercion was essential to keep people in their places."[45] They note the "coercive side of state intervention," especially for "poor white and free black families," which continued to prevail despite the eventual introduction of the contractual model of domestic relations into the South in the postbellum period.[46]

In the Progressive Era, several conservative legislators (mostly southern) now presented white supremacy and patriarchy as American family ideals, whose preservation in the face of nonwhite proliferation similarly warranted positive national state intervention. Senator Nathan Bryan (D-FL), for instance, identified "loose morals in the home" as common to nonwhite groups, such as "Asiatics" and "negros," to justify their active political exclusion as American citizens, claiming, "They have one element in common, and that is they have loose morals in the home. They do not know what home life is as we understand it"; instead, he said, "American civilization is what the American home has made it."[47] For such legislators, values defined a home, and American family values were first and foremost racially inscribed: the values of a white (Christian) family. This racialized Soul ideal and its policy preoccupation with preserving traditional family values persisted and developed in policy discussions, extending beyond its original southern home (although it continued to be most prevalent there) to the agrarian West.

Conservative congressmen from western states, for instance, facing large-scale Asian immigration, attacked the marriage practices of immigrant groups as illustrations of their diminished values and there too presented them as threats to American traditional family values.[48] Celebrating marriage as "more than a civil contract," they underscored its Christian white character, valorizing it as a "public institution established by God himself . . . recognized in all Christian and civilized nations . . . essential to the peace, happiness, and well-being of society."[49] These legislators attacked the practice of picture-bride marriages among Japanese farmers, for instance, to advocate for strict policies regulating immigration. Picture-bride marriages were solemnized in Japan between a bride and the picture of a man, the latter residing in the United States and unable to travel abroad without risk to reentry. Legislators using a Soul family approach condemned the practice of marriage sight unseen and its consummation with a surrogate in Japan as abhorrent to the standards of "civilized" white American family morality/values. At other times, legislators highlighted other immigrant/ nonwhite family practices, such as the treatment of wives by husbands, birthing practices, and household division of labor, to emphasize these groups' "dubious" family values as a basis for their active policy exclusion from American political and social life.

Conservative legislators also expressed alarm over changing mores of sexuality in other less racial contexts too, such as in instances of funding of public recreation areas. During the turn of the century, courtship had moved beyond home parlors and parental supervision to dance halls and social clubs for the lesser-affluent, urban, often immigrant families.[50] In a hearing on a D.C. appropriation bill, some congressmen, using a more materialist Hearth lens, viewed government funding of such dancehalls benignly as "reaching a class of our people that are unable to provide for themselves." Others, such as southern Democrat Thomas Sisson from Mississippi, however, were quick to express deep alarm over these "questionable dance halls" because, they said, "girls were not properly supervised," such that "they were no good for them or their community," and vehemently opposed the use of government monies for this purpose.[51]

Yet nowhere was the prevailing Soul concern with sex and white supremacy more visible than in the era's crusade against interracial marriage. Miscegenation was particularly noisome to members from the South who viewed sexual practices as inextricably bound to race and the preservation of white supremacy. By 1909, twenty-eight states and territories had laws proscribing and punishing intermarriage between whites and nonwhites, most often blacks. However, southern congressional delegations were alarmed by what they saw as a growing incidence of intermarriage in cities such as the District of Columbia, where such marriages were not illegal[52]; they also condemned the practice more generally in the permitting states of the North. Starting from the 59th Congress in 1906 and for every Progressive Era Congress examined thereafter (up to the 66th Congress, 1919–1920), southern members introduced antimiscegenation bills for the District of Columbia and occasionally offered constitutional amendments banning the practice of intermarriage.[53] Their remarks on intermarriage and interracial sexuality illustrate the fundamentally racial origins of the Soul family values approach. Like immigration restrictions, here too they sought positive intervention by the national state, actively curtailing and penalizing these practices.

Antimiscegenation legislators, such as Georgia Senator Seaborn Roddenberry (D-GA), consistently emphasized the American-ness of same-race (white) sexuality/marriage and its moral supremacy, claiming that "intermarriage between whites and blacks is repulsive and averse to *every* sentiment of pure American spirit. It is abhorrent and repugnant. It is subversive to social peace. It is destructive of moral supremacy."[54] Legislators from states such as Illinois, which permitted incidences such as the highly publicized intermarriage between "negro pugilist" Jack Johnson and "unfortunate white woman" Lucille Cameron, were urged "in the name of girlhood and womanhood . . . to take action."[55] Failing action by state legislatures, they pointed to purported American sentiment against intermarriage to demand constitutional amendments "prohibiting forever the marriage of whites and negroes."[56]

Members' arguments against intermarriage also display an enduring belief, as a carryover of the organic domestic ideal of the slave South, that reproducing a desired social order is a defining family feature worthy of the highest public attention.[57] Southern delegations advocated for strict laws prohibiting and preventing intermarriage to "let . . . each race know that there is no chance of social equality, no danger of destroying the Caucasian race by mongrelization."[58] For these members, the reproduction of white supremacy and its racially stratified social structure pivoted on the strict regulation of family sexuality. Here active government intervention, through regulatory policies, was considered essential—to restrain tendencies of promiscuity in nonwhite races and sexual lapses among whites. Senator William Milton (D-FL), for instance, warned against the mixing of "the idle rich" who had "exhausted the pleasures of wealth" and now "naturally seek animal pleasure" with the "human animal of mixed race" who is "often exceeding handsome and highly seductive." Unless "restrictive measures are taken," he said, "a saturnalia of vice will here reign . . . and the danger grows."[59]

The southern faction's continued preoccupation with race, sex, and the threat of nonwhite and mixed families to the traditional white patriarchal family structure is evident in the data from committee hearings. As mentioned, the largest bloc of family cases (24 percent) using a Soul family values approach discussed issues of sex, sexuality, and biology. Also, 41.1 percent of all Soul family cases emphasizing values were nonwhite, as opposed to merely 11.8 percent of all Hearth family references that stressed economics. Presaging a politics to come, legislators disproportionately highlighted family values, not family economics, when discussing nonwhite families.

In sum, the immigration and intermarriage debates demonstrate the extent to which the reproduction of white supremacy and a stratified racial-sexual order was a central *family* policy concern, illustrating the racial origins of the Soul family values approach. Constrained sexuality within the (white) family was viewed as a vital *American* family cultural practice that warranted public or government intervention. Thus, in Soul conservative discourse, a family's intimate behavior, marriage, and sex, far more than their economic conditions, were quintessentially "public" insofar as these alone reproduced or threatened white supremacy and the social structures embedding it. Nonwhite families and sexuality were thus disproportionately discussed as Soul family values concerns and much less as targets in need of material Hearth programs.

Among more progressive members of Congress who focused more on families' economic conditions, concern over problematic sexuality was limited to impoverished conditions in which it flourished or its public health implications. For instance, they stressed the need to control "bad reproduction," asserting the national importance of producing a better, healthier American stock.[60] In this period, legislators who preferred the Hearth family economic frame were also racially biased inasmuch as they privileged native-born white American standards of health, fitness, and fertility practices as the universal standard for constructing welfare programs and services.[61] However, their arguments for positive state intervention in these areas were not directed at instating white supremacy but at producing a healthy American population. They thus proposed several policies advocating federal government programs, both welfare and regulatory, to enhance the physical vitality of the population. They called for federal aid for universal physical education in all schools for children from six to eighteen years of age.[62] Health and educational programs for the protection of maternity and infancy as well as the mandate for a federal children's bureau were all presented as part of the evolving Hearth position that the national government had a legitimate interest in family health, including sexual health, as in promoting healthy motherhood and the reproduction of healthy babies.[63]

In sum, the emerging Hearth and Soul family ideologies found in congressional debates and committee hearings invoked a wide range of varied, intertwined, ideational principles—from ideas about gender, race, and sex to family structures and ideas of state. Liberal Hearth advocates highlighted a family's material condition as central, folding their concerns with family values (sexuality and moral family behavior) into this larger frame of family economics and material well-being. On the other hand, another faction— the conservative Soul group—highlighted the (southern) patriarchal white family ideal and its associated values, emphasizing gender and racial traditionalism and a rigid separation between family and state except in the case of sex and marriage, thereby upholding an alternative frame of family values. These emerging differences are summarized in Figure 11.

The next section turns to how these sectional family ideologies impelled coherent policy differences, underscoring the partisanship and sectionalism of their advocates in Congress.

Republican-Hearth and Democratic-Soul Policy Systems

During committee hearings, legislators used family examples to focus policy attention on four broad family policy categories, each encapsulating distinct family qualities.[64] This section assembles the four family policy types and uses them to analyze legislators' policy positions in the Progressive Era; the same family policy typology will be used recurrently in the chapters to come, documenting their changes and evolution across the twentieth century. The four kinds of family policy were the following:

1. Ascription: In one set of policy concerns, in 13.5 percent of family cases, legislators addressed *biological* ("ascriptive") qualities of the family and directed policy attention at family biology and reproduc-

Gender Relations

Common Belief—Gendered spheres: feminine moral/domestic sphere and masculine amoral/political sphere

Central Ideational Dichotomy—
- Hearth ideal: Gender equality
- Soul ideal: Gender hierarchy/paternalism

Associated Policy Dichotomy—
- Hearth ideal: Policies facilitating greater participation of women in politics and in the development of policies
- Soul ideal: Policies protecting the home and preserving the isolation of women from political participation

Family Structure

Common Belief—Classist; ideal family structures both drawn from upper-class (native-born, white) families

Central Ideational Dichotomy—
- Hearth ideal: Egalitarian family structure, focused on the creation of companionship, nurturing and emotional support among family members
- Soul ideal: White patriarchal family structure, focused on the reproduction of stratified social relations

Associated Policy Dichotomy—
- Hearth ideal: Policies recognizing and facilitating greater interrelationship between feminine-domestic and masculine-political spheres
- Soul ideal: Policies preserving traditional family self-regulation and rigid boundaries between domestic and political spheres and exclusion and regulation of nonwhite families

Role of Government and Public Policy vis-à-vis Families

Common Belief—Public policy must sustain and/or encourage idealized family structures and gender relations

Central Ideational Dichotomy—
- Hearth ideal: National interest is paramount; necessitating active government intervention into the family through material assistance, programs, and regulation of unhealthy family practices and material conditions
- Soul ideal: Self-regulation is paramount; necessitating limited government intervention, upholding parental authority and agency. Except in the case of race and sexuality, where positive regulatory state action is necessary.

Associated Policy Dichotomy—
- Hearth ideal—
  Policy target: socio-economic conditions of families, regulating adverse impacts of industrialization
  Policy form: expert-driven, centralized, standardized uniform policies
- Soul ideal—
  Policy target: patriarchal (white) family values, policies preserving and facilitating the continuance of traditional (white) familial practices, particularly vis-à-vis sex, sexuality, and reproduction
  Policy form: localistic, community-based, preservationist policies

Figure 11. Emerging principles of Hearth and Soul family ideological divisions in the Progressive Era, 1900–1920.

tion. This included issues of intermarriage and race, "blood" affiliation or "family lineage" concerns such as in the case of reservation eligibility of Native Americans, and policies pertaining to sex and sexuality.

2. Autonomy: Through a second set of policy concerns, in a comparable 11.9 percent of family cases, members also engaged with policies to focus on *private*, internal qualities of a family, emphasizing its separateness from the national state; these included policies to preserve parental rights and parental choice, limits on government intervention, and traditional gender relations.

3. Regulation: Through a more salient third set of policy questions, raised in 34 percent of all family cases, Congress members targeted forms of family behavior seen as contrary to the success and well-being of the nation. This category invoked the following policy issues: compulsory schooling/education, juvenile institutions for delinquent children, immigration policies and Americanization of foreign families, control of liquor/gambling and of addictive/abusive behavior, marriage registration and divorce, and wives' equality in suffrage/citizenship policies.

4. Welfare: By far the most salient set of policy issues, invoked by members of Congress, in 40.6 percent of all family cases, was social welfare and focused policy discussion on some aspect of the *economic* conditions facing families, raising issues such as health and living conditions of the family, labor/work conditions, housing, child labor, wage policies, and veterans' pensions.

Legislators in their interrogations and remarks during committee hearings thus raised four interrelated yet distinct *public* aspects of family, those to which they directed policy attention; these were (1) family as a unit of biological reproduction, (2) family separateness or autonomy, (3) economic family welfare, and (4) regulation of harmful family behavior. The most highlighted of all, welfare, was squarely economic (Hearth) in its focus on material conditions. Yet other concerns, raised in a quarter of family cases invoking family ascription and autonomy, illustrate an alternative attention to family values (the Soul family approach) at this time. The fourth policy focus, regulating undesirable family practices, encompassed concerns that were mixed, Hearth and Soul: involving attention to a family's discrepant values along with attention to its deprived economic context. These divisions and their categories are summarized in Table 3.

Table 3. Typology of Family Policy, as Assembled from Committee Hearings, 56th–66th Congresses (1900–1920)

Family Quality	Corresponding Policy Issue Illustrated Through Remarks on Family Cases	Policy Category	Policy Approach
Family as biological unit, reproducing extant social structures	(1) Sexuality/reproduction (2) Family lineage (3) Race	Ascription	Soul
Family separateness from the state	(1) Limited government (2) Property/wealth (3) Parental rights (4) Traditional gender relations	Autonomy	Soul
Economic family welfare	(1) Living conditions (2) Child labor (3) Wages (4) Housing (5) Labor conditions	Welfare	Hearth
Undesirable family behavior as harmful to national interest	(1) Compulsory education (2) Juvenile institutions (3) Immigration (4) Americanization (5) Women's equality (6) Uniform marriage/divorce (7) Liquor/gambling (8) Law and order	Regulation	Hearth/Soul

Whereas members from both parties focused policy discussion on Hearth-based, family welfare significantly, this was so more for Republicans than Democrats. In 45.8 percent of their family cases, Republican members stressed welfare policies, in comparison to Democrats, who cited welfare concerns in 30.6 percent of their family references. Republicans were equally preoccupied with regulation policies, also a (quasi) Hearth concern, raising these also in 45.8 percent of their family cases, whereas Democrats were far more circumscribed in this regard, mentioning Regulation policies in the least number of their family cases, only 11.1 percent.

More than welfare, Democrats raised Soul family values concerns through family ascription policies, citing these in 34.7 percent of cases; they also raised policies to preserve family autonomy, another Soul policy type, in a significant proportion of their cases (23.6 percent). In matters most directly involving family values, Democrats far surpassed the Republican delegation, the latter citing autonomy policy concerns in only 5.8 percent of their family references and ascription policies in a mere 2.5 percent.

Republicans and Democrats thus alternatively privileged family economics or family values as foundational to their family policy visions, more aligning respectively with the Hearth and Soul family systems. Democrats combined a focus on family economics, seen in their high interest in social welfare policies, with a keen interest in preserving family values, such as through family ascription and autonomy-focused policies; for them, as some have argued, policy interest in family economics was legitimate only insofar as it supported distinct cultural relations, such as patriarchal and racialized social relations.[65] For Republicans, however, interest in family values was folded into their overarching policy focus on family economic conditions, illustrating more directly the Hearth family approach. Column proportions and chi-square tests confirm that partisanship and policy type bear a statistically significant relationship, with significant differences between the parties in relation to all four of the policy categories: Democrats discussed significantly larger proportions of ascription and autonomy-related policies, and Republicans referenced significantly more welfare and regulation policies.[66] The Democratic-Soul and Republican-Hearth family alignments that emerged in the Progressive era thus manifested in distinct policy configurations[67] (Figure 12).

The emergence of the partisan-family alignments can be traced to specific congresses (Figure 12). Starting with the 61st Congress (1909–1911), the Democratic Soul alignment began to combine a focus on welfare policies with ascription and autonomy policy concerns. The alternative configuration also emerged in the form of the Republican Hearth family alignment, beginning with the 61st and 62nd Congresses: that is, around the turn of the first decade, family welfare policies were first configured along with a more long-standing concern with regulation policies. In later congresses (64th through 66th), Republicans articulated more consistently this Hearth policy configuration with which we are familiar today, combining welfare and regulation policies to solicit active state intervention into (predominantly economic) family affairs.

Not unlike today, sectionalism, even more than partisanship, defined politics and family political alignments. In terms of numbers and seniority,

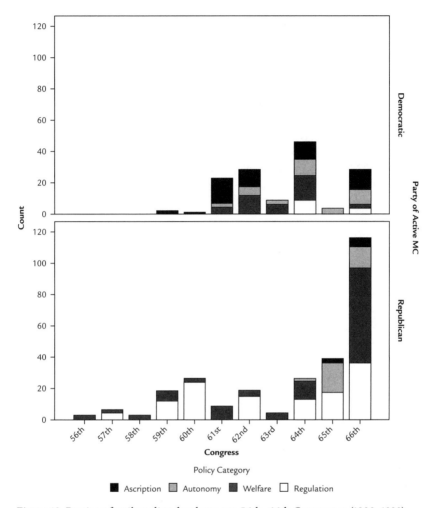

Figure 12. Partisan family policy development, 56th–66th Congresses (1900–1920).

southern congressmen were prominent players in the Democratic Party for the congresses investigated (56th to 66th). Their strength during this period is reflected in the distribution of (active) members of Congress who referred to family cases during hearings. The above partisan distribution mirrors the prevailing regional bases of the two parties—the agrarian South for Democrats and the manufacturing North (Northeast and Midwest) for Republicans. Almost three-quarters (65 percent) of all Democrats who cited or

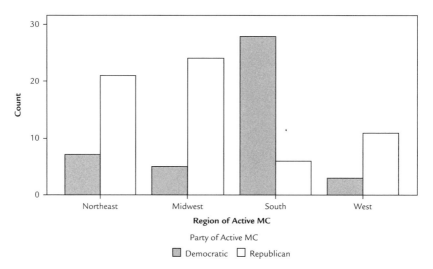

Figure 13. Region and party of active MCs, committee hearings, 1900–1920. The unit of analysis is member of Congress who made reference to family case(s).

addressed family cases were from the South, whereas many more Republicans from the Midwest and Northeast were active in this way.[68]

Southern Democrats most strongly asserted the Democratic-Soul family configuration, combining a focus on ascription and autonomy policies with welfare (Table 4A). They consistently brought up perceived threats to the traditional structure, sex, and morals of white supremacy by focusing policy discussions on miscegenation, intermarriage,[69] and extramarital sexual relations.[70] The southern faction was at the heart of the Democratic-Soul family alignment, containing their party's interest in family economic conditions into a broader, more consistent emphasis on preserving (racial and patriarchal) family values.

On the other hand, northern Democrats from the Northeast and Midwest espoused a Hearth ideology more similar to that of northern Republicans than the Soul ideology of their (mostly southern) Democratic colleagues. Relative to their party, this northern Democratic faction used significantly higher proportions of family cases than average to highlight family economic welfare and regulation policies, suggesting that they too had an economic (Hearth) understanding of the family.[71]

Although Republicans who raised and discussed family cases during hearings were more regionally dispersed than Democrats, within the GOP too, sectional patterns are evident, pointing to the largely northern character

Table 4A. Democratic Family Cases by Policy Category, 56th–66th Congresses (1900–1920)

| | Region of Active MC | | | | | | | | | | | | |
| | Northeast | | Midwest | | South | | West | | Total | |
	Count	Percent	Count	Percent	Count	Percent	Count	Percent	Count	Percent
Ascription	2	18.2	5	27.8	34	33.7	9	81.8	50	35.5
Autonomy	3	27.3	1	5.6	28	27.7	1	9.1	33	23.4
Welfare	3	27.3	8	44.4	32	31.7	0	.0	43	30.5
Regulation	3	27.3	4	22.2	7	6.9	1	9.1	15	10.6
Total	11	100.0	18	100.0	101	100.0	11	100.0	141	100.0

Table 4B. Republican Family Cases by Policy Category, 56th–66th Congresses (1900–1920)

	Region of Active MC														
	Northeast		Midwest		South		West		Total	
	Count	Percent	Count	Percent	Count	Percent	Count	Percent	Count	Percent
Ascription	1	1.1	3	2.6	2	25.0	1	1.8	7	2.6
Autonomy	9	10.3	4	3.5	2	25.0	1	1.8	16	6.0
Welfare	39	44.8	66	57.4	2	25.0	12	21.8	119	44.9
Regulation	38	43.7	42	36.5	2	25.0	41	74.5	123	46.4
Total	87	100.0	115	100.0	8	100.0	55	100.0	265	100.0

of the Republican-Hearth family alignment. In contrast to the southern-dominated Democratic Party, northern (midwestern and northeastern) Republicans raised the most family cases in committee hearings (Table 4B). In so doing, they referenced a much larger (than average) proportion of cases that stressed welfare and also addressed regulation. Regulation policies, while important to northern Republicans, were the most important to Republican members from western regions.[72] It is also worth noting that compared to all other Republicans, northeastern Republicans emphasized autonomy in a disproportionately large percentage of their cases. This seeming (partisan and sectional) anomaly was to become the Republican norm in the post–New Deal midcentury era, when the Republican Party switched to an autonomy-based negative state Soul family approach instead of their welfare-oriented positive state Hearth one. On the whole, however, during the Progressive Era, the northern-dominated Republican Party was far more likely than southern-based Democrats to stress the Hearth family configuration, emphasizing welfare and regulation policies over all others.

Despite their sectional and partisan divergences, legislators in Congress most converged in the level of policy attention they paid to family economic welfare. Even the staunchest conservative Soul faction in the Democratic Party, southern Democrats, used large proportions of their family cases to highlight welfare policies. Instead, partisan factions differed more significantly in their understanding and attention to family values. Within the southern Democratic-Soul family system, parochial family culture, values, and morality associated with native-born white families called for active state preservation.[73] However, within the northern Republican-Hearth family system, more focused on economics, members by and large addressed family values in a more nationalist way, often tied to a family's economic condition. Their limited concern with family values was intermixed with their preoccupation with family economics, and as in the case of families battling alcohol and gambling, negative family values were associated closely with poverty.[74] Underlying these partisan family ideals and policy approaches were sectional demographic differences in the lives and practices of families they represented across the United States, to which the final section now turns.

Underpinning Demographic Family Conditions

The sectionalism of the emerging partisan Hearth and Soul family alignment extended beyond the regional affiliations of their members in Congress but also manifested in demographic differences among the families they repre-sented. The Democratic Party and the Republican Party espoused Soul and Hearth family ideologies, respectively, relying on family characteristics en-demic to their respective regional bases.

Members of Congress were divided in the kinds of demographic data they highlighted in their policy discussions as well as in how they put that data to use. Hearth members, stressing greater national state intervention into material family life, valued the collection of systematic family data as a basis for advocating uniform, standardized, family-related policy across the nation.[75] Several members and their witnesses cited rising divorce rates as cause for great alarm, often as a rationale to galvanize federal standardized laws on marriage and divorce.[76] Based on its exceptional divorce rate, the populous western state of California was repeatedly decried as the "greatest divorce center," and other "small, smutty, western" towns such as Reno were also bewailed as the "divorce Mecca of . . . the rest of the Union." Ten mid-western states were also cited to bear the "supremacy of guilt in granting di-vorces" insofar as they accounted for "more than half of all . . . divorces . . . granted in the forty years from 1867 to 1906."[77] National and state census figures were cited extensively to illustrate that even conservative northeast-ern states, such as Massachusetts, had seen a growth in divorce "three times as fast as the population in Massachusetts from the years, 1860 to 1915."[78]

During the 56th to 66th Congresses (1899–1920), thirty-three bills and resolutions were introduced in the House and Senate proposing uniform marriage and divorce laws across the United States. The majority of mem-bers introducing these measures were from the Republican Party, represent-ing northern (midwestern and northeastern) states, the regions with rapidly climbing divorced and single-parent families. These members also cited changes in birth and death rates to advocate "public protection of maternity and infancy" through federally funded prenatal health care for mothers and children such as the Sheppard-Towner program.[79] In this instance as well as in numerous others, Hearth members of Congress, their witnesses, and con-stituents used changing family demographics (and statistics), particularly in their regions, to propose interventionist welfare and regulatory programs.

Other changes in family demographic behavior, also occurring more rapidly in the industrializing North than elsewhere, were the increasing rates of women's wage labor and their new dual burden of homemaking and em-ployment, swelling rates of urban migration and foreign immigration, and alterations in family living arrangements (changes in housing quarters from single-family to tenement housing, for example). These too were emphasized by Hearth advocates, who underscored changing material conditions as grounds to seek national state intervention—such as for Federal Home Economics programs for women, immigration reform, federally funded housing, and reconstruction policies.[80] For the period under consideration (1899–1920), sixty-two such bills and resolutions pertaining to services and programs for immigrant families, female wage earners, and mothers were introduced in Congress. Here too, Republican members from northern states were the most active sponsors, and Democratic members from northern regions were also very active.

Southern Soul members were less preoccupied with the material changes in family demographics cited by their northern colleagues. However, they were more likely to use demographic data to emphasize the distinctiveness of southern family behavior from all other regions, illustrating the deep sectional (southern) roots of the Soul family approach. For instance, when challenging the necessity for uniform marriage and divorce laws across the country, Soul members emphasized the continued lower rates of divorce in their own states and stressed the significance of enduring, often religious, moral codes of conduct among southern families. Representative Whaley (D-SC) stressed South Carolina's distinctive marriage and divorce patterns in this way:

> Do you not believe where you have a provision for divorce it places a premium on people not getting along together, and that where you do not have divorce laws that it works the other way? That has been our experience in South Carolina. We have not got any divorce law down there, and we have very few separations. I do not believe we have had more than seven in the whole States, with a million and a half population. You never hear of them going to other States and getting divorces, very few of them. . . . We have a high standard and live up to it.[81]

In fact, of all the other regions in the United States, the South indeed had the greatest proportion of married men and women, and this comparative excess increased from 1900 through 1920.[82] Higher proportions of married populations in the South were not limited to women (as was the pattern in some other regions); southern men too married in higher proportions than elsewhere. For every single southern man in 1920, there were almost two married men (1.82); this ratio—and the preponderance of married men proportions over single men in the South versus other regions—continued to grow through the Progressive Era.[83]

In contrast, by 1920, the most urbanized region, the Northeast, had the highest proportions of single and combined single and divorced populations. The Northeast continued to have higher proportions of single women than in any of the other three regions from 1900 through 1920, and the comparative excess in single women proportions in the Northeast became more apparent through this period. In terms of fertility too, the agrarian South far differed from (exceeded) the North in the early twentieth century. After the Civil War, the South and West had substantially higher fertility rates than the North (Northeast and Midwest), as the Midwest moved from being a region with large families to mirror the low fertility rates of the Northeast.[84] Through the late nineteenth century and Progressive Era, changes in the demographic patterns, particularly in the northern regions, left families in industrializing regions increasingly smaller and less married than those in the more agrarian regions of the South (and West).

Southern Democratic members also emphasized the ongoing distinctiveness of the South's racial composition (notably their high proportion of blacks), questioning the ability of nonsoutherners to contemplate the "race question" when, as they claimed, "in two counties in Georgia there [were] 101,000 [negroes]—more than in the whole nine suffrage states put together."[85] Southern demographic differences in family living conditions, as well as their lower levels of industrialization and wealth distribution, were frequently cited in defense of southern states' rights and local community self-regulation.[86]

In sum, northern Hearth members of Congress focused on rising divorce rates, increasing women's employment, overcrowded familial living/housing conditions, and high infant and maternal mortality rates that were reflective of their own crowded urbanizing regions to propose enhanced national state intervention into family behavior and redistributionist policies and programs for economic assistance. In contrast, Soul members of Congress were less interested in changing family demographic patterns; instead, they emphasized the demographic distinctiveness of the South vis-à-vis national divorce rates, race composition, child occupation statistics, and lower family wealth and income to argue more for states' rights and preservation of southern white family values.

North-South differences in family conditions also conditioned partisan variations in the kinds of family cases used by members to illustrate their policy preferences.[87] Democratic members of Congress used families residing in the South to most illustrate *positive* cases, to be emulated in family policies (64.7 percent of all Democratic positive family cases were from the South), while Republicans disproportionately used northeastern families as such positive examples (45.5 percent of all Republican positive cases). However, when illustrating *negative* families, the two parties switched; Democratic members emphasized northeastern families as negative case examples (40 percent of all negative Democratic cases), while Republicans' negative family cases were predominantly from the South (35.3 percent of all Republican negative cases). Controlling for positive and negative case examples, the relationship between family region and party of member associated with that family example is statistically significant. Families from the South disproportionately formed positive case examples for Democrats but negative examples for Republicans. And, families from the Northeast were mostly positive case examples for Republicans but negative illustrations for Democrats. Democratic family examples also tended to reside in either small towns or small cities with populations of less than 10,000; Republicans drew on families in small cities, but the largest proportion of their family illustrations was more urban and resided in metropolises (mostly New York City and Chicago), with populations of over 100,000.[88]

Subdividing the parties into their regional factions finds that parochialism went even further. Across both parties, legislators generally drew on family examples from their own regions as positive cases. Democrats from the South disproportionately used southern families as positive examples (almost 80 percent of their positive cases were from the South), and northeastern families comprised almost 90 percent of northeastern Republicans' positive examples. However, when illustrating *negative* families, northeastern Republicans mostly cited families from the South (almost 44 percent of the times), and southern Democrats, while still using southern families to illustrate negative cases, nevertheless cited many more northeastern families as negative rather than positive cases (40.9 percent of all southern Democratic negative family cases were from the Northeast as opposed to 5.6 percent of their positive cases). Members of Congress thus tended to draw on family examples from their own regions more than from any other region, and they used parochial family examples more as positive than as negative illustrations of families. The relationship between region of member of Congress (MC) and region of family example was found to be statistically significant at a level of .05 for both Republicans and Democrats.

Table 5. Demographic Characteristics of Family Case Examples, Democrats and Republicans, 56th–66th Congresses (1900–1920)

| | | Party of Active MC | | | |
| | | Democratic | | Republican | |
		Count	Percent	Count	Percent
Marital condition*	Single/separated	6	6.0	16	12.7
(chi-square = 2.87,	Married/widowed	94	94.0	110	87.3
$p = .092$)	Total	100	100.0	126	100.0
Family's race**	White	74	65.5	124	93.2
(chi-square = 29.9,	Nonwhite	39	34.5	9	6.8
$p = .000$)	Total	113	100.0	133	100.0
Parents' nativity	Native born	87	79.1	96	71.1
(chi-square = 2.04,	Foreign born	23	20.9	39	28.9
$p = .153$)	Total	110	100.0	135	100.0
Income status**	Lower income	72	78.3	70	56.0
(chi-square = 11.62,	Middle income	10	10.9	27	21.6
$p = .003$)	Upper income	10	10.9	28	22.4
	Total	92	100.0	125	100.0
Mother's employment	Housewife	20	50.0	28	47.5
(chi-square = .062,	Employed	20	50.0	31	52.5
$p = .80$)	Total	40	100.0	59	100.0

* $p \leq .1$. ** $p \leq .05$.

When looking at the demographic characteristics of Republican and Democratic family cases, one finds that Democrats and Republicans were significantly divided in the marital condition, race, and income status of the family cases they referenced; however, they were not significantly different when it came to the families' nativity or the mother's employment status (Table 5).

Unlike now, both Democratic and Republican members overwhelmingly used families in which the parents were either married or widowed (94 percent of Democratic versus 87.3 percent of Republican cases); however, Republican legislators drew on single-parent/separated family examples more significantly than did Democratic members. Also, Democratic legislators used significantly more nonwhite family cases than did Republicans (34.5 percent of Democratic cases vs. 6.8 percent of Republican) and emphasized lower-income family cases more than Republicans, who used larger

Table 6. Demographic Characteristics of Negative Family Examples, Democrats and Republicans, 56th–66th Congresses (1900–1920)

| | | Party Sponsor of Family | | | |
| | | Democratic | | Republican | |
		Count	Percent	Count	Percent
Marital condition	Single/separated	5	12.2	14	21.2
	Married/widowed	36	87.8	52	78.8
	Total	41	100.0	66	100.0
Family's race	White	30	66.7	66	100.0
	Nonwhite	15	33.3	0	.0
	Total	45	100.0	66	100.0
Income status	Lower income	31	77.5	51	79.7
	Middle income	3	7.5	8	12.5
	Upper income	6	15.0	5	7.8
	Total	40	100.0	64	100.0

Note: Appraisal of family = negative family.

proportions of upper- and middle-income families. Democrats emphasized lower-income families in greater proportion as positive cases, while Republicans highlighted upper-income families in this way.

Among negative cases, only race (and not income or marital condition) was significant to party: Democrats used larger proportions of nonwhite cases as negative examples. However, in terms of income, legislators from both parties disproportionately emphasized lower-income families as negative cases. Similarly, members from both parties focused on single/separated-parent families as negative case examples, even though more Republican cases exhibited that characteristic (Table 6).

To summarize, the Democratic positive family ideal underlying its Soul family values approach was southern, rural (from villages and small cities), married, and lower income and included many nonwhite but always single-race families. The Republican positive family ideal that was at the core of their economics Hearth family approach was northeastern, urban (many from metropolises), also married but more upper income, and almost exclusively white. Republicans, much more than Democrats, were concerned with single-parent (separated and unmarried) families that they presented as negative families in need of policy assistance, and Democrats were correspondingly more focused on nonwhite families, which they, in turn, highlighted as both positive and negative examples.

The characteristics of the family examples used and discursively highlighted by legislators reflected the actual demographic conditions of families from those regions. The southern family was indeed more rural, married, lower income, and racially diverse than the northern family. The family cases cited by members from the two parties thus can be said to be fair representations of the family conditions prevailing from those regions. Finally, the analysis suggests that during the Progressive Era, race (first) and income differences (second) among North-South families appear the most salient to partisan divisions in family ideology and policy preferences. Thus, at the heart of the emerging partisan Hearth and Soul family approaches lay two very different sectional families, embedded in starkly different material contexts and embodying alternative cultural values. These two families, their lives and values, would continue to condition divergent policy responses by the parties that came to represent them.

Conclusion

During the Progressive Era, northern Republicans constituted the most consistent Hearth bloc in Congress focused on family economic issues, while southern Democrats predominantly espoused a Soul family values approach. Each partisan set espoused different ideational visions of the family. This chapter has suggested that these family ideological variations conditioned policy divisions. The Hearth ideal of a gender-egalitarian family was centered on its economic condition, in which the welfare of children was paramount. On the other hand, the Soul ideal of a white patriarchal family was centered more on its moral supremacy, where welfare of the family was largely determined by its racial and gendered values.

Demographic differences underpinned the Hearth and Soul family ideologies of the era, and the two family ideologies mirrored sectional demographic divisions in family condition, such that the parties' espousal of one or the other ideology was to a large extent shaped by their regional constituencies. For instance, Democratic members from the South were more likely to support a racialized Soul family ideology, reflecting family demographic conditions (lower income, high marriage rates, more racially diverse populations) in that region, and Republican members from the Midwest and North were more likely to support a Hearth family ideology, consonant with the demographic family conditions (more single-parent smaller families, higher income, more urban, less racially diverse) of the electorate there. Bottom-up, society-centered phenomena, such as North-South variation in family demographics, shaped partisan clashes over family ideology and policy during the first two decades of the twentieth century.

Despite the prevailing constitutional boundaries on the powers of the national state in the Progressive Era, competing family ideologies thus roiled members of Congress even in this period, infusing numerous battles over woman suffrage, intermarriage, social welfare, child labor, and even citizenship. Varied sectional ideals and practices of gender, race, sexuality, and class intertwined in numerous ways to produce either a more economic or valuational focus to the parties' family agendas.

As the nation moved into the periods of Depression and World War II, these clashes over family would evolve and recur. The next chapter picks up the story of family political development in the next significant era as identified by platforms: the period following World War II, after the constitutional reordering of the New Deal and the transformation of party politics by Franklin Delano Roosevelt, as American family life responded to new conditions of peacetime prosperity as well as uncertainty and fear accompanying the onset of the Cold War.

Chapter 3

Post–World War II Era: Haven in a Heartless World

The decade following World War II was fraught with uncertainty and contradictions. On one hand, the nation entered a period of unprecedented material prosperity, with the average household income almost doubling during a postwar boom.[1] However, demobilization and the emerging Cold War also led to a pervasive sense of vulnerability and unease. In 1952, 64 percent of those polled admitted to worrying "a lot" or a "fair amount," as opposed to 37 percent who said they only worried "a little" or "not at all."[2] When asked again two years later in 1954, 49 percent further acknowledged that they "worry more now than [they] used to."[3] It is under such circumstances of nationwide unease that family first moved onto the national stage of American politics. Far from being the inevitable result of a return to peace and prosperity, as historian Elaine Tyler May demonstrated, the 1950s nuclear family was in fact the result of the "first wholehearted effort [at] creat[ing] a home."[4] Aptly characterized as "homeward bound," Tyler May describes the new postwar politics of domestic containment that elevated family as the first line of defense against social stress.

The postwar preoccupation with creating a domestic ideal is well evidenced in policy discussions in the decade following World War II. During that period, legislators in Congress accorded family a pivotal role in offsetting postwar and Cold War uncertainty, attempting to deploy both welfare and regulatory policies to instantiate it within American society. However, just as in the Progressive Era, there were considerable differences in the kinds of family ideals that were harnessed by various legislative factions and embedded in their policy positions and debates. Whereas most Democratic legislators in postwar Congresses used the Hearth family approach to focus public policies on family *economic* welfare, they also began to acknowledge the importance of family *emotional* and psychological well-being and sought to expand existing social services and programs on both grounds. On the other hand, the Republican minority embraced a Soul family approach to emphasize private, increasingly free market–oriented family values, constructed at this time in more racially neutral terms than before—the values of liberty, self-regulation, and autonomy. They used these family values to resist the expanding national state and regulation of the economy. A third, intermediate faction of southern Democrats adopted a mixed approach, combining their abiding attention to parochial, private family values with a concerted public focus on family economic conditions. In all cases, however, either for its economic, emotional, or valuational qualities, family for the first time was collectively viewed as a keystone of *national* social order.

This chapter argues that the post–World War II decade marked a new stage in family political development, when legislators first approached the American family as central to the well-being of the nation and thus an appropriate, necessary element of national policy. This was vastly different from the Progressive Era, when family occupied a contested space within national (as opposed to state) politics, and so the midcentury marks the beginning of our own, current family political stage. There were also crucial aspects that distinguish the postwar family party alignment from its later iteration. Unlike in the culture wars of the late twentieth century when family became a central locus of partisan competition, political differences over family following World War II were very firmly contained within partisan cleavage over the national state. Moreover, unlike the more polarized partisan politics of the late twentieth century, at this earlier time, the presence of conservative southerners within the Democratic Party and their volatile accommodation within the New Deal alliance engendered three, not two, family political ideologies. Most Democrats and most Republicans espoused Hearth and Soul family positions respectively, but southern Democrats occupied a third ideological space: sometimes advocating Hearth and sometimes Soul family ideals. These family party developments came in the aftermath of World War II and must be viewed in the context of the social dislocations that war and then demobilization brought to the lives of American families.[5]

During World War II, several million families had been uprooted from their homes and from familiar and kinship networks as they traveled to war-boom towns in search of employment or to army bases to stay close to servicemen-husbands. After the war, these families faced residential and economic uncertainty with the closure or reduction of war-related industrial jobs and the service discharge of millions of veterans. Also, a large proportion of veterans' marriages and families had been formed in haste prior to the war and were often strained by the interim (wartime) marital infidelity by one or both spouses. In the immediate aftermath of war, the rate of divorce, 24 per 1,000, was the highest it had ever been, underscoring the great instability of these war-forged families.[6]

World War II also brought the first large-scale incorporation of women (particularly mothers) into the workforce, significantly destabilizing gender norms within families.[7] During demobilization with the return of male veterans, a sizable proportion of women workers returned to their homes and relinquished their roles as breadwinners.[8] However, belying expectations, a vast majority of women retained their jobs.[9] Married women's paid employment became one of the "many changes created by the war [that] became permanent once the nation . . . readjusted to peacetime living,"[10] reordering families' lives significantly. As historian Karen Anderson writes, "Rather than providing clear-cut alternatives to previous sex role definitions, the war years generated contradictory tendencies, confusion, insecurity, and anxiety." Whereas war "offered women new opportunities for independence and role flexibility and challenged conventional stereotypes regarding women's physical and emotional makeup, it also promoted considerable apprehension about family stability."[11]

Anxiety over the family continued into the 1950s along with the large-scale adoption of the nuclear male-breadwinner family.[12] As new domestic electronic appliances revolutionized family living, consumerism increased, further enhancing (material) incentives for some women and their families for paid employment; other women found themselves compelled to work due to family upheavals, such as death, divorce, or desertion by the male breadwinner.[13] Despite the increasing trend of women's wage work or perhaps because of it, working mothers were much castigated; they were blamed for a rising divorce rate, child neglect, increasing juvenile delinquency, and numerous other social ills.[14] The terrors of the Atomic Age, Red Scare, and fear of subversive activities yielded a pervasive sense of national insecurity during the Cold War that engendered a preoccupation with family conformity and the need to re-create a social equilibrium.[15] In 1955, in a statement to a congressional committee, social observers such as Dr. Grace Sloan Overton (a nationally known youth counselor) were cited, cautioning, "If we are not careful in America . . . within 3 generations, possibly 2, the homelife as we know it will not exist any more. The idea of family will be over and done with."[16]

Policy makers in Congress displayed much concern over the emergence of postwar family disruptions. They discussed the bona fides of servicemen's marriages and debated the extent to which pension laws and dependents' benefits could contribute to fraudulent marriages.[17] They also proposed new enhanced dependent allowances to encourage marriage and family life among the lower ranks in the military.[18] They began to debate the expansion of public assistance, most particularly welfare programs to families (Aid to Dependent Children) and public housing projects, on grounds that they either strengthened family ties or encouraged its disruption.[19] Juvenile delinquency also received widespread media and congressional attention. In 1953, the Senate established a Subcommittee to Investigate Juvenile Delinquency in the United States. Through the 1950s, the subcommittee conducted over seventy hearings in twenty cities across the country on a variety of topics such as comic books, television, pornography, and plural marriages, all of which were seen to threaten existing social relations and traditional (nuclear) family norms. Senator Hendrickson (R-NJ), the original sponsor, told the *New York Times* that the subcommittee was formed in response to the alarming 30 percent increase in juvenile crimes in the five years since 1948.[20] In all of these hearings, family instability was repeatedly cited as having a profound impact on postwar society. Child development experts pointed to family breakdown and delinquent parents: deserting fathers who shirked their breadwinning responsibility and, more often than not, preoccupied, uncaring working mothers.[21]

To instantiate the nuclear family, legislators advocated the policy configuration of welfare and regulation policies with which we are familiar today, combining a system of programmatic benefits with more coercive policies to foster (nuclear male-breadwinner) family behavior. This "carrot-and-stick" system of policies, begun in the Progressive Era but developed more fully in the postwar period, illustrates what political scientist Priscilla Yamin has described as an enduring pattern of "rights and obligations" that constructs marriage (and family) as an American political institution.[22] On one hand, postwar legislative proposals expanded the rights and entitlements of (married) nuclear families to certain social services and veterans' benefits, whereas other regulatory policies obligated those already in such family arrangements to perform their family roles in specified ways. In either case, either through rights-driven benefits and/or obligations-focused regulation, postwar legislators sought to quell potential disruptions to the (married) two-parent nuclear family ideal.

In the Progressive Era, legislators and social groups advocating family welfare had focused their arguments on children—stressing their unique vulnerability to social and economic stress and the inability of individual families and private or local relief groups to adequately provide for many of them. The postwar era, despite upholding these child-centered ideals, also marked a shift in policy focus—from attention to the impoverished material conditions in which children lived (the erstwhile focus)[23] now to parents and their crucial affective role in child development. Many legislators in the early postwar period thus proposed expanded welfare policies that were much more parent centered; they called for new "constructive" family services (including counseling, referrals, and guidance) to instruct parents in parenting and also for greater regulation policies to coerce delinquent parents to step up and fulfill their family responsibilities. Reflecting the prevailing postwar therapeutic approach to family and child development,[24] the enhanced focus on parents was accompanied by greater awareness and emphasis on the emotional and psychological components of family and child welfare. Legislative social welfare policies now invoked a new child-focused model of affective parenting, reflecting what has been noted by family historians Mintz and Kellogg as the postwar family's ardent embrace of "the (suburban) notion that you must eternally give to your children, otherwise you are not a loving parent."[25] The new attention to parents and to child and family affective welfare was juxtaposed with the more enduring focus on material family welfare—expanding the liberal Hearth family state to what we are familiar with today.

In opposition to the call for greater state intervention, other legislators deployed a Soul family values framework to present societal and family valuational vulnerability as symptoms of illegitimate or excessive national state intervention. On these grounds, they opposed expansions to national health and welfare services without a means test, claiming that the lack of a means test would "foster excessive dependence on government and discourage individual self-reliance."[26] In a tone that came to resonate loudly in the late twentieth century, they asserted that the paternalistic national state occluded free-market, voluntary, and local communitarian action and generated a climate of dependency and diminishing family and social responsibility. For example, Senator William Purtell (R-CT) expressed alarm over "the idea that down in Washington there is a thing called a Great White Father who creates wealth" and linked "that very philosophy channeled down to the kids" to the prevailing "delinquency problems," asserting that "the removal of responsibility from communities to the Federal Government [has] something to do with the laxity in those communities in solving their own problems."[27]

This position was in some ways a continuation of a similar Soul oppositional stance in the Progressive Era, when economic regulation and national state intervention in policy areas such as child labor and compulsory schooling were also opposed on grounds of diminishing local and family autonomy and private decision making. Unlike those earlier times, when these values were distinctly local and parochial and harnessed to preserve white supremacy, particularly in the South, in the postwar period, these family values were less racially charged, more market centered, and vested with larger, more nationalistic meaning. Thus, "private initiative" and "family autonomy" were now imbued with a *national* character, as *American* family values in direct contrast to un-American totalitarianism or socialism. Private market-based family values were now, for the first time, national in scope and application—another political framing from the postwar era that has endured in politics to our present day.

This chapter will reveal how legislators in their policy debates drew on the ideological legacies of the Hearth and Soul family approaches inherited from the early twentieth century and modified them to address wartime and postwar experiences, the constitutionally reconfigured national state, and the rising concern with family disruption and delinquency. Hearth advocates grafted the new concern over family affective well-being onto their long-standing preoccupation with family economic welfare and used this to advocate for state expansion. For other legislators, aligned with the Soul approach, family values continued to be the *central* policy focus, which in turn they used to advocate against state expansion in favor of the private market.

The narrative to follow first discusses the impact of War World II and the New Deal on the developing state ideals of the Hearth and Soul party factions in Congress, demonstrating how support or opposition to the national state became the central axis dividing the two partisan systems at this time and engendering a third, intermediate one. Next, it reveals how competing state ideals accommodated contrasting and developing ideals of *family,* showing how a democratized companionate family ideal centered on the experiences of suburban and urban families was now at the center of the postwar Hearth system's interventionist national state and a more traditional family ideal still situated within a vision of organic social and community relations was at the core of the postwar Soul system's more market-driven, minimal state ideology. The concluding section draws comparisons between the complex postwar Hearth and Soul family party alignments and their later incarnations, seen in the "culture wars" of the late twentieth century.

Demobilization, the Postwar State, and the Evolving Hearth and Soul Family Ideologies

In the 1930s, the New Deal dramatically altered the constitutional role of the American national state in such a monumental way as to constitute, what political scientist Theodore Lowi famously called, a second founding of a new Republic.[28] In response to the Great Depression, Franklin Delano Roosevelt and his Democratic supporters redefined constitutional boundaries between federal and state prerogatives, successfully clearing the way for an expanded national state.[29] As revealed by James Sundquist in his classic work on party systems, a new line of cleavage in party competition for and against the national state's activist domestic measures developed in the 1930s, replacing the previous line of cleavage between the parties for and against the gold standard.[30] John Gerring similarly observes a coincident turn in Republican Party ideology, starting with Herbert Hoover's campaign in 1928, when the GOP embraced individualist neoliberalism, professing a new antistatism unlike before.[31] World War II and demobilization instantiated this pattern, expanding the New Deal national state still further and entrenching partisan divisions over it.

In many classic and recent accounts, the post–World War II period is characterized by a continuing liberal consensus within the American electorate in favor of a greater role for government.[32] The fact that Democrats held the presidency for twenty consecutive years till 1952 is seen to indicate the prevailing strength of the New Deal Democratic coalition, despite internal squabbles and occasional electoral setbacks.[33] Within this perspective, social welfare issues cast a long and dominant shadow during the postwar era, with foreign affairs coming in second.[34] Whereas the Democratic Party was widely presumed by voters to be more in tune with public preferences on social welfare, the electorate viewed Republicans as more competent on foreign affairs. The midcentury electoral success of the Democratic Party is thus attributed to the fact that the public continued to place a much higher priority to issues of social welfare.[35]

Much of this electoral consensus is also tied to the differential size and composition of Democratic and Republican coalitions. The postwar Democratic Party represented a larger blue-collar coalition, featuring working-class Americans across regions, a few multiclass ethnic minorities (notably Jews and Catholics), and, most important, the entire solid South. The Republican Party at this time was instead aligned with a smaller, white-collar coalition, comprising middle-class Americans. Organized labor, at its peak at the start of the 1950s, was the mainstay interest group of the postwar Democratic Party, and the Republican counterpart was small business.[36] Typically, the political fortunes of the GOP in the period from the 1930s to the 1960s are thus understood to have been bleak; barring a small proportion of forceful dissenters, described as "committed conservatives [who] had not given up . . . their efforts to make a case against expanded government," the GOP itself is seen to have moved toward a more moderate course, accepting the triumph of "the Democratic Party's argument that [national] government should play a strong and active role in society."[37]

The analysis in the following chapter reveals this picture of postwar liberal dominance to be only partially true, supporting work that instead highlights diverse coalitions within the two parties at this time.[38] In terms of family, policies focused on social welfare (the mainstay of the liberal Democratic regime) were expectedly by far the most salient policy type advanced in Congress, but other policies—notably regulation and autonomy—were also significant in committee discussions and in sponsored bills, suggesting much less than complete acquiescence to the Democratic liberal agenda. There were also consistent, statistically significant, partisan differences among legislators in the kinds of ideologies of state, economy, and family that they invoked. Thus, instead of an across-the-board postwar liberal consensus, the findings support the more complex view that recognizes differential partisan dynamics at play among the levels of congressional versus presidential party politics. As party scholar Byron Shafer observes, while the "presidential Republican party *did* accept the social welfare consensus [i]n congressional contests . . . the situation . . . was strikingly different."[39] He writes, "Many seats remained reliably Republican, thus obviating the need for social welfare accommodation. Many of the rest were reliably Democratic, such that accommodation (or not) was irrelevant. Lacking much incentive then, few successful Republicans moderated at the congressional level."[40] This was especially evident in the case of family.

Congress members from both parties used a majority of their family cases to articulate Hearth principles: stressing a structural view of family material and affective well-being and calling for an expanded welfare state. Across both parties, 81 percent of family cases illustrated Hearth family economic ideals, compared to 75 percent in the Progressive Era and 78 percent in the contemporary period. However, while Democrats disproportionately used their cases, almost 85 percent of all, to illustrate Hearth ideals, many more Republican cases, almost 40 percent of them, articulated Soul family values principles, emphasizing market-based private family values over family economic conditions and advocating instead for a minimal welfare state.[41] Thus, although social welfare issues and the Hearth family ideology were undeniably central to postwar party politics, they were not unanimously accepted. The ideological differences in Congress held firm for the five (and a half) congresses examined in the immediate postwar era.[42] This party dynamic drew upon previous political developments—the New Deal's expanded responsibility to families, World War II, and increasing national state involvement in family, now in terms of family psychology, affect, and values in addition to family economic conditions.

In the social insurance and public assistance programs contained in the landmark Social Security Act of 1935, the national state had assumed responsibility for the first time for the public dependency of destitute children, the unemployed, and the elderly. Public works programs and numerous New Deal agencies led to an exponential increase in the size and expenditure of the federal government. Regulation of financial markets and support of workers' collective bargaining rights were further ways by which Democratic New Dealers expanded the reach of the state into the economy and the lives of people.[43] The enhanced national state and its entrenched interest groups became the new normal, now largely seen as a positive good by a majority of Americans and not merely a necessary evil.[44]

What is often overlooked in standard accounts of the New Deal is that the newly active national state was predicated on a new civic conception of family, reconfiguring "the protection of family" as a legitimate *national* public responsibility, hitherto confined to the police powers of states. Family newly emerged as a viable portal through which state programmatic expansion took place.[45] In the historic 1936 election, in which FDR (and his New

Deal policies) received a resounding 60.8 percent of the vote, the Democratic Party platform asserted the "Protection of the family and home" as the first of three new public obligations, a part of a "self-evident truth . . . that government in a modern civilization has certain inescapable obligations to its citizens."[46] Compared to the Progressive Era, there was a vast increase in the number of sponsored postwar bills directly addressing families. In comparison to an average of forty-two bills invoking families in each congress in the Progressive Era, there were eighty-eight such bills per congress from 1945 to 1955.[47]

For Democratic Hearth liberals more focused on the economic insufficiencies of families, World War II unequivocally demonstrated the need for an active, interventionist national government. The war had revealed many lapses in family life, which, they claimed, could not be met by individual states or private charities alone. In particular, the health of citizens, especially that of children, illustrated the national significance of families' own deficiencies in providing for their members. Seven months into his presidency in November 1945, Harry S. Truman sent a presidential message to Congress proposing a new national health care program, poised to become a central priority of his Fair Deal agenda.[48] In that message, Truman pointed to the widespread rejections by the Selective Service System (the draft) during the war, which had classified 30 percent of all registrants as unfit for service. This, he claimed, was stark evidence that the health of children should now be a "public responsibility," its national ramifications warranting the assistance of the national state. "The health of the Nation," he wrote, "is a national concern" and "the health of all its citizens . . . of American children . . . deserves the help of the Nation"; "by preventing illness, by assuring access to needed community and personal health services, by promoting medical research, and by protecting our people against the loss caused by sickness, we shall strengthen our national health, our national defense, and our economic productivity."[49]

Illustrating the era's growing awareness of affective issues in addition to economic ones, several Democratic members of Congress, such as Claude Pepper (D-FL), described the wartime discovery of widespread health defects as a wakeup call to the fact that individual families alone could not buy good medical and emotional health for their children.[50] To them, the financial burden of good medical care for chronic or catastrophic illness even prevented families with comfortable incomes from providing full medical care to their children.[51] Others pointed to the "terrifying" national implications of "defective manpower" in times of war and ongoing preparedness as further grounds for national state action for family assistance.[52]

Many policy makers highlighted the success and ongoing relevance of temporary federal services developed for families of servicemen and war workers during the war, arguing for their permanence in the postwar period. For example, the Emergency Maternal and Infant-Care program enacted during the war in 1943 had provided servicemen's wives with federal medical care throughout their pregnancy, during childbirth, and thereafter, also providing care for their children during the first year of their lives.[53] Another program, established by the Lanham Act, provided temporary federal funding for public daycare centers to enable mothers to work in wartime industries. Housed in public schools, the federal daycare centers were established as a universal public service similar to public education, available to working mothers across income groups contrary to a relief program.[54] The emergency medical and daycare measures were set to expire six months after the official end of the war. Democratic proponents in Congress called for them to be made permanent, arguing that "we can not say to the mothers of this Nation that we value their lives and the well-being of their children in war, but think little of them in peace."[55]

The legacy of the war also included extraordinary regulatory measures undertaken by the federal government to reduce sexual delinquency and maintain social conformity. "Victory girls" (also called "khaki-wackies" and "free girls" by the media) had received much attention by public officials and private citizen groups, intent on preventing female "sex delinquency" and safeguarding public morals and health.[56] In contrast to Rosie the Riveter (the much-celebrated, patriotic woman who left home to work in wartime factories), victory girls were derided for performing sexual services for servicemen out of a sense of patriotic duty.[57] The May Act of 1941 established a Social Protection Division (SPD) administered by the Federal Security Agency, which was charged with the responsibility of "protecting" servicemen from the spread of venereal disease by suppressing "lewdness, assignation and prostitution."[58] Unlike previous efforts, the act focused on suppressing prostitution and regulating extramarital female sexual activity while eliminating punitive measures against servicemen who contracted venereal disease.[59] Under the guidance of the SPD, all women arrested or held for investigation on various morals charges were to be detained for mandatory testing for venereal disease. This led to widespread changes in morals laws across several states, broadening them to allow the apprehension of a wider range of suspect female behavior. As the SPD repeatedly noted, commerce was not essential for sexual regulation; a prostitute was, in effect, "any woman who was sexually active in the absence of 'sincere emotional content.'"[60] Recognizing the May Act as extraordinarily effective in suppressing "prostitution" and venereal disease, members in postwar congresses recommended that it too be made permanent.[61] Forged in times of war, the national state thus began to actively promote/construct the boundaries of appropriate moral and sexual behavior within and without the family.

These wartime regulatory measures articulated the prevailing concern with national regulation of women and their sexuality during times of social stress, which then continued into the postwar years as part of the growing preoccupation with creating a moral and also materially successful family. For several policy actors, deviant female sexual or moral behavior and the negative values it illustrated were tied to family poverty and insufficient welfare services. They claimed, "It was because most of our counties failed to provide adequate services that many immature girls from poor homes found their way to army camp communities during the war years."[62] Thus, sexuality and moral values, also within the public responsibility of the Democratic liberal national state, were interlinked with its enduring focus on family economic well-being—the less the material resources, the greater the likelihood of moral/behavioral deviance—a position that regained much prominence in debates over welfare and sexual/family behavior of the poor in the later decades of the twentieth century. For much of the immediate postwar era then, family policy debate in Congress for many Democratic-Hearth legislators predicated an enhanced, expanded national state centered on wartime experiences and the perception that families were increasingly unable to absorb and address new economic and emotional needs.

Yet World War II (and the Great Depression before it) did not obliterate the alternative, Soul, approach; its emphasis on private family values as separate from and more crucial than public economic assistance lent credence to the renewed insistence on a limited, much less active, peacetime national state. With the cessation of hostilities, Soul conservatives in Congress—now predominantly from the Republican Party—renewed their call to scale back government, instead urging the resumption of private enterprise, market freedoms, individual initiative, and voluntary activity in American economy and society. Republican-Soul advocates claimed that American families, like private enterprise, had relinquished much of their autonomy during the war and argued that government should make way for autonomous decision making and voluntarism.

Policy debates regarding the postwar housing crisis are particularly revealing of the differences in state and market ideals between Democratic-Hearth and Republican-Soul family proponents. One set of legislators, emphasizing the continuing emergency of the time, stressed the importance of government initiative to provide housing for veterans and their families. Another set emphasized the return of more peacetime conditions and called for easing restraints on private capital and on individual family initiative. Privileging family free-market values over economic assistance, its autonomy, choice, and liberty, this faction vehemently claimed that the "time had come" to remove the national government "from the business of constructing homes." For example, Republican Congressman J. Harry McGregor (R-OH), in a committee hearing on Housing for Distressed Families of Servicemen and Veterans with Families, asserted, "A man and his wife want to design their own little home," and highlighted that "there is a good deal of pride in self-designing so that they can provide for the necessary things they want in the home that they want to live in all their lives."[63] In contrast, Democratic Committee Chairman Fritz Lanham (D-TX) claimed that even though "that is the normal disposition of every person," the proposed federal distressed housing program dealt with "veterans who cannot do that."[64] Another committee member, Mrs. Helen Gahagan Douglas (D-CA), similarly stressed government involvement in the case of returning veterans, as they "are not on their feet yet. They do not know where to turn. They are confused, and there is a kind of carryover from the war."[65] Republican McGregor, on one hand, and Democrats Douglas and Chairman Lanham, on the other, presented divergent interpretations of what constituted the postwar housing problem. For McGregor, it was primarily values, diminished opportunities for private initiative, and individual family self-determination, and for Lanham and Douglas, it was interlinked with more tangible economic deprivation—the economic inability of the millions of returning soldiers to independently obtain housing for themselves and their families.

Additionally, the widely acknowledged problem of health deficiencies prompted Republican advocates to propose a health care program that again was more attentive to values, character, and private initiatives than public economic assistance. Unlike the dominant (Truman-backed, Murray-Wagner-Dingell) Democratic bill, which was universal in scope and provided for compulsory national health insurance, the conservative Republican bill recognized, "in a free society most real wealth and all goods and services are primary the product of individual initiative and personal effort" and that "a national health program, consistent with this way of life, must encourage the individual to provide health protection for himself and his family through his own effort."[66]

Thus, for a distinct oppositional faction in Congress, the war was not a legitimate ground to alter what they considered a traditional American way of life and its goals—all valuational (Soul) in character: freedom, private initiative, and personal responsibility—as distinct from and more important than material need or public economic assistance. In the context of peacetime and the emergence of the Cold War, these neoliberal values were raised to greater, more national significance, calling for an enhanced vigilance against an expanded/expanding national state.[67]

A third ideological faction embracing a mix of Hearth and Soul family approaches also existed within postwar party politics. The analysis of committee hearings finds that Hearth and Soul family ideals now clustered around three, not two, overarching sectional factions. Through their family cases, Republicans in the Northeast and Midwest articulated the Soul family values approach the most. By far, midwestern Republicans were most staunch in their Soul ideology. Conservative Republican Senators Robert Taft from Ohio and Homer Capehart from Indiana repeatedly raised free-market family values, such as self-sufficiency and maintenance of individuals' and families' autonomy from the national state, to advocate for policies such as voluntary private health insurance, opposing federal involvement in public housing, and favoring a means tests to limit eligibility of families to federal social services.[68] On the other hand, Democrats from all regions outside of the South exclusively espoused economic Hearth family ideals through their family cases: a full 100 percent of cases by Democrats from the Northeast, Midwest, and the West illustrated such ideals. And yet another distinct sectional faction, the southern Democrats, formed a third family ideological division, separate from both Democrats and Republicans. Unlike other Democrats, those from the South used a significant proportion of their family cases to illustrate a Soul family values approach, but they did so in different ways and less frequently than Republicans, all the while also displaying preferences for Hearth family economic ideals, so cherished by nonsouthern Democrats.

The peculiar, intermediate position of southern Democrats' family ideology illustrates that faction's distinctive, important position within postwar congressional politics. By 1937, a group of conservative Democrats in

Congress had become politically hostile to the New Deal. These conservative Democrats mostly came from the South and coalesced with Republicans in a so-called Conservative Coalition to block the tide of liberal New Deal programs.[69] During the war years, southern Democrats constituted the largest regional bloc of the Democratic Party, also displaying the most coherence in their legislative voting records. Through the decade following World War II, by taking advantage of institutional rules such as the seniority rule, which enabled them to assume powerful committee chairmanships and ranking positions, and their mastery of parliamentary procedures, southern Democrats became a formidable faction within their party and within Congress.[70]

Their power also came from the fact that they were vital to Democratic dominance of Congress through the postwar period, barring which both parties would have been competitive.[71] Starting from 1940, the Democratic Party was increasingly beholden to the southern vote to carry presidential elections, the South thus being critical to the party's hold on the White House till 1952. GOP prospects in House elections, too, were much brighter than is usually assumed: in 1938 in all regions outside the South, Democratic vote percentages had fallen to 50 percent or less, giving Republicans a tie or electoral advantage there—their improved prospects finally resulted in Republican control of both houses of Congress in 1946.[72] Although Democrats regained control in 1948 and formed majorities in four of the six postwar congresses from 1946 to 1956, postwar congressional party politics was, for the most part, competitive, suggesting the Democratic Party's indispensable need to placate the southern faction to keep it within its fold.[73]

Of the three factions, southern Democratic centrality to congressional politics at this time and their abiding preoccupation with family are evidenced in the number and frequency by which they cited and interacted with the family cases during committee hearings. Southern Democrats invoked 222 family case examples in the six postwar congresses studied (from 1945 to 1956) compared to nonsouthern Democrats' 132 cases and Republicans' 105 family cases. Through these family cases, southern Democrats evidence much preoccupation with social welfare; 78 percent of their family cases referenced economic Hearth family ideals, which was (at this time) centered on social welfare. Some southern Democrats, such as Claude Pepper (D-FL), who strongly championed family economic issues, were far from being conservative and in fact asserted Democratic New Deal Hearth positions as strongly as their nonsouthern colleagues.

More typically, however, southern Democrats were moderate to conservative, who supported the expansion of national social welfare programs *despite* their opposition to a strong national state. They justified their pragmatism on grounds of regional inequalities, the South's agrarianism and poverty, and the region's increasing share of the nation's elderly and children. For example, in support of variable federal grants to states for public assistance depending on a state's ability to finance its own relief, Representative Sidney Camp (D-GA) recounted the case told to him by a mail carrier in his district of a blind man on his route, aged seventy-five, and his wife. The mailman recalled that the blind man's children had gone to Detroit to work in the automotive industry and had left their aging and disabled parents at home. Representative Camp thus asserted that only a variable grant program would facilitate reaching such remote areas and circumstances such as these, common to several southern states.[74]

At another hearing on Social Security revision when conservative Republican Senator Eugene Millikin (CO) expressed disdain for a bill for aid to crippled children, southern Democratic Senator John Connally (TX) responded emphatically,

> One of the reasons these things come to Washington is the unjust and uneven economic situation in the United States whereby there are funneled to the rich centers like Chicago and New York, the problems and the emoluments that come from all over the United States. . . . The people out in the States see the injustice of paying these enormous profit incomes into these rich centers and then having the rich centers holler, "Oh, States' rights. We cannot do this. You must go back and do it at home." When you try to force some little State right now to put on these programs alone, without outside aid, it is simply unworkable, and in a way tyrannical. . . . My sympathies are all the other way so far as the governmental theory is concerned. *But the governmental theory is one thing, and digging down in your pocket and getting the money is another thing.* However, you cannot disassociate them . . . if you look back over the roll calls, you will find that a lot of southerners who believe in State rights, and all that, every once in a while vote for these bills putting the responsibility on the Federal Government, and the reason is just founded in what I have said in this statement.[75]

Yet southern Democrats, more like Republicans, also displayed a preoccupation with family values. Whereas Republicans referenced values in 80 percent of the family cases they cited during committee hearings, southern Democrats did so in 76 percent of their own family cases and nonsouthern Democrats in 69 percent of theirs. The high percentages of values across family cases for all three factions illustrate the legislators' preoccupation with family values, morals, and character in addition to its material well-being.

However, significant statistical difference between the three groups is evidenced in the *kinds* of values they invoked. By far, southern Democrats were the most moralist, referencing religion and traditional sexual and gender relations (coded as "moral values") in almost half of their family values cases (48 percent of all their family cases that invoked values cited moral values specifically). Belying their free-market ideology at this time, Republicans were more secular in the values they invoked, citing values such as family autonomy and private initiative more than religious/traditional ones: when they did invoke values in almost 60 percent of such family cases, Republicans made reference to nonreligious, nonmoralistic, "secular" values. Southern Democrats thus occupied their own ideological space *between* nonsouthern Democrats, on one hand, and Republicans, on the other, espousing a more moralistic mixed version of both Hearth and Soul family approaches.

Southern Democratic family ideology in the postwar era was a continuation of their stance from before. Southerners even in the Progressive Era had played a central role in the Democratic Party's then Soul family values approach. Their insistence on white supremacy, local autonomy, limited national state, patriarchy, marriage, and hierarchical social orders was channeled into an insistence on the preservation of (white, moralistic) family values in policies such as intermarriage bans, opposition to woman suffrage and to child labor regulation, and so on. Issues of race, segregation, and white supremacy, inextricably tied to family through sex and reproduction, continued to remain all-important for southern congressmen in the New Deal and postwar eras as well.[76] However, local control over newly instated federal welfare programs served to institutionalize the paternalistic control of southern white elites over rural blacks and poor whites, enabling the South as a region to reproduce its racial politics on its own during this period without having to approach Congress directly.[77] Indeed, southern Democrats aligned themselves with more liberal Democrats only on the condition that the racial hierarchy of the seventeen segregated southern states was preserved.[78]

However, the growing civil rights movement in the 1940s and 1950s, the increasing northward migration of southern blacks, Harry Truman's presidential actions favoring civil rights, and a strong civil rights plank in the 1948 Democratic Party platform intensified southern Democratic dissatisfaction with their party.[79] In the Dixiecrat Revolt of 1948, South Carolina Governor Strom Thurmond made a strong showing as a third party candidate, carrying four of the eleven ex-confederate states away from Harry Truman, the Democratic nominee. Although southerners returned to the Democratic Party in the next several elections, their position within the Democratic Party was increasingly unstable in the postwar period, as they moved further away from their party's liberal Hearth family position.

The postwar ideals of state upheld by the nonsouthern Democratic-Hearth family faction, the Republican-Soul faction, and the southern Democrats' mixed faction are summarized in Table 7. Through the postwar decade, there was an increasing divergence in family ideologies among legislators. In the 1950s, legislators increasingly invoked the Soul (secular and moral) family values approach when they referenced real-life family cases in committee hearings. When discussing these families, although legislators were more likely to invoke an economic focus, the Hearth approach, as seen in Figure 14, as the postwar period progressed away from World War II and into the 1950s, more members used family cases to articulate Soul family values principles rather than more economic Hearth ones.

Paired samples t tests reveal that "Congress" and "family ideology" (Hearth or Soul) were negatively correlated, indicating that family cases in later postwar congresses were more likely to illustrate Soul ideals than those in earlier congresses.[80] Thus, we see that members of the 79th Congress (1945–1946) exclusively used family cases to articulate a Hearth family ideology, and the family economics approach was dominant up until the 83rd Congress (1954–1955); however, we also see a few family cases illustrating the Soul approach in the 80th and 81st Congresses, which increases through the 1950s, peaking in the 84th Congress (1955–1956), with much more emphasis on family values and character.

In sum, contained within postwar Democratic-Hearth and Republican-Soul contests over state ideals was an ongoing difference in the kinds of

Table 7. Ideals of State, as Dividing Hearth and Soul Family Alignments in the Postwar Period

---

State Ideal: Democratic-Hearth Family Framework

STATIST, REDISTRIBUTIONIST PHILOSOPHY

Ideological foundation: New Deal active national state

Immediate interpretive context: World War II, Cold War continuing material emergencies and shortages

Ideals: Alleviation of human suffering (economic focused)

Threat perception: Spread of poverty; social breakdown; increased human suffering

---

State Ideal: Republican-Soul Family Framework

ANTISTATIST, ANTI-REDISTRIBUTIONIST PHILOSOPHY

Ideological foundation: Opposition to New Deal state

Immediate interpretive context: Return of peacetime conditions, fight against communism

Ideals: Autonomy, self-reliance, private initiative (neoliberal values focused)

Threat perception: Tyrannical government, social breakdown, loss of liberty

---

State Ideal: Southern Democratic-Hearth and Soul Family Framework

---

ANTISTATIST PHILOSOPHY WITH SOME REDISTRIBUTIONIST CONCESSSIONS

Ideological foundation: States' rights, local control

Immediate interpretive context: Southern poverty and agrarianism, civil rights movement

Ideals: Autonomy, white supremacy, traditional social hierarchies (moral values focused)

Threat perception: Regional inequalities and distribution of income, upheavals to racial order

---

family ideals upheld and politicized by their members. Republican-Soul advocates primarily assigned political value to free market–based family *values* such as personal initiative, responsibility, and independent choice, thus advocating minimal state presence. In contrast, Democratic-Hearth proponents viewed affect and values as intertwined with more tangible, more fundamental, *material* goods such as provision of health care, housing, and other services, calling for an expanded state. Southern Democrats,

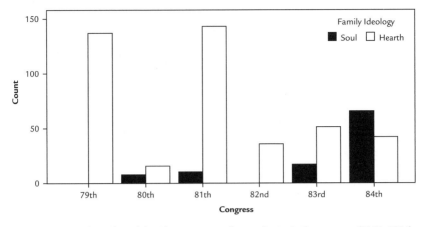

Figure 14. Hearth and Soul family case examples, 79th–84th Congresses (1945–1956). Data compiled by author, from congressional committee meetings, 1945–1956.

a third increasingly powerful group, displayed early support for liberal Democratic family economic ideals but, as the postwar period wore on, became more aligned with the Republican Soul approach.

The intervening events of the Great Depression and World War II did not obliterate (or unify) the two recurrent state philosophies. Despite the widespread popularity of the interventionist state among the majority of the American public, a distinct faction of members of Congress and their constituents continued to embrace the ideal of a limited state privileging valuational, not economic or service, goods. The next section shows how the prevailing Hearth and Soul state ideals were dependent on underlying, diverging *family* ideals.

Postwar Family Trends and the Development of Political Family Ideals

The post–World War II period witnessed widespread upheavals in how Americans practiced and thought about family life. Universal aspiration for ("modern") companionate families, rejection of traditional family practices, increasing reliance on relationship experts rather than kin, ambivalence over changing norms of motherhood, and a heavy onus on parental responsibility were some of the developments that marked the era's preoccupation with family life and welfare. These social trends made their way into legislators' ideologies and policy approaches unevenly, in large reflecting their region and the families that formed their core constituencies. The northern urban (and suburban) wage-earning nuclear family lay at the heart of the liberal Hearth family faction who focused on external, economic, and structural factors to address family in policy. Other legislators, who expressed more concern with family values and moral life, centered their policy approach instead on a (southern or midwestern) local family, one that was still embedded in thick community networks and reliant on their own independent source of income. Regardless of their differences, postwar legislators in common turned to a policy configuration that endures to this day, combining *welfare* and *regulation* policies to contain family deviance and to encourage nuclear family norms.

In earlier times, so-called companionate family ideals, such as the need for affection, intimacy, companionship, and child-centeredness in family life, could be pursued only by the affluent. In the prosperous postwar era, however, the companionate family was democratized,[81] insofar its once elusive goals became possible for millions of American families.[82] Families, across regions and now even across income groups, sought companionate ideals of love, togetherness, and personal fulfillment.[83] The enlarged appeal of the companionate family ideal, particularly its emphasis on emotions, psychology, and family-based affect, made its way into legislative debate and policy approaches.

Democratic legislators and their surrogates were deliberate in their pursuit of companionate affect in their policy agenda. They began to incorporate a language of family needs, underscoring the principle established first in the New Deal that family need was a legitimate public responsibility of the national state. Robert L. Doughton (D-NC), for example, a southern Democrat and chair of the powerful Ways and Means Committee, in reference to proposals to expand Old Age Insurance, remarked, "If it were not a question of need, none of these pension plans, either by Government or by private industry, would be required at all. . . . [need is] the paramount consideration in these pension plans."[84] Arthur J. Altmeyer, commissioner of Social Security, a Roosevelt appointee, and central figure in the drafting of the Social Security Act, also highlighted the programmatic significance of growing family needs, explaining, "Since the [public assistance] program is designed to provide for persons in need, it contracts or expands as need increases or diminishes. . . . Since VJ-Day the extent of need has been on the increase in the United States. Many factors, among them lessened work opportunities for submarginal workers with the return of servicemen to civilian life, and the inflationary trend, have been responsible for the steady rise in public assistance rolls and in payment levels."[85]

Needs were increasingly defined as both material and emotional, particularly in light of prevailing national and international conditions. The existing Democratic alliance claimed that the national state had a responsibility to meet diverse needs across the nation given its regional disparities, as George Ehinger, from the Child Welfare Commission of the American Legion, asserted, "Because a child is born in Alabama and another child in New York, Uncle Sam is equally responsible to see that each child gets at least the minimum of this physical needs . . . [and] to see that each child is entitled to a minimum of his mental needs."[86] The presence of communism and the Cold War also served to highlight the growing interest in emotional and mental needs. A signature event in the history of children and family policy development was the Midcentury White House Conference on Children and Youth in 1950, where for the first time the emotional welfare of children was made the top priority and mental, emotional, and spiritual qualities of children were stressed as essential to individual happiness and responsible citizenship.[87] In his address to the over 6,000 delegates to the conference, President Truman emphasized the threat of communism and the ongoing war in Korea as "the serious crisis in world affairs overshadowing all we do" and underscored the "struggle . . . [to] preserve the elements of our American way of life that are the basic source of our strength." The "ideology of communism," he said, "is a challenge to all the values of our society and our way of life" such that "the moral and spiritual dangers that flow from [it] are a much more serious threat to freedom than are its military power." In this context, Truman asserted that the "single most important thing our young people will need to meet this critical challenge . . . is moral strength—and strength of character."[88]

The preoccupation with mental, psychological, and emotional toughness within the family impelled proposals for a whole slew of additional psychological or emotional welfare services, such as relationship advice, guidance, referral, and active instruction in childrearing and other directed family practices. The director of the Bureau of Public Assistance, Jane Hoey, another key Democratic appointee since the Roosevelt administration, told Congress, "People in increasing numbers are looking to the local welfare department not only for financial aid but for other services unrelated to immediate financial aid," as "records of the welfare agencies . . . show that many families do survive when they get the kind of help they need at the right time." "Sometimes," she said, "the help that they need is financial . . . [but] many families are emotionally in conflict to the point where they do not see how to go on living together as a group . . . if such a family can find a skillful and understanding counseling service, they can find a way through their emotional confusions to a sound basis of mutual understanding and relationship that makes it possible for them to continue to live successfully as a family group."[89]

The "whole child" approach, first advanced by the Children's Bureau in the 1910s and further pushed by welfare officials in the postwar period, demanded a coordinated outlook that combined economic, physical, mental, and spiritual needs of children.[90] This approach, as well as its acknowledgment of the once overlooked dimension of emotional and behavioral problems, was now resurrected to advocate assistance to even higher-income families.[91] Katharine Lenroot, chief of the Children's Bureau, first appointed by Roosevelt in 1934 and in her position until 1951, told the House Committee on Labor, "Experience has shown that children from all economic groups may have these [emotional] problems, that many parents want help and advice in dealing with them, and that service should be available without feeling that to receive help from a child-welfare worker carries any disgrace or stigma."[92]

The increased attention to a family's psychological and mental needs brought with it an enhanced appreciation of the role of professionals and expert advice in guiding family development and success. Historian Elaine Tyler May affirms in *Homeward Bound*, her authoritative work on Cold War families, that postwar America was *the* era of the expert.[93] In an atomic age rife with uncertainty, in which children were born in a world unfamiliar to their parents, families increasingly looked to professionals to tell them how to manage and lead their lives. The tremendous popularity of books such as Benjamin Spock's *Baby and Child Care* and Norman Vincent Peale's *The Power of Positive Thinking* illustrates the postwar disposition of young Americans to turn to the advice of experts in their quest "toward a radically new vision of family life [by] trying self-consciously to avoid the paths of their parents."[94]

Members of Congress too came to rely heavily on professionals, calling on social scientists, doctors, psychologists, and social workers in formulating their family policy ideas. At postwar committee hearings, professional witnesses provided 57 percent of family case anecdotes presented before

Congress, in contrast to merely 33 percent of all family anecdotes supplied by experts in the late twentieth-century period and 53 percent in the Progressive Era. In contrast to later in the twentieth century, professionals were thus much more likely than private citizens to play a central role in postwar family policy discussion. Whereas professional experts have always played a pivotal role in the formulation of liberal Hearth family policies, making the case for greater state programs in partnership with families, in 25 percent of their cases, postwar expert witnesses also articulated Soul family principles, stressing in those cases family values rather than government material services.

Heightened attention to family also brought with it an increased standard for parent involvement in child development and rearing. Considerable proportions of both Hearth and Soul cases mentioned "irresponsible parents" such that there is no statistically significant difference between the two family alignments in this regard. Twenty-six percent of Soul and 21 percent of Hearth cases expressly mentioned the irresponsibility of parents. This is illustrated in numerous discussions of deserting fathers. Midwestern members in particular, such as Gerald Ford (R-MI), Andrew Jacobs (D-IN), and Louis Rabaut (D-IN), proposed multiple regulatory bills in successive congresses making abandonment of dependents a federal crime. These bills were designed to enforce child support orders across state lines, regulating the "illegal meanderings" of husbands who failed to provide for their families. The bills were nicknamed "runaway pappy bills" and gained much public attention.[95] Many members stressed the legitimacy for the involvement of the federal government in such cases, arguing that "this is a matter which vitally affects the national interest in that the strength of American families is of the utmost importance to the strength of America."[96]

Hearth advocates, following the approach of welfare officials, again viewed the problem of nonsupport as part of a larger intertwined, complex problem: "Where family relations are so strained, where the husband and father is not only separated from his wife and children but fails to provide for them, support is but one of a multiplicity of problems."[97] They thus proposed expanded welfare and counseling programs in addition to regulation and child support enforcement.[98]

For another group of congresspersons, however, paternal responsibility represented *the* keystone to family integrity; to them, the phenomenon of deserting fathers demonstrated the erosion of fundamental human values and the diminution of family self-sufficiency, threating the very fabric of social order. These legislators were far more categorical in their punitive appraisals of deserting fathers and in their condemnation of the family's subsequent public dependency. They roundly derided them as the "vilest segment" of the population,[99] as "buzzard bait" who had "proven that [their] fatherly affection is of not much value."[100] Representative Andrew Jacobs (D-MI) cited Judge Niblack in his district in Michigan as illustrating "the best brand" of psychology, recounting, "He would say, 'Did you work last week?' and the offender would say, 'Yes, but I had a payment to make on my car.' The judge would say, 'Your payment on your car is not nearly as important as your children. Put him in jail over the week end and we will see what he is able to do next Saturday.'" Representative Jacobs concluded, "That kind of psychology is tops because it works"; "these fellows," he said, "are unfit to bring children into the world. I do not think you need to hold them on your knee too much or coddle them."[101]

Just as deserting fathers received heightened attention by the postwar national state, in part reflecting the inward turn to family psychology and relationships, the problem of delinquent mothers now also assumed salience in policy debate at this time. For long, mothers had been viewed as central to their family's and children's health, given their primary role in caregiving and in food preparation;[102] however, in the postwar period, mothers were seen as fundamental to an individual's long-term psychological and emotional development, impacting adulthood in new, multiple, and long-lasting ways. Professionals emphasized the problems that could result from a mother displacing her own frustrations onto her children. This pattern of maternal behavior was then linked to various psychosociological disorders in adults, such as schizophrenia, homosexuality, identity diffusion, and an inability to assume the commitments of adulthood.[103]

At its core, as many have now shown, the concern over the bad mother was a concern about maintaining traditional gender norms, which had been threatened by the large-scale entry of women into the workforce during and since World War II[104] and the converse fact that vast proportions of other mothers (suburban housewives) were now raising their children with an exclusivity and in an isolation without parallel in American history.[105] Unlike today, when the companionate family has assumed an egalitarian form in which the roles of male and female spouses are more interchangeable, the postwar companionate family was strongly prescriptive of traditional gender norms, prescribing a supportive, subordinate role of the mother and wife.[106] This was also in contrast to the earlier 1920s, when popular readings of new psychological theories were used to justify freer sexual expression for women and men; after the war, however, "psychology was beginning to serve the interests of those seeking to inhibit sexual and social freedom for women. . . . psychologists and social workers were [now] being delegated the primary responsibility for adjusting women to more repressive standards."[107]

Through the 1950s, the traditional roles of wife and mother thus resumed dominance as pivotal cultural values to be upheld. In the case of women, the era's emphasis on companionship and individual satisfaction was firmly contained within the domestic sphere, enhancing and complementing but not challenging a woman's paramount roles as mother and wife. As a witness to a Subcommittee on Juvenile Delinquency observed, "Too often mothers go to seed within the four walls of a little home allowing the thousand and one repetitive and never ending duties to completely absorb them and to wash all the sparkle out of their personalities." Instead, he claimed "parent-education classes" would provide mothers with "opportunities to renew their growth as important, unique, and interesting personalities in their own right" and help them realize that "a vital, interesting, well-informed mother is a much better companion for the husband, and mother for the children than a half-dozen household martyrs."[108]

During committee hearings, defective mothering was invariably at the center of most accounts of social ailments, the cause of juvenile delinquency, sexual precociousness, and uncontrollability among adolescent girls and lack of moral backbone and indiscipline among boys.[109] The bulk of family cases mentioned "married mothers" (see Table 8). However, "widowed mothers" featured prominently also, more so to advocate the Hearth approach rather than Soul.[110] The family cases displaying the Soul family values approach made numerous references to "remarried mothers," demonstrating the previously stated preoccupation with family self-sufficiency and marriage as private solutions to dependency.

Soul cases also disproportionately referenced "irresponsible mothers," often using this to illustrate the drawbacks of irresponsible state programs. Some of the first references linking the national state's own irresponsible welfare services to family irresponsible behavior, notably moral indiscretions and deliberate dependency, appear at this time in committee transcripts. In this period as in later decades, some legislators and their witnesses challenged the expanding national welfare state by claiming that such state intervention encouraged extramarital childbearing and irresponsible behavior by

Table 8. Characteristics of Mothers, Illustrated in Hearth and Soul Family Case Examples, 79th–84th Congresses (1945–1956)

| | | Family Ideology | | | |
| | | Soul | | Hearth | |
		Count	Percent	Count	Percent
Mother's marital status	Unmarried	1	1.3	10	2.6
	Married	66	83.5	290	76.1
	Widowed[a]	3	3.8	46	12.1
	Deserted	4	5.1	24	6.3
	Remarried[a]	4	5.1	4	1.0
	Dead	1	1.3	7	1.8
	Total	79	100.0	381	100.0
Mother's characteristics	Involved	27	57.4	71	44.9
	Irresponsible[a]	18	38.3	32	20.3
	Ill[a]	2	4.3	46	29.1
	Dead	0	.0	9	5.7
	Total	47	100.0	158	100.0

Source: Data compiled by author from committee hearings, 1945–1956.
[a] Values in the same row are significantly different for Soul and Hearth cases at $p < .05$ in the two-sided test of equality for column proportions. Tests assume equal variances.

mothers. Some witnesses, such as Catholic and other charity organizations, cited such cases as examples of the inefficacy of large public relief programs as opposed to more local, private relief efforts.[111]

The emphasis on curtailing defective parenting and encouraging "responsible" motherhood and fatherhood downplayed, even devalued, parents' traditional, intuitive knowledge. Experts instead celebrated the ongoing postwar cultural shift in which parents were more willing to devote themselves to being "good" parents and to learn new family methods and practices. As Thomas Van Sant, director of the Division of Adult Education in Baltimore, told the Senate Subcommittee on Juvenile Delinquency, "Parents do not already know those things which will assure them of being wise and judicious in all situations. Parents themselves are the first ones to admit this."[112] According to Van Sant, reliance on professional advice was more needed than ever to guide families in "our rapidly changing technological age" and because of the "ever growing imbalance between advancing science and lagging social behavior."[113] For several liberal Hearth family proponents in Congress and their surrogates, external expert knowledge, not local, community, or traditional sources, would thus better guide families toward the new family ideals that postwar society seemed to wholeheartedly covet.

However, for others in Congress, new companionate ideals of family, love, affection, and personal fulfillment, although important, were still secondary to the preservation of more traditional family values such as moral discipline, parental respect, obedience, and personal responsibility. Some family examples thus demonstrated a continued reliance on traditional family supports such as religion, church, community, and parents to ensure family success and well-being. For example, Mrs. Mary Bittinger, wife of the church pastor and social worker at the Presbyterian Child-Placing Service of the Presbyterian Church in Nashville, Tennessee, testified before the Senate and offered the example of her twenty-three-year-old son, John, his marriage to Marge, and their new family in the following way, as an illustration of the enduring appeal of more traditional, religious, and community-based family relations. Senators Estes Kefauver (D-TN) and William Langer (R-ND) applauded these ideals and, like many others, acknowledged the importance of "closely united religiously-oriented homes."[114]

> When these children were asked to delay their marriage a year, John replied: "You know I wouldn't do anything you forbid." Marge's statement was, "I wouldn't want to marry without your consent and blessing." They were obedient to the request made of them. They later enjoyed all the loveliness of a church wedding in the church of the groom, ceremony performed by the groom's father. Their request as a request from the groom's father was an autographed Bible to take with them to their new home. The first Sunday they were in Knoxville they sought out Sequoia Hills Presbyterian Church where they placed their membership, and where they are active worshippers and workers. It is a relationship as this that every American boy and girl should be able to enjoy.[115]

From committee data (see Table 9), we find that members often invoked morals and values while illustrating both Hearth and Soul approaches through their family examples, but as already discussed, the kinds of family values they illustrated were often different. Soul cases, which evidenced the preeminence of family values above economic conditions, were more likely to refer to traditional moral, community, and free-market values, in contrast to

Table 9. Religion and Values Illustrated in Hearth and Soul Family Case
Examples, 79th–84th Congresses (1945–1956)

| | | Family Ideology | | | |
| | | Soul | | Hearth | |
		Count	Percent	Count	Percent
Value emphasized by policy*	Liberty/self-sufficiency	32	41.0	13	5.1
	Equality/inequality	0	.0	38	15.0
	Social justice	0	.0	48	19.1
	National gratitude	0	.0	29	11.5
	Democracy	0	.0	59	23.3
	Parents' irresponsibility	20	25.6	53	20.9
	Irresponsible business	26	33.3	13	5.1
	Total	78	100.0	253	100.0
Type of values*	Secular	31	34.8	193	75.4
	Moral	58	65.2	63	24.6
	Total	89	100.0	256	100.0

Source: Data compiled by author, committee hearings, 1945–1956.
* The chi-square statistic is significant, $p \leq .000$.

Hearth family cases that demonstrated (even then) more secular-humanist values, such as democratic participation or equality. Sixty-five percent of family illustrations of Soul ideals invoked moral values in contrast to 25 percent of Hearth family examples.

Of the Soul cases that mentioned specific values, 41 percent referred to individualist private values of "liberty" and "self-sufficiency" unlike Hearth cases, where only 5 percent did as much; also, a larger proportion of Soul cases focused on irresponsible businesses such as comic books, television stations, and so on as negatively impacting family life and morals.[116] In their descriptions, many of these businesses were local enterprises, negatively impacting the moral fiber of communities in which they were based. In comparison, Hearth family cases emphasized instead secular-humanist values of "democracy" (23 percent), "social justice" (19 percent), and "equality" (15 percent) in their descriptions.

The qualitative difference in the kinds of values illustrated through the Hearth focus on family economics and the Soul emphasis on family values cases is statistically significant. It demonstrates the onset of what has become an ongoing divide between the family values of "two Americas"—one, a secular-humanistic set associated with more "modern," expert-driven, companionate families often at home in urban and suburban areas, and the other, moral and private market values linked to more "traditional," community-embedded, local families (still) firmly grounded in the fabric of small-town America and small business.[117]

Even in the postwar era, at the heart of Soul (political) family ideology was small business and its vision of an interdependent, organic society.[118] Through small family-run businesses, legislators described a Jeffersonian-like society in which individual family units, employers, churches, and local groups remained cohesively interconnected to one another, unimpeded by external government intervention. This picture, of course, stood in stark contrast to the Hearth portrayal of "modern," discrete, suburban family life, with families always on the move with little community life or shared connections, or of urban families also with minimal commonality or connection to their neighbors.

The Soul organic vision of society permeated arguments for the removal of federal government programs and reinstatement of local organizations at the center of all (public and private) family welfare and assistance. Neighbors and local communities, closely interlinked and cohesive, were shown to better administer, monitor, and assess welfare and provide solutions to social problems than state or impersonal agents. As Senator Eugene Millikin (R-CO) strongly asserted, "Why do we come to Washington . . . and ask for a solution of a problem which, by its nature, is local? . . . after all, if a person is sick, he is sick in the town of Squedunk; or if disabled, he is disabled in the town of Squedunk. And that has a direct impact on his family and on his neighbors and on the community, and in a dozen other directions, the most of which are local."[119] Similarly, Senator Edward Martin (R-PA) underscored close-knit communities, with close interactions among members, all of whom possessed intimate knowledge of one another: "The people in the community know the people that ought to have assistance, and they know the ones that can spend the money to their advantage and those who cannot. They know where there is a father that will go the taproom [or not]."[120]

Conflicting ideals of society and economy also underpinned policy debates over national wage legislation. Some contended that low wages and economic deprivation were at the heart of a "trifling attitude" and unhappy home life, and thus a decent wage was necessary to "make it possible for a man with a family to raise his children."[121] In these narratives, society comprised discrete family units, where the very success and quality of an individual's family life, his own self-worth and personal value, depended in large part on fair remuneration of his wage work. Illustrating this position in support of an increase to the minimum wage, Solomon Barkin, director of research at the Textile Workers of America, for example, cited the far-reaching affective and behavioral impact of higher wages in the South on the lives of southern textile families. He described workers' material, working conditions as formative of their very experience of family and community:

> You will find that when people are undernourished, when people do not have good conditions of living, work just does not matter because in cotton mills, for example, until a few years ago you could work a whole week and come out with a blank check because all the money was spent in the company store and you paid the company or the employer for his home and his services . . . and other debts. . . . Under that set of conditions . . . people did not have any interest in jobs. . . . They were indifferent and we used to say, back in 1939, that we had never seen a textile worker walk about the town except in denims. . . . His wife would be going into the mill wearing her print cloth dress, usually secured at the remnant shop in the mill out of the company store. She would come in walking downtown with tufts of cotton lint about her. She did not care about her appearance. The town was unimportant, her home was unimportant, nothing mattered.
>
> Now . . . visit a southern cotton textile town . . . there has been a tremendous improvement. They used to pay 25 cents a room a week, now southern textile workers are paying $35 a month but they now have modern homes. . . . Why you could not go to the Southern community on Sunday and find anybody in denim; they are all wearing store suits and white shirts. They have a new bearing, they have a new independence . . . just because we raised the minimum wage and the wage of those textile workers.[122]

For this witness and the congress members who supported him, standardized higher wages and income determined the independence, work ethic, and the very motivation to pursue happiness among workers.

Opponents to the standard, nationwide, minimum wage claimed that it reduced other—more traditional—values within communities, turning traditional humanism and cooperation between employers and employees into materialistic contractualism and distrust. They instead privileged organic qualities such as cooperation, interdependence, and community cohesion above all and separated from coarse materialism. For example, a representative of the southern lumber industry opposed the minimum wage increase, saying, "The wage-hour law . . . has destroyed that amiable and cooperative employer-employee relationship that made American industry the greatest of any in the world." He lamented, "The wholesome security of the family atmosphere, so typical of the South and Southern industry for generations, has been dissipated by the Fair Labor Standards Act and, in its place, has been substituted a venom of skepticism, distrust, and in some cases, actual animosity between men on whose cooperation the survival of both depend."[123]

Another witness, an owner of an auto service plant from Columbus, Ohio, cited a personal case of generosity to a mentally challenged worker and his family, referring to "a moron who loafed in my blacksmith shop day after day." The owner reported saying, "Well, if he can sweep we will put him on the pay roll at 25 cents an hour, and give him $10 a week, because he is in here all the time anyway . . . he has been there for 5 or 6 years." In this way, the worker, although a special case, was able to "get $500 to $600 a year," which "helped his father."[124] However, Irving McCann, general counsel to the investigating committee, went on to describe state regulatory obstructionism, whereby the Wage and Hour Division held the owner guilty of violating law because he had not applied for a handicapped worker exception. After he was found guilty, they permitted him to employ "this fellow as a man who was deficient at a reduced rate." Representative Wint Smith (R-KS) underscored the inefficiency and mismatch between government bureaucracies and small business by pointing out that it took the owner three months to get that permit. "The inspector made two trips by air to Cincinnati out to this man's plant to find out whether he could hire this moron at $10 a week." Representative Smith concluded, "Here is the Government stepping in and telling you [a small business owner] how much to pay, and we have always thought that wages were based on the productivity of that labor."[125]

In sum, even in the postwar era, there were two prevailing central ideals of family espoused by groups of legislators in Congress. Whereas some proponents stressed companionate family ideals of love, child-centeredness, and reliance on expert knowledge, others espoused a more traditional family ideal in which responsibility, discipline, and obedience were more central.

Table 10. Postwar Imbricated Ideals of Family, Society, and Economy

Hearth Approach (Nonsouthern Democrats, Sometimes Southern Democrats)
<u>Family ideal type</u>: Companionate nuclear family
<u>Ideals</u>: Love, spousal affection and companionship, child centered, expert reliant
<u>Society conception</u>: Discrete family units; working (material) conditions dictate home life
<u>Economy conception</u>: Regulated employer-employee relations, standardized, fair to workers
<u>Core constituency</u>: Mobile, urban and suburban, laboring families

Soul Approach (Republicans, Sometimes Southern Democrats)
<u>Family ideal type</u>: Hierarchical family
<u>Ideals</u>: Parental authority, moral values, religious, obedience, discipline, antiexpert
<u>Society conception</u>: Organic society, with interdependent and localized family units, cooperative social relations
<u>Economy conception</u>: Free exchange between employer and employees, subjective, interpersonal
<u>Core constituency</u>: Small business family, family farm

The Hearth family approach was imbricated with a distinct conception of society and economy, in which families were discrete social units, and the success of family life was much dependent on wages, income, and other material conditions at work and at home. In contrast, the Soul family approach continued to assume a more cohesive, organic conception of society and economy, built on cooperation, free exchange, and trust between interdependent social units. These ideals, summarized in Table 10, underpinned and informed the alternative approaches to the welfare state and to social policy at large. The three identified delegations of legislators (southern Democrats, nonsouthern Democrats, and Republicans) adopted these approaches differentially and in differing degrees.

Contrasting legislators' alignments with one or the other of these family ideals are strikingly suggested by the characteristics of the family cases used by the three groups of legislators during committee hearings. Family cases referenced by members from the three ideological factions were significantly different in terms of the family's race, mother's marital status, and mother's other characteristics; no statistical difference was found in regards to family

Table 11. Characteristics of Family Cases by Active MCs' Ideological Faction, 79th–84th Congresses (1945–1956)

		Ideological Faction					
		Southern Democrat		Nonsouthern Democrat		Republican	
		Count	Percent	Count	Percent	Count	Percent
Types of values*	Secular	89$_a$	53.0	86$_b$	92.5	49$_a$	58.3
	Moral	79$_a$	47.0	7$_b$	7.5	35$_a$	41.7
	Total	168	100.0	93	100.0	84	100.0
Family race*	White	207$_a$	91.6	113$_b$	75.3	62$_b$	71.3
	African American	9$_a$	4.0	5$_a$	3.3	0[1]	0
	Foreign/ white ethnic	6$_a$	2.7	30$_b$	20.0	1$_a$	1.1
	Other	4$_a$	1.8	2$_a$	1.3	24$_b$	27.6
	Total	226	100.0	150	100.0	87	100.0
Family structure	Nuclear	222$_a$	87.7	152$_b$	95.6	99$_{a,b}$	92.5
	Extended	31$_a$	12.3	7$_b$	4.4	8$_{a,b}$	7.5
	Total	253	100.0	159	100.0	107	100.0
Income status	Lower income	153$_a$	79.3	92$_b$	66.7	63$_{a,b}$	69.2
	Middle income	36$_a$	18.7	33$_a$	23.9	22$_a$	24.2
	Upper income	4$_a$	2.1	13$_b$	9.4	6$_{a,b}$	6.6
	Total	193	100.0	138	100.0	91	100.0
Mother's marital status*	Married	164$_a$	71.9	126$_b$	85.7	66$_{a,b}$	77.6
	Widowed	34$_a$	14.9	10$_a$	6.8	5$_a$	5.9
	Deserted	11$_a$	4.8	11$_a$	7.5	6$_a$	7.1
	Other	19$_a$	8.3	0[1]	0	8$_a$	9.4
	Total	228	100.0	147	100.0	85	100.0
Mother's characteristics*	Involved	53$_a$	47.3	25$_a$	52.1	20$_a$	44.4
	Irresponsible	25$_a$	22.3	3$_b$	6.3	22$_c$	48.9
	Ill or dead	34$_a$	30.4	20$_a$	41.7	3$_b$	6.7
	Total	112	100.0	48	100.0	45	100.0

Source: Data compiled by author, congressional committee hearings, 1945–1956.
Note: a, b subscripts report the results of column proportions tests with a significance of .05. Each significant pair is marked by differing subscripts; those with identical subscripts have no significant difference.
* Chi-square significant at $p \leq .05$.

income or structure (Table 11). Whereas a vast majority of cases across the three groups were drawn from white families, the families referenced by southern Democrats were the most white, nonsouthern Democrats referred to the highest proportion of foreign or white ethnic families, and Republicans spoke of the largest proportion of Hispanic and Native American families.

The racial composition of family cases reflects, to a large extent, the constituent bases of each legislative delegation. From the end of Reconstruction up until the Voting Rights Act of 1965, African Americans in the South were effectively disenfranchised, their interests peripheral to southern white members of Congress. However, southern Democrats in the Progressive Era cited black families with much greater frequency than other legislators. As discussed in the previous chapter, southern Democrats did this as a way to distinguish the South from the rest of the country and to press for the establishment of white supremacist policies at the national level, such as nationwide intermarriage bans and ascriptive immigration policies. Southern Democratic focus on predominantly white family cases in the postwar period instead reflects both demographic shifts and political changes that had occurred in the region since the Progressive Era. Whereas in the period following World War II, the South was still the region with the largest African American population, the increasing mechanization of cotton growing was displacing millions of black tenant farmers who were migrating out of the region in search of employment. From 1940 to 1970, five million African Americans migrated northward, to more industrial urban centers, greatly diminishing their presence in the South.[126] Further, in order to retain the South within its coalition, the Democratic Party deliberately accommodated the South's claim to white supremacy by upholding its prerogative to reproduce, at the local level, its own racialized social order. In this way, the issue of race and instantiation of white supremacy was relegated in many ways to a more subterranean, local level.[127] Thus, it is not surprising that southern Democrats in the postwar period almost exclusively referenced white families as illustrations of their (national) policy concerns and preferences.

Outside of the South, though, Democrats had been gaining a strong foothold among white ethnics, first- and second-generation immigrants who were themselves or had parents who were foreign born. This constituency was reflected in the higher than average mention of foreign-born, immigrant, or white ethnic families among the family cases referenced by nonsouthern Democratic members and their witnesses. The large proportion of "other" race families referenced by Republican members reflects Republicans' stronghold in mountain states such as Utah and the Dakotas, where Native Americans were found in larger numbers.

As postwar Democrats sought to universalize "family need" and assist all families, emotionally, psychologically, and materially, regardless of income, they referenced more middle- and upper-income families (32 percent combined). Table 11 also indicates that this expansive approach was more prevalent among northern Democrats, as southern Democrats continued to highlight lower-income families. Republican-referenced families were not dissimilar from those referred to by any of the two groups of Democrats with regard to family income, as there is no statistical difference in their proportions of lower- or upper-income families. Finally, the data suggest that the families invoked by the legislative factions also varied in terms of the mother's marital status. Whereas nonsouthern Democratic cases focused most on married mothers (86 percent of all nonsouthern Democratic cases contained references to married mothers versus 71 percent of southern Democratic cases), southern Democrats were more likely to reference "other" mothers (i.e., mothers who were either "unmarried" or "remarried" or "dead"). Republican cases were not statistically different from either southern or nonsouthern Democratic cases in regard to the mother's marital status. It bears noting that across the three groups, a substantial proportion of cases referenced widowed mothers. Widows were central to much of the post–World War II veterans' and social security legislation, and this focus diminished over the rest of the century, as evidenced by the falling percentage of widowed family cases in later periods to a fraction of its postwar high.

Among the cases that make mention of the characteristics of mothers, both Democratic factions had comparable proportions of cases that stressed the illness or deceased status of mothers (30 percent of southern Democratic cases and 41 percent of nonsouthern Democratic cases versus 7 percent of Republican cases). Republican cases, most concerned with family values, disproportionately stressed "irresponsible mothers" in 49 percent of their cases; southern Democrats mentioned irresponsible mothers in 22 percent of their cases; and nonsouthern Democrats, demonstrating the greatest preoccupation with structural family conditions, were the least concerned with irresponsible mothers, mentioning them in the lowest proportion (6 percent) of their cases.

In brief, nonsouthern Democrats were more likely to reference secular values in white and white ethnic families, from both lower-income and upper-income groups, with nuclear family arrangements in which mothers were mostly married and actively involved in family rearing, with some in-capacitated by ill health or deceased. These kinds of families were at the core of the postwar Hearth family economic ideology that stressed state expansion into families. Southern Democrats, on the other hand, almost exclusively focused on white families, more often from lower-income groups and with extended family networks, in which, compared to their Democratic colleagues from the North, more mothers were remarried or unmarried and a good proportion was seen as irresponsible, along with a sizable proportion of those who were ill or deceased. Among these cases, one sees a mixture of Hearth and Soul characteristics, where the focus on economic deprivation is combined with culturally traditionalist concerns over irresponsible mothering and family moral values. Finally, Republicans were the most likely to stress private values through family cases; their families included those of racial minorities in addition to white ones, extending across income groups, with an overwhelming focus on the mother's married status and a preoccupation with the "irresponsible mother" to the exclusion of a mother's incapacitation through death or disease. The Republican family picture seen through these cases reveals a stronger emphasis on private Soul qualities of a family in which values and the mother's involvement and marriage status were vital to family economic independence, free markets, private initiative, and their opposition to an expanded state.

The data on family cases also point to the sectional differences that continued to underpin the political family ideology of the three legislative factions. There is an observable, statistically significant relationship between the region of the member of Congress and the region of the family case that he or she referenced during committee hearings.[128] The sectional schism in the Democratic Party at this time can be seen in the regions from which they most drew their family examples. Nonsouthern Democrats disproportionately drew on families from the Northeast (in 41 percent of their cases) while southern Democrats referred to a much higher proportion of families in the South (51 percent of cases). Republicans, in (statistically significant) contrast to both kinds of Democrats, were more likely to reference families in the West (Table 12).

It bears noting that Republicans drew their largest proportion of cases from the South. This would seem to suggest that for Republicans, their Soul family ideology was not reflective of the lives of their (majority) constituents, since the South was solidly Democratic at this time and had almost no Republican representation in Congress. Republican reliance on families in the

Table 12. Family Cases by Region and Ideological Faction of MC, 79th–84th Congresses (1945–1956)

		Ideological Faction					
		Southern Democrat		Nonsouthern Democrat		Republican	
		Count	Percent	Count	Percent	Count	Percent
Family region	Northeast	53[a]	23.9	54[b]	40.9	22[a]	21.0
	Midwest	39[a]	17.6	15[a]	11.4	16[a]	15.2
	South	113[a]	50.9	42[b]	31.8	34[b]	32.4
	West	17[a]	7.7	21[b]	15.9	33[c]	31.4
	Total	222	100.0	132	100.0	105	100.0

Source: Data compiled by author, congressional committee hearings, 1945 to 1956.
Note: a, b subscripts report the results of column proportions tests with a significance of .05. Each significant pair is marked by differing subscripts; those with identical subscripts have no significant difference.

West is more reflective of a bottom-up story since many districts in certain Rocky Mountain states were reliably Republican.

Conclusion

In the post–World War II era, legislators for the first time began to concern themselves with family values, affective dynamics such as emotions and psychology, and the national policy significance of family disruption. Far from reflecting a period of idyllic family relations, members of Congress from both parties and diverse ideologies articulated an underlying anxiety over the stability and certainty of the nuclear family. Depending on prevailing state ideologies, the alarm over family breakdown came to be aligned with calls for the expansion and/or curtailment of the welfare state, a development that continued and deepened in the late twentieth century.

Postwar family policy dynamics were, however, different from later ones in two important respects. First, in the postwar period, while the proponents of Hearth and Soul approaches emphasized different qualities of families in their family policy ideals (moralistic vs. secular, parent vs. child centered, etc.), they both commonly assumed a nuclear family form. In contrast, as seen in the next two chapters, in the late twentieth century, Hearth and Soul advocates diverged sharply in their very assumptions of family form, with Hearth proponents eschewing the dominance of one form/structure and

Soul advocates staunchly supporting the nuclear family form as the only legitimate family form.

Second and more important, in the postwar period, welfare state expansion and its opposition centrally shaped the development of partisan family ideologies. Thus, social welfare (its expansion or curtailment) was the dominant policy axis through which members of both parties addressed family issues. This is unlike later periods, including our own, when divergent family ideals themselves have shaped party competition. While both Hearth and Soul family policy approaches coexisted during the postwar period too, their politics were less clearly divided by party, and the two family ideals were more overlapping and far less culturally polarizing than they came to be in the late century, an unprecedented period of family political development to which the next two chapters now turn.

Chapter 4

Late Twentieth-Century Period: Family Transformations and Policy Shifts

Starting in the late 1970s, the two parties began to vie to hold the mantel of family in their campaign slogans and policy agendas, typically by promising to deploy the national government to "strengthen families," which meant targeting family values, culture, and morality just as much as family economic conditions and material well-being.[1] Jimmy Carter was the first president to make strengthening of family a goal for his administration.[2] Then, during Reagan's presidential campaign in 1980, the Republican platform called for sweeping reforms to "restore the family," and President Clinton in his 1994 State of the Union address declared that the country's problems were rooted in the breakdown of families and communities.[3] In the same year, Republicans emphasized family in their Contract with America, with four of their ten proposals addressing families. Less than two years later, Democrats rallied around strengthening families in their "Families First" Campaign in 1996, with Bill Clinton and Republican candidate Robert Dole battling to be the bearer of family in that election. In the 2000 election, Democratic presidential candidate Al Gore called for a family lobby as powerful as the gun lobby, and in 2004, George W. Bush's reelection was widely attributed to the turnout of (conservative) "values voters," for whom conservative family values, such as opposition to same-sex marriage equality, had become a clarion call.

Promotion of family strength and family stability as explicit policy goals rose to prominence in the late 1970s in liberal-Democratic social welfare policies such as Title XX social services (1975 Social Security Act), the Supplemental Security Income program (consolidating Aid to the Blind, Aid to the

Disabled, and Old Age Assistance), and the earned income tax credit for working poor families. In these policies, economic deprivation and family strength were viewed as intertwined, and a stated policy goal was to strengthen family by enhancing its economic resources.[4] Soon, however, the valuational approach to strengthening family began to loudly rival the economic one, seen most clearly in the organization of the White House Conference on Families (WHCF) in 1980.

In 1980, the Carter administration organized a White House Conference on Families, sponsored by a coalition of twenty-eight family-related nonprofit organizations and comprising of a series of three conferences held in three cities: Los Angeles, Minneapolis, and Baltimore. During the conference, conflagrations among attendees pointed to the deep ideological rifts that were emerging among conservatives and liberals in their approaches to family. In Baltimore, prolife groups staged walkouts in opposition to proposals favoring abortion and the Equal Rights Amendment, claiming that the conference had been "rigged" to support more government involvement in family instead of less.[5] In Minneapolis, conservative groups similarly staged a walkout, but this time they were met by liberal dissenters who countercharged the conservative caucus of being racist, claiming that less government in family life implied less policy assistance for black families. In Los Angeles, the National Pro-Family Coalition asserted that the conference had been skewed to reflect the views of social work professionals and federal bureaucrats with vested interests in expanded government involvement and spending.[6]

The policy goal of strengthening family thus also began to emerge as a conservative emblem for retrenchment of federal programs, leaving most family services and economic assistance to private and local devices.[7] This was most evident during the 1980s, when the Reagan administration aimed at getting government "off the backs of families" and called to greatly reduce government responsibility for family economic life. In the 1990s, however, conservative moralists (or paleo-conservatives), a key Republican faction, reengaged the national state and turned to public policy to *promote* conservative family values and goals. A central development that followed was the Republican programmatic turn toward affirmatively protecting the traditional two-parent, nuclear, heterosexual family and engineering traditional values of stable marriage fused with free-market goals of self-sufficiency through federal programs.[8] Furthermore, regulatory/punitive policies were devised to instill family responsibilities through punitive measures such as wage garnishment for failure to pay child support payments, and public service programs were used to encourage marital family formation and promote responsible fatherhood and working parenthood.[9] Still other measures hoped to encourage traditional families by pressing adoption over foster care.[10]

And yet the liberal Hearth approach, targeting family economic conditions, did not by any means disappear from party agendas. Instead, Hearth advocates began to use the language of values to expand their rationale for support services for work and family life, family health care, affordable childcare, and higher wages and benefits.[11] They now invoked secular-humanist values that focused on quality-of-life issues, such as gender equality and opportunities for individual choice, to continue to stress interventionist policies and programs related to economic security.

In the last three decades of the twentieth century, it is thus fair to say that national political actors were exponentially more attentive to family values, thereby deploying the state to address family in ways unimaginable to previous generations. This enhanced family-state relationship pivoted on increasingly divergent family political ideals, as family surfaced to independently structure party competition in contrast to its lesser significance in previous periods. Postwar competition over family conceptions, for example, had been contained within the parties' competing ideologies of state: northern Democrats had called for state expansion to provide family economic assistance and services, and Republicans and often southern Democrats had sought to limit the state to protect private family values (market and moralistic, respectively). The late twentieth-century period was distinctive insofar as "family values" exploded into political significance and were articulated by all legislative contingents. As part of this phenomenon, differences over the family and the importance of policy approaches directed primarily at values and/or economics now began to drive party competition itself.

The parties, however, did not align neatly to one or the other family ideal and/or policy approach. For instance, although the Republican Party began to actively promote the Soul family values approach, prominent factions within the GOP disagreed over whether family values should limit or activate the state. On one hand, the neoliberal faction continued to uphold the party's long-standing market-based family values, privileging parental autonomy and individual responsibility as a primary doorway to combat state expansion. On the other hand, an emerging religious faction now aimed to use state machinery and programs to positively instate traditional family values and Christian morality. The two factions within the GOP Soul tent thus came to form an uneasy alliance over their divergent state ideals and in the kinds of family values they hoped to uphold. They united, however, in their common disavowal of redistribution and the national state's intervention into family *economic conditions*, jointly opposing the Hearth policy approach that was advanced by key factions within the Democratic Party. The Democratic Party, now comprising both "old" and new Democratic factions, persisted in upholding the more redistributionist economics-centered Hearth family approach, but it too began to be more attentive to family values, albeit secular-humanist (not moralistic or neoliberal) ones.

The late twentieth-century battle over family exudes the kind of image since instilled in American imagination by the term "culture wars," where two partisan Goliaths enter the political arena to battle for the soul of the country. Missed within this evocative depiction focused solely on new clashes over values/culture is the extent to which this development drew on previous political battles over family ideals and underlying differences over state and economy in addition to values and culture.

This chapter will demonstrate that in the late twentieth century, political parties polarized explosively not only over the substance of family values but also, more enduringly, over the relationship of family values to family economic conditions. The period's increasing polarization over family, while stark in its enhanced clashes over alternative family values, did not unsettle underlying, enduring partisan battles over family economics or longstanding differences over the relationship of family to state, society, and the economy. Instead, family values were deployed more fully to repackage family economic issues into valuational forms, highlighting issues such as taxes, public assistance, housing, and health care as matters of self-sufficiency and hard work, as well as connecting market-based economic values more deeply to traditional family values, such as to parental control and marital sexuality. Much like in the Progressive Era, when Soul family values also had heightened political appeal, battles over gender, race, and sex strongly underpinned differences over family political ideals.

Historian Robert Self, in his book *All in the Family*, notes the increasing politicization of family values in the late twentieth century in contrast to the midcentury's unidimensional emphasis on family economics. He writes that, whereas the "liberal political project" of the midcentury was one where "social welfare liberals . . . from the New Deal to the Great Society . . . hoped to assist families economically," by 2004, "family was a conservative emblem" wherein "conservatives endeavored to defend families from moral threats."[12] This chapter and the next analyze what this development reveals about party dynamics in the late twentieth century by asking why and how family values emerged as a central partisan project, in many ways directly recasting family economics and revising party agendas.

By way of an answer to these questions, the narrative developed in the next two chapters identifies the growing sectional polarization in family policy debates. It demonstrates that the conservative Soul family approach, pursued by most Republicans in Congress, centered on distinctly *southern* family values, such as preeminence of marriage, religion, family authority, and parental autonomy, which matched prevailing southern public opinion and which Republicans increasingly invoked in policy debates by drawing upon family examples from smaller southern towns. And the liberal Hearth family approach, articulated by most Democrats, evoked *northern* more secular-humanist values, such as gender equality, personal choice, and self-fulfillment, that they, in turn, depicted through stories of northern, urban, and often lower-income families.

This research thus reveals that politicized GOP family values grew out of highlighting family realities practiced and felt in the South and that these were largely contrastive to family lives in the urban North. Partisan family polarization thus accompanied sectional demographic divisions, reflecting the parties' shifting strength and increasingly divergent electoral bases. As the Republican Party shifted southward, it turned to southern family values, such that the growing prominence of the Soul family values approach among Republicans *and* Democrats in late twentieth-century politics reflects the electoral ascendance of the GOP and the rising political importance of the South. The southernization of partisan family approaches and the enhanced emphasis on family values were thus shaped by a perfect storm of late twentieth-century demographic and political transformations. Soul family ideals, long championed by southern congressmen, now became starkly prominent in Republican and then national policy discourse—shifting political attention toward family values and forcing Hearth proponents to reenvision their focus on family economics in valuational terms.

In this way, the explanation connects the story of late twentieth-century southern realignment to family political development. A vast body of literature convincingly ties the southward movement in the GOP and conservative ascendance in American politics to the rightward political turn in race and gender agendas,[13] and this chapter demonstrates a missed dimension of this now familiar story: how and why southernized party politics also aligned, very deeply, with issues of family. In many ways, the emergent Soul family values focus described here accommodated (southern) conservative ideals of race and gender long present but rejuvenated at this time. The narrative also points to a more formative role of family now than previously. No more mere subtext, family now became the very issue through which the parties came to directly assemble, modify, and split over ideals of state, economy, race, and gender.

The present chapter discusses the enabling conditions that shaped transformed family party dynamics in the late twentieth century. It first analyzes changes in demographic family structure that occurred after 1960 and the regional variation of these changes, demonstrating that the South came to experience the most dissonance between family change and its persisting values; the next section analyzes the use and adaption of family political approaches by Democratic and Republican legislators in Congress in crafting policy responses to the period's watershed family changes. In particular, the section finds that "autonomy" policies gained unprecedented appeal among Republicans while "ascriptive" policies also made a comeback, albeit more reservedly. The following final chapter then connects family demographic and policy changes to party politics and the dramatic realignment of parties in the late twentieth century, demonstrating how the southward shift of the GOP and the northward movement of the Democratic Party manifested in the parties' increasing polarization over family.

Late Twentieth-Century Family Transformations

Writing in 2005, family historian Stephanie Coontz observed that marriage and family had changed more in the past thirty years than in the past five thousand.[14] This section describes the monumental changes occurring in the family in the waning decades of the past century, which produced new sets of family issues and allowed for the politicization of family values more than ever before.

By all accounts, the nuclear family began to rapidly unravel in the late twentieth century. Whereas in 1960, over 70 percent of all American households were made up of a breadwinner father, homemaker mother, and their biological children,[15] three decades later, such "traditional" nuclear families accounted for less than 25 percent of the nation's households.[16] Described as a massive "demographic transition," the United States moved from a period of higher fertility to one with rising ages at marriage, growing rates of cohabitation, increases in single-person households, declining remarriage rates, fertility postponement, and higher rates of childlessness.[17] In contrast to the earlier family shift that occurred during the industrialization of the United States, demographers distinguish this recent postindustrial transition by pointing to the enhanced role of nonmaterial, cultural shifts, such as the rise of expressive individualism, the celebration of individual self-fulfillment over duty and obligation, and the redefinition of social norms that organize family life.[18] Changes in family behavior, such as the postponement and reduction in childbearing, are also explained as a "function of more pressing competing (individual) goals such as prolonging education, achieving more stable income positions, increased consumerism, realizing a more fulfilling partnership, keeping an open future etc."[19] In many ways then, the massive family demographic shift of the late twentieth century was as much a watershed in cultural norms, values, and affective goals as it was a structural phenomenon.

Four shifts in particular marked the unparalleled transformation of family: decline in married-couple families, marital instability, shifting gender roles, and extramarital childbearing.[20] Starting in the 1970s, a growing proportion of families began to extend beyond the traditional two-parent household and into several other households due to divorce, remarriage, and single and unmarried parenthood.[21] Among family households,[22] the proportion of married-couple households with children declined significantly—from 40 percent of all households in 1970 to a mere 23 percent in 2003, whereas the proportion of children living with one parent doubled (see Figure 15).[23] Children were more likely than ever to have their biological parents separated, divorced, and/or remarried and often shared with stepsiblings.

Marriages became much less enduring. Beginning in 1974, divorce far outpaced death as the more common ending of a marriage. In 1900, 10 percent of marriages ended in divorce; the divorce rate then rose gradually through the century but doubled in the decades between 1960 and 1980, such that 50 percent of all first marriages and 60 percent of remarriages typically ended in divorce in 2007.[24] Unmarried fertility also became increasingly common, with many more children conceived and reared in extramarital arrangements. The sequence of marriage first and childbearing later was largely unsettled, particularly among African American women.[25] In the 1930s, 82 percent of

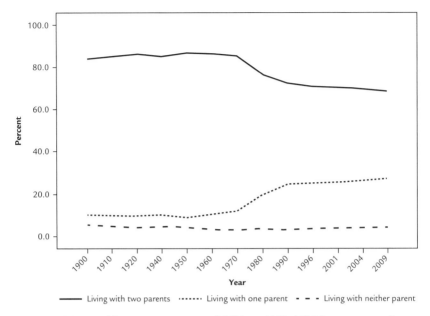

Figure 15. Historical living arrangement of children, 1900–2004 (in percentages).
U.S. Census Bureau, Current Population Survey, Historical Table CH-1.

first births were conceived after marriage, compared to 47 percent of such births in the 1990s. From 1930 up to the 1960s, 50 to 60 percent of unmarried women married before the birth of their first child, but that number fell to a low of 29 percent by the mid-1980s and has leveled off at around 33 percent since the 1990s.[26]

A final development that marked the watershed late twentieth-century change in family life was the widespread incorporation of mothers into the workforce. In the early part of the twentieth century, when production sites moved outside the home and married women lost their "productive" economic roles, the norm of a separate domestic sphere emerged in which women would concentrate on motherhood and household management and men on outside work and public affairs.[27] Starting in the early 1960s, this norm of privatizing the role of women to the domestic sphere came undone as unprecedented proportions of wives and mothers joined the paid workforce.[28] In 1948, only about 17 percent of married mothers were in the labor force; by 1995, their rate of workforce participation reached 70 percent.[29]

The increased participation of mothers in the workforce not only called into question traditional assumptions regarding family division of labor between fathers and mothers but also affected the capacity of family units to absorb several of their previous functions independently—such as care of elderly and sick family members and, especially, daylong care of children. Maternal employment and the disproportionate responsibility still shouldered by mothers for family care[30] thus raised several new issues of work and family conflict. Such issues were previously marginal when mothers were wholly occupied in the domestic sphere.[31]

Although these trends of monumental family change occurred nationally, they had distinct regional patterns. In 1900, the majority (62 percent) of the U.S. population lived in either the Northeast or the Midwest. However, by the end of the century, the majority (58 percent) of the population resided in either the South or West, such that the mean center of the U.S. population shifted southward.[32] Southern and Western populations grew in proportions and in forms different from the more northern regions east of the Mississippi. Whereas states in the Northeast as well as those on the West Coast and along the Great Lakes began to exhibit the liberalizing family formation and fertility patterns described above, much of the South, the Great Plains, and some Mountain states continued traditional family patterns of early marriage and higher childbearing but now with higher teen and nonmarital fertility.[33]

Marriage continued to play a central role in organizing life in the conservative states of the South and Mountain West. Census data reveal the comparative universality of marriage among southern and western populations in relation to those from northeastern and midwestern regions.[34] While all four regions followed similar marriage trends—registering cycles of increase and then decline in marriage through the twentieth century—differences between the two sets of regions remained apparent in the *rates* of marriages practiced.[35] Through the past century, marriage rates in the West and South far bypassed those in the Northeast and Midwest (see Figure 16), somewhat converging in 1960 and then moving apart once again. The South now surpassed the West, with the highest marriage rate of all.

Survey data also find that more than any other regional group, southerners continued to place a higher than average value on marriage and family as social institutions; for instance, they expressed greater levels of disapproval for cohabitation before marriage and more frequently viewed homosexual, premarital, teenaged, and other extramarital sexual relations as

Figure 16. Marriage rates averaged per decade by region, 1940–2000. Compiled from monthly and national vital statistics reports (rates per 1,000 population).

always wrong.[36] Also, unlike other regions, in the South, childbearing continued to be strongly associated with marriage. Although southern, religious (evangelical) states have the highest levels of teen pregnancies and early births, pregnancies in the South were much less likely to result in abortions and far more likely to lead to marriage, and thus the South registered the lowest levels of nonmarital fertility than elsewhere (along with higher reliance on grandparents and subsequent divorce and remarriage).[37]

Thus, whereas in the previous postwar period, the regions converged in their nuclear family practices, all registering drops in age of marriage, increased fertility, and rising teen birthrates, the subsequent liberalizing family transformations—decline in fertility, increased age at marriage, higher rates of cohabitation—were more regionally dispersed. These changes occurred more thoroughly and dramatically in the Northeast and more slowly in the South, the Mountain West, and the Plains. As legal scholars Naomi Cahn and June Carbone demonstrate in their book, *Red v. Blue Families: Legal Polarization and the Creation of Culture*, the late twentieth-century family demographic transition thus began to map a "cultural divide," with liberal northern states displaying more rapid liberalization of family life and the more conservative southern (and western) ones exhibiting slower change and continued attachment to traditional family behavior and attitudes.[38] As a region pivotal to late twentieth-century American politics, the South thus remained far more conservative in its family practices and views, rendering a distinctly conservative influence on partisan family battles.

In the next section, we see how polarized policy divisions took form in Congress, more deeply dividing congressional legislators as they tried to make sense of the cataclysmic family changes occurring throughout the nation. We see how one set (conservative traditionalists) approached public policies as vehicles to reverse these "liberalizing" trends, aiming to restore the traditional nuclear family as a model of private values such as self-sufficiency and of highest moral worth. Liberal congressional members espousing Hearth ideologies, on the other hand, were unconcerned with behavioral reversal but instead approached public policies more as a means to fill the (emerging economic) gaps in family's functions. Now as always, the two camps articulated their divergent partisan (family) differences through policy but with far fewer overlaps than ever before.

Hearth and Soul Policy Responses in Congress

Drawing on familiar Hearth and Soul frameworks, Democratic and Republican legislators in Congress began to interpret the late twentieth-century demographic transformation of family in vastly different ways. Most Democratic members of Congress continued to uphold the Hearth view and focused on economic, structural, and material changes that accompanied family transformations, calling for continued and enhanced state programmatic assistance. Among the many reasons cited for the creation of the House Select Committee on Children, Youth, and Families in 1983, Chair George Miller (D-CA), for example, emphasized "the dramatic and permanent changes in the living situations of families and children" in which "more children were born into poverty, more were raised in single-parent families," with problems such as "increased stress, family violence, abuse, family poverty."[39] Patricia Schroeder (D-CO), a long-term advocate for family and children's issues, also asserted that the House Select Committee was established "because members recognized how profoundly social and economic trends are impacting on families and children" and emphasized that an "obvious fundamental change has been that the economics of family life are new: both parents are working now, not just one, while at the same time the costs of housing, food, transportation, health care, and education are rising beyond peoples, [*sic*] means." "Economics," she said, "has as much to do with keeping a family well and together as any other factor."[40]

Democrats repeatedly voiced increased economic vulnerability over altered family values and attitudes as a public policy concern. Representative George Miller (D-CA) went so far as to provide his own family experience as an example of the limited impact of values and character in the face of cold economic realities, talking about an episode when he was young and first married and, as he put it, "took off and went to Alaska to go fishing, to make my fortune." On his return two months later, he recounted, "My wife asked me if I had made any money. I said no, but geez, what a great experience. I said I never worked so hard, and I met all these people, and it was just a great experience. And she said, why don't you take some of that experience to the grocery store and see what you can put on the table for dinner."[41] Hard economics and not ideals were the bread and butter of the Democratic approach.

Democrats, attuned to the increased ranks of feminists, civil rights activists, and other egalitarians among them, were in fact sanguine about late twentieth-century family changes and stressed the increased love, amplification of women's choices, and opportunities to call for enhanced state programs to offset families' increased economic vulnerability. Julie Matthaei, associate professor of economics from Wellesley College, an invited witness to the Democratic Select Committee's hearing on work and family, described the "emerging reality" of a "more egalitarian marriage" as an "increasingly valued ideal." "Greater equality within marriage," she asserted, "has allowed women to speak out against wife battering, and has inspired social concern as to the extent of spouse and child physical and sexual abuse within the family," and it also has permitted more people to "live in nontraditional family forms, from living together without marriage, to living alone, or collectively, to living with a member of one's own sex." Like many Democrats, she urged Congress to "develop new remedies more consistent with the egalitarian family" and to remove impediments endemic to the prevailing "economy structured to complement separate spheres marriage," advocating improved women's access to male-dominated jobs, paycheck equity, childcare and family leave measures, and antipoverty programs.[42] These structural remedies resemble the expanded housing, employment, health, and Social Security measures proposed by liberal Democrats in the postwar era to enhance and strengthen the economic foundations of the nuclear family.

On the other hand, late twentieth-century Republicans emphasized anew their postwar vision focused on family values and attitudes, now interpreting late twentieth-century family changes as the outcome of desperately degenerating moral values. Republicans claimed that declining family values were unraveling "natural" private family supports (such as marriage, women's role in family care, extended families), which, in turn, generated economic strain and public expenditures.[43] For Republicans, declining values led to enhanced economic deprivation, not the other way around. Senator Jeff Sessions (R-AL), for example, advocated that marriage is essential to "general welfare" in large part because "divorce and unwed childbearing create substantial public costs borne by the taxpayers."[44]

Elected to the House in 1980 and presaging a long career in the Senate, Dan Coats (R-IN) offered his own district in the Fort Wayne metropolitan area as an example of deteriorating private values as leading to family economic decline. He described his district as middle of the road, where during the decade of the 1970s, there was a great growth in prosperity; yet, he said, "our increase in one-parent families was nearly twice the average." He concluded that the cause of the dramatic increase in one-parent families was "not the economy and it was not the recession"; instead, "the increase in one-parent families resulted from a *change in attitudes* on the part of people in terms of what the family unit should be." Pointing to a "cycle of economic and social trends" that, he said, was emerging among one-parent families, he explained, "there is only one wage earner, that wage earner is probably female without adequate work experience and therefore unable to qualify for high-paying jobs."[45] At another hearing on "Diversity and Strength of American Families" in 1985, Coats thus took issue with Chairman George Miller's (D-CA) economic position, claiming instead, "If another drumbeat should sound, it ought to be a drumbeat on attitude, the importance of a family, the centrality of the family, the need for commitment."[46] Republican legislators thus repeatedly characterized economics as the symptom and values as the fundamental cause.

The enhanced focus on family values set in play a tectonic shift in family political discourse, in many cases reframing even family economic policies in Soul terms (i.e., into a language of values and morality). Tax reform, welfare programs and services, farm subsidies, homeownership incentives, and health care were now often discussed as questions of family values or family morality. For example, Representative Donald Manzullo (R-IN), in a hearing on estate tax reform, cited estate tax as the one tax issue "raised to the level of a moral issue," passionately arguing, "It is immoral in this country for people to have to pay taxes in order to pass the result of a lifetime of earnings on to their children."[47] Frank Wolf (R-VA), in another hearing, talked about tax reform and raising the personal exemption as "part of the magic which allows moms and dads to keep more of their own money to spend on whatever they want to spend it on" and " to spend more time with their families," for "if moms and dads are not home with their children," he said, "it is very difficult to teach . . . values and it is very difficult for the children to catch those values."[48]

The late twentieth-century ascendance of the valuational, Soul approach to family and the increased polarization of the two parties over the centrality of Hearth or Soul frameworks can be seen quantitatively as well, in data on bill sponsorship and committee hearings from the 1980s to 2004. The percentage of sponsored family bills citing family values increased tenfold from postwar to the late twentieth century, from a mere 4 percent in the immediate postwar decade to almost 40 percent in the last decade of the twentieth century.

However, the heightened policy attention to the Soul family values approach had a distinct partisan distribution. Whereas 83.7 percent of family bills sponsored by Democratic members of Congress stressed economic aspects of family life, 65.1 percent of Republican-sponsored family bills emphasized values. Moreover, during committee hearings, a vast majority (97.2 percent) of family cases referenced by Democratic members highlighted economic Hearth principles, and a sizable majority (53.4 percent) of family cases invoked by Republican committee members alluded to Soul family values. These differences are statistically significant.[49]

As seen in previous chapters, typically four main types of policies have been historically advanced to address family-related problems: welfare policies, which seek to augment families' economic conditions; regulatory policies, aiming at regulating undesirable family behavior; autonomy policies, to promote family self-sufficiency and independence; and finally, ascriptive policies, encouraging the (typically white, heterosexual) traditional family through reference to biological ("ascriptive") characteristics, such as race, sex and sexuality, and gender. In the post–World War II era, building on the reconfigured New Deal national state, liberal Hearth Democrats and conservative Soul Republicans, as well as mixed Hearth-and-Soul southern

Democrats, directed their attention primarily to social welfare and regulation policies. Ascriptive and autonomy policies received minimal attention. In contrast, the late twentieth-century period began to resemble the earlier, Progressive Era, insofar as there was a significant resumption of interest in ascription and autonomy policies. Legal scholar Barbara Bennett Woodhouse argues that late twentieth-century conservative family policy resonated with policy positions in the Progressive Era insofar as both sets of policies stressed family ascriptive rights and parental autonomy over children, first raised in the earlier period in opposition to child labor bans, compulsory education, vaccination mandates, and services targeting child abuse.[50] Unlike the Progressive Era, though, the more recent period had to contend with vastly expanded state machinery, to be used to either advance family rights or be dismantled in favor of family autonomy.

Three policy developments marked the late twentieth-century era more acutely than others: first, autonomy policies began to actively compete with social welfare policies. Second, even the familiar Hearth configuration of welfare and regulation policies began to be used routinely to encourage parental responsibility, even though their primary focus remained families' economic augmentation. Finally, starting in the 104th Congress (1995–1996), members of Congress became far more divided by party along Hearth and Soul lines than ever before, with much less overlap.

We see these developments first in congressional hearings.[51] As seen in Table 13, there remained distinct policy configurations in the late twentieth-century Hearth and Soul approaches. Legislators highlighted the economics-based Hearth approach mostly through family anecdotes that referenced welfare and/or regulation policies, while they stressed a valuational Soul approach in other family examples that mostly discussed ascription-based and autonomy policies. However, Republicans also still continued to highlight welfare policy issues, using 47 percent of their family cases to reference such policies. This partly suggests that the focus on family's economic circumstances was still popular (and relevant) among members of both parties, in conjunction with the dramatic ascendance of Soul principles. Yet the partisan (Republican) turn toward Soul ascriptive and autonomy policy concerns is also unmistakable.

Temporal patterns are also evident, as seen in Figures 17A and B. In particular, the 1990s was a critical period during which legislators increasingly referred to Soul family values by highlighting autonomy policies, stressing the importance of family self-sufficiency and independence from the state.

Table 13. Policy References in Hearth and Soul Family Case Examples, Committee Hearings, 97th–109th Congresses (1980–2006)

		Family Ideology			
		Soul		*Hearth*	
		Count	*Percent*	*Count*	*Percent*
Policy category	Ascription[a]	29	11.7	9	1.1
	Autonomy[a]	134	54.3	16	1.9
	Welfare[a]	47	19.0	624	73.4
	Regulation[a]	37	15.0	201	23.6

[a] Values in the same row are significantly different for Soul and Hearth cases at $p < .05$ in the two-sided test of equality for column proportions. Tests assume equal variances.

In almost two-thirds of Soul family examples cited in the 104th and 105th Congresses in the mid-1990s, legislators highlighted the valuational approach through discussion of autonomy policies. Following which, in more recent congresses, legislators advancing a Soul approach began to use family examples to highlight ascription policy, such as sex and sexuality issues. Family examples illustrating Hearth family economic ideals continued to make reference to welfare and regulation policies, advocating for enhanced state assistance and regulation on material grounds.

This policy reconfiguration in the 1990s is also evidenced in congressional bills. An analysis of a sample of bills[52] introduced from the 100th to the 106th Congresses (1989–2004) reveals that the greatest proportion of family bills in fact invoked Hearth principles, approaching family issues primarily as family economic conditions. However, this proportion began to decline in relation to bills illustrating Soul valuational approaches, mainly through increased sponsorship of autonomy bills (see Figure 18). The upswing in Soul bills occurred in the 1990s; this trend was more pronounced in the 104th Congress (1995–1996), following the historic 1994 election and the Contract with America.

The bills were further coded based on whether they addressed one of five recurrent family frames—family sexuality, family structure, parenting, family property/wealth, and public assistance. This analysis reveals another interesting development in late twentieth-century family politics—*parenting* became a dominant focus of all bills across all four categories. Even among welfare and regulation bills, a large proportion now addressed family assis-

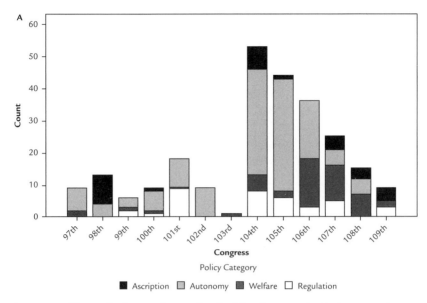

Figure 17A. Types of policies referenced in Soul family examples during committee hearings, 97th–109th Congresses.

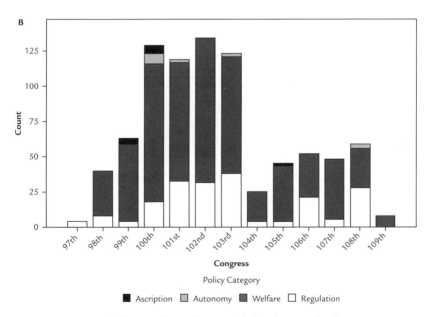

Figure 17B. Types of policies referenced in Hearth family examples during committee hearings, 97th–109th Congresses.

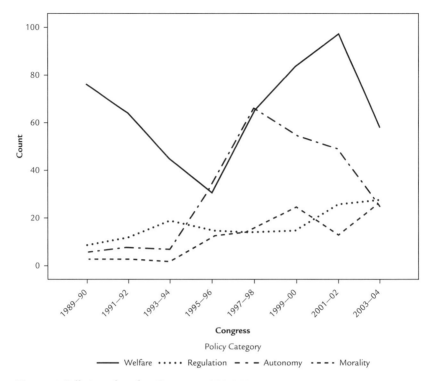

Figure 18. Bills introduced in Congress, 1989–2004.

tance and regulation through the frame of parenting. In fact, the single largest proportion of regulation bills were those that addressed parenting as the primary frame of concern.

The largest proportion of autonomy bills focused on issues of family wealth and property (such as tax breaks and deductions, repeal of estate taxes, family savings provisions), but here too there were a sizable proportion of "parenting"-focused autonomy bills. This suggests the duality in the existing valuational Soul framework that privileges both economic and social (parental) values: self-determination in matters of property as well as increased parental rights over their children. These are encouraged through both negative state action (keeping the state out, for example, by repealing estate taxes) but also through positive state benefits such as tax deductions and programs to encourage or "teach" parental responsibilities and rights.

The emphasis on "parenting" marks late twentieth-century family political development in very particular ways. As seen in Chapter 3, in the postwar era, members of Congress were preoccupied with the regulation of "deficient" parental behavior and the creation of welfare programs to educate and reform such parents. Numerous "runaway pappy" bills and programs for "parent education classes" indicate that then too the legislative construction and reification of norms and ideals of parenthood were central to the politics of family. However, as the analysis of bills from the 1990s show, late twentieth-century legislators' preoccupation with parents extended beyond these concerns. Instead, parental *autonomy* and parental *rights* now emerged to highlight the autonomy aspect of parents' policy significance, and legislative proposals now firmly tied ideas of parental responsibility to antistatist market values of private choice *and* to cultivating socially conservative ideas of parental supremacy and traditional family hierarchies.

State programs to instruct parents were now directed at encouraging parental autonomy, privatizing parental choice, and limiting parents' need of the state. For instance, a witness at a hearing on "Building Assets for Low-Income Families," Michelle Simmons from Norristown, Pennsylvania, was invited by Senator Rick Santorum (R-PA) as "one dramatic example of how faith, hard work, the charitable community, and strategic use of government incentives . . . can make a significant difference in people's lives." Simmons, a graduate of the Self-Employment Training Program and the Family Savings Account, told of how she went from a "hope-to-die dope fiend, living out of a cardboard box on the streets of LA" to learning about and practicing budgeting and saving, transmitting the norms, values, and culture of savings to her children while also enabling her to own her business. She recounted, "My children used to be like, 'Ma, why are you rushing down to the bank?' I said, 'because I have to get it in by the 31st.'" By repeatedly telling her children, "You have to save every month," she claimed, "they just learned discipline from that."[53]

Thus, through a variety of proposed programs much like those that hoped to create a "culture of savings," conservatives such as Rick Santorum began to find ways to harness government, ironically, to engineer both market ideals of self-sufficiency along with social-traditional ideals of strong, disciplining parents and parental/family autonomy from state.[54]

Conclusion

In the late twentieth century, as the parties increasingly divided over the primacy of family values versus economic conditions to explain family demographic changes and frame policies, the Republican Soul family approach burst into political significance, now dressing even economic welfare issues in a valuational garb. Why did this happen? Why did the Republican Party, long a stalwart of individual values, free markets, and limited government, embrace moralistic family values and a state-expansivist Soul agenda? Why did the Democratic Party acquiesce and also in part reimagine its policy approach in terms of family values while also diverging more sharply from the GOP in its continued insistence on family economic security? The next chapter turns to uncovering the connected pieces of these empirical puzzles. It suggests that the rise of the conservative Soul family values approach, its wholehearted embrace by the Republican Party and its lukewarm incorporation into Democratic agenda, as well as the increased polarization of the two parties over the family, was a vital part of a broader southern-centered conservative ascendency and a deep-seated southernization that was under way within late twentieth-century American politics. Party politics, the content of the next chapter, was at the heart of this phase of family political development, a crucial part to completing this century-long story.

Chapter 5

Family and Party Change

Late-Century Party Developments:
Southernization and Sectional Family Values

In its last two decades, twentieth-century party politics underwent a complete metamorphosis—as the New Right emerged and galvanized Republican party leadership, the GOP and the center of gravity of American party politics shifted decisively right. The rightward turn in late twentieth-century politics and the impact of the New Right on the Republican Party are well documented by political scientists and historians.[1] Described by some as "movement conservatism," the New Right began to take form in the late 1950s, the result of an amalgam of factors such as Senator Joseph McCarthy's anti-Communist crusade, the intellectual collaboration of influential conservative thinkers such as William F. Buckley Jr. and Russell Kirk, the launch of important magazines such as the *National Review* as a forum for conservatives, and the emergence of grassroots organizations focused on recruiting like-minded conservatives.[2] Over the course of the next three decades, the New Right marginalized moderates within the GOP and relentlessly sought to transform the Republican Party into an arm of conservative ideology.

By reversing the GOP's long-standing liberal position on race, women, and civil rights and combining principles of economic conservatism with social traditionalism, the New Right found a new electoral base in the suburban South and Southwest among socially conservative white southerners and religious fundamentalists who were long wary of the national state and were now increasingly troubled by the civil rights and cultural liberalism progressively espoused by the Democratic Party.[3] Starting with the victory of one of their own, Ronald Reagan in 1980, the New Right steadily consolidated GOP control of Congress, through the efforts of Newt Gingrich and other southern Republican members.[4]

In the late 1960s, another new political faction, the New Left or New Politics Democrats, brought with them their own valuational concerns, this time into the Democratic fold. New Politics Democrats arose out of the middle-class suburbs,[5] formed on university campuses, and mobilized in opposition to the Vietnam War. In contrast to the old Left (the Liberal-Labor Democrats of the postwar), the New Left advocated a new strain of cultural liberalism, calling for a New Politics focused on "dealing with the quality rather than just the quantity of life"[6] and emphasized "choice rather than constraint . . . rights rather than responsibilities."[7]

Unlike organized labor, for which redistributional interests were paramount, middle-class college-educated Democrats and their party activists were also concerned with values and principles and pushed for their greater salience.[8] Importantly for family politics, New Politics Democrats were motivated in large part by specific causes (such as women's rights, rights of gays and lesbians, and environmental conservation).[9] Democratic advocacy of economic programs and services to families thus began to also invoke a language of values, and issues such as individual sexual autonomy, reproductive choice, self-fulfillment, and/or race and gender equality in the family began to be addressed.[10] By altering presidential candidate selection rules, instituting institutional reforms within Congress, and creating "public interest" consumer and other groups, New Politics Democrats successfully reconfigured the Democratic Party and altered its agenda to reflect their own cultural liberalism, adding to (but not displacing) the party's long-standing economic liberalism.[11]

The 1970s thus marked the onset of reconfigured party competition. On one hand, economic concerns continued to be salient to both political parties and their dominant factions, particularly among Democrats.[12] However, on the other hand, other issues—mostly those that came to be labeled "social issues" (also Vietnam)—ascended to the forefront of national politics, reorganizing party politics.[13] The South played a pivotal role in this transformation of parties, from programmatic entities focused on economic redistribution and a primarily Hearth family view to those incorporating an explicit political language of values, morality, and Soul family perspectives.

Since 1938, southern Democrats had been an anomaly within the New Deal and postwar party system. Central to Democratic electoral success but skeptical of their party's growing statism and ever watchful of federal government infringement on states' rights, white supremacy, and a so-called southern way of life, southern Democrats (in Congress and their constituents) were precariously accommodated within the postwar Democratic Party.[14] With the influx of counterculturalists, civil rights activists, and women's and gay rights activists into the party in the late 1960s, southern Democrats, like moderate Republicans, found themselves marginalized within their party.

As their power was waning in the Democratic Party, a reactionary political coalition with appeal for the South emerged within the Republican fold. That faction comprised religious conservatives, notably evangelical Protestants. Up until the 1970s, they were largely apolitical and traditionally Democratic.[15] They then reentered politics as the New Christian Right, motivated by developments they viewed as antithetical to their values: in particular, the moral relativism and secularism of cultural liberals and Supreme Court decisions removing school prayer from public schools and legalizing abortion, among others.[16] "Personal salvation" and "leading a godly life on earth" were signature characteristics of evangelical Protestantism,[17] which raised the stakes among these Christian groups for why traditional family values and practices had to be preserved. In the evangelical perspective, the movement away from the married nuclear American family illustrated a broad-based moral degeneracy. The preservation of traditional families and traditional family values hence became the clarion call by which evangelical elites mobilized followers.

Through meticulous organizational efforts as well as systematic overtures by conservative Republican strategists,[18] leaders of the Christian Right, such as Jerry Falwell, Pat Robertson, and Jim Bakker, effectively used conservative Soul family ideals to bring evangelical Protestant voters into the Republican tent, helping to elect Ronald Reagan to the presidency in 1980. Across the 1980s, historically Democratic congressional districts began to elect Republicans for the first time in the twentieth century. Several erstwhile southern Democrats now ran as Republicans in congressional elections, and along with Republican transplants to the South, such as Newt Gingrich (R-GA), they successfully transformed the once-solid Democratic South, "southernizing" the GOP and American party politics.[19] Family was central to this late twentieth-century southernization.

Whereas the individual was at the center of new Democratic cultural liberalism and its focus on individual rights and personal freedoms,[20] family was at the core of the New Right and Republicans in Congress. Under the banner of traditional family values, Republicans could all at once oppose the liberal state, challenge moral relativism, and privatize family responsibilities and social problems and develop a neoliberal market rationality.

In a hearing on AIDS and teenagers, Republican Congressman Clyde Holloway, newly elected in 1986 from Louisiana's erstwhile Democratic eighth district, took issue with a Democratic witness who advocated respect for individual preferences and personal civil rights of AIDS patients. Holloway instead asserted the New Right's family-centered religious view, stating, "There is a total breakdown in our environment today and I blame it on the fact that we have no family life any more in this country . . . we need to bring some common sense back to our country and some religious beliefs and strong beliefs to get our family life going again."[21] Frank Wolf, another Reagan Republican elected in 1981 from a former Democratic district in Virginia, also similarly lamented, "Regrettably, the trend in American policies has been to focus laws on individuals, thereby discouraging cooperation in the family, to undermine the family foundations through the regulatory process and to erode parental authority by limiting the very rights of parents in raising their children."[22] And in a hearing on "Divorce and Its Impact on Children and Families," Thomas Bliley Jr., a southern Democrat turned Republican elected in 1981 from another previously Democratic Virginian district, also emphatically denounced "the growing cultural change . . . that marriage need not be permanent." He said, "Individual happiness is important," yet he emphasized the joys and responsibilities of married family life and marital childbearing, stating, "Marriage asks a sacrifice of us and has responsibilities which accompany it. These responsibilities are not without their headaches . . . but they also have joys no single person could begin to understand."[23]

With the influx of cultural conservatives and newly elected southern Republicans, Republican Party platforms through the 1980s now asserted the family-centered view, claiming to "redefine and broaden the debate by transcending the narrow terms of government and the individual"[24] and instead pledged to "reemphasize those vital communities like the family . . . which are found at the center of society, between government and the individual." The platform asserted, "The family is the foundation of our social order . . . we insist that all domestic policies, from child care and schooling to social security and the tax code must be formulated with the family in mind."[25] As historian Robert Self notes, "family had quite suddenly and powerfully joined communism and civil rights as the battlegrounds on which conservatives would wage war on liberalism."[26]

The New Right's turn to family reflected and accommodated the Republican Party's changing electoral base—namely, its shift to the South—a region with its own distinct political culture.[27] Late-century southerners as a social and electoral group continued to share a conservative political identity, their policy preferences distinct from Americans in the North and Pacific Coast.[28] Election results and survey research data demonstrate political divisions between white and black southerners, but they also suggest marked continuing differences between North and South, evidencing that southerners as a group appeared to be more socially conservative, nationalistic, and religious than nonsoutherners and were better satisfied, regardless of class, race, or party, with their states and communities than is true of other Americans.[29]

Despite widespread economic changes and alterations to the regional population, the late twentieth-century South was thus a region that inhabited two worlds. Writing in 1986, Richard Gray, scholar of literature, observed, "While its material culture has changed substantially since the Second World War, its non-material culture, although altered, still enables southerners to think and talk of themselves in terms of their regional identity, the inherited codes . . . southernness continue[s] to embody an undeniable core of shared meanings, understandings, and ways of doing things."[30] Sociologists and survey data reveal that the attachment to place and to family as a cultural characteristic continued to make southerners distinctive from other Americans, and the themes of place, family history, localism, and community were found to have special enduring meaning for most southerners.[31]

Southern family ideals and beliefs overlapped with the New Right's Soul family approach in the following four ways—in their common approach to (1) religion, (2) race, (3) marriage, and (4) authoritarian structures. First, the South, long drawn to Soul family ideals and religious moralism, had become increasingly fundamentalist in the postwar period.[32] As early as in 1962, Samuel S. Hill, a scholar of southern religion, observed that orthodox religion was "so pervasive" and "so intimately connect[ed] with other elements of life" that it may be characterized as "Culture-Protestantism."[33] Evangelical themes such as the inherent immorality of the soul, individual salvation, and nascent human imperfectability fortified long-standing southern skepticism of federal government.[34] These themes also echoed neoliberal concerns, such as personal morality or individual responsibility, further harnessing white southern opposition to the welfare state and building on their preference for local (parental and community) autonomy over federal state intervention.[35]

Family stories recounted and sponsored by Republican legislators in committee hearings through the 1980s, 1990s, and early 2000s evidence many of these aforementioned religious/evangelical themes, often illustrated by southern families. A central evangelical belief in human imperfectability, in human suffering and misery as the natural order of human condition,[36] recurred extensively in Republican family stories. Family examples emphasized forbearance in the face of continual economic hardship through cultivation of character strengths, such as self-reliance, faith, and personal merit and hard work and not through state programs or external assistance. The (married, heterosexual, nuclear) family was presented as crucial for the reproduction of such character traits across generations, ensuring personal success despite ongoing adversity.

One family so celebrated was that of Timothy Vann, an unusually named woman. Along with eight other families, the family of Mrs. Vann, an African American widowed mother of ten children from St. Paul, Minnesota, was honored in 1983 by Nancy Reagan and the evangelical American Family Society as a "Great American Family." Mrs. Vann testified before the Senate Subcommittee on Family and Human Services and was introduced by Senator Denton (R-AL) as an illustration of "what keeps a family together and . . . what makes them joyful."[37] In telling her story, Timothy Vann repeatedly made reference to ongoing adversity and the importance of time-honored values to get her family through trying times. She said, "Not all has been smooth, and my family has had the same difficulties that anyone else has had but we hung in there together." In addition to "serious sickness . . . cancer, school problems and peer problems," as African Americans, she said they faced more than the "usual problems of ordinary people"; they were "met with racial, education, housing, military and job discrimination." Yet, she declared, "the pains and insults of discrimination were counteracted with constant reminders [to her children] that they were made in the image of God, and they were endowed with . . . potential greatness if they tried the best they could."[38]

Republican members of Congress increasingly turned to self-described, evangelical southern family values to address family problems. Far more family cases discussed by Republicans during congressional committee hearings referred to God, religion, and religious-based values—almost 50 percent of Republican family examples mentioned religion in some way compared to 61 percent of Democratic cases that did not, a statistically significant difference. Moreover, two statistically significant groups of legislators—southerners and Republicans—used many more family cases than did others to highlight religious-based themes, and the families that illustrated religious themes also mostly came from the South.[39] Evangelicalism thus provided the New Right with a new religious language by which to appeal to the South, simultaneously melding religious family values and individualist market-based ones into a common cause, in opposition to state-sponsored economic assistance.[40]

Second, along with religion, race too played a decisive role in the so-called southern family strategy of the New Right and in the growing appeal of the GOP in the South. Starting with Goldwater in 1964 and continuing through Reagan, the Republican Party shifted its long-standing defense of civil rights, accommodating southern segregationists such as Governor George C. Wallace of Alabama.[41] Evangelical leaders who proclaimed principles of American exclusivity and racial conservatism did so with tacit GOP approval, enhancing their appeal and that of the Republican Party to conservative white southerners (and alienating moderate Republicans from the northeast).[42] Race and racial backlash according to a growing corpus of literature was central not only to the rise of southern Republicanism and the movement of white southerners from the Democratic to the Republican column but also to the ascendancy of conservatism, more generally, in the late twentieth century.[43] Through its Soul family approach, Republicans were able to mollify white southerners' anxieties over racial transformation while appealing to their preferences for limited (federal) government and traditional social order.

Conservative Soul family values and practices were long those of white middle America, demonstrated most clearly in the GOP's late twentieth-century crusade against welfare.[44] Democratic witnesses, such as Harvard University Professor Tamara Hareven, repeatedly pointed this out, saying, "Attitudes towards family life in American society have been governed too often by stereotypes of the 'ideal family,'" illustrating the "tension between the ideals of family behavior imposed by the dominant culture and the traditional patterns of black families and of immigrant families."[45] Other witnesses pointed to studies on "economically secure black fathers" described as "an often maligned group" who "represent the 50 percent of black males in this country who remain in their homes with their wives and children." These fathers were "moderately strict," "warm and loving," "shared child-drearing tasks with their wives," and "expressed the belief that their children should be as educated as possible." "In short," said John McAdoo, associate professor at the University of Maryland, "the child-rearing values that these men hold and express are solid, basic American values." He thus concluded that "economic security," the Hearth approach, "appears to play a more positive role in the successful child-rearing activities within black families."[46]

Legislators such as Dan Coats (R-IN), however, continued to stress the importance of attitude and values in addressing black family problems and sometimes squarely addressed the racially charged nature of their arguments. Coats, for example, recalled a Bill Moyers special on the black family and a subsequent statement made by Moyers to Caroline Wallace, a director of inner-city youth, saying, "These things that you are saying, that is, that people have to take responsibility and attitudes have to change. Bill Moyers can't say these things, the Governor of New Jersey can't say these things, a white man can't say these things." Wallace, recounted Coats approvingly, "looked right back at [Moyers] and said, 'Why not? If you start saying them, and if I say them, and if we all start saying them, and everybody in their own corner starts saying them, it will become a drumbeat. And when the drumbeat starts beating, then maybe we can change some attitudes here.'"[47]

African American Democratic Representative Eleanor Norton from the District of Columbia, in a hearing on "Black Men & Boys in the District of Columbia," expressed similar concerns about black family "norms" of non-marital childbearing and absent fathers. She posed a question that she described as "perhaps the most difficult of all": "if we let in the African-American community so much water roll over the hill, with people having children without even thinking about marriage . . . even if we get to the point where opportunity is available, even given the fact that for many young African-American middle class men opportunity is available . . . if it becomes an acceptable way to have and raise children, at some point will it matter that some members of the community in fact have opportunity?"[48]

Black families were repeatedly emphasized as the forbearers of what lay in store for all American families, demonstrating the ill effects of declining family values. Several professional witnesses asserted, "The biggest problem facing blacks in America today is the absence of the father from the home and the role reversals found in the black family. [These] observations now are beginning to apply equally to all families, whether they are black or white or other racial origins."[49] Citing various research studies, they declared, "If you have a well-structured home life, your chances of being a normal person and being out of that ghetto in a few years is extremely high."[50]

In discussing black families, legislators and their witnesses thus used culture "values" and "attitude," the Soul approach, disproportionately more than in their discussions of white families. Almost 48 percent of African American family cases referenced during committee hearings addressed the importance of family values compared to, for instance, 41 percent of white family examples. Far more than white families, black family examples were drawn from those on welfare with an extramarital family structure. Thirty-two percent of black family examples were those that received welfare, compared to 5 percent of white family stories and 13 percent of black and other nonwhite family anecdotes told of nontraditional family structures in contrast to 7 percent of white families. Moreover, a full 50 percent of black family examples were from the South, compared to 43 percent of white family cases. All these differences are statistically significant. Significantly, legislators from both parties used comparable proportions of (poor) black family examples in this way to highlight the Soul family values approach, evidencing its continued racialized character and commonly accepted cultural image across partisan groups but emphasized most through southern family examples by southern legislators.

Third, the Republican Soul emphasis on the sanctity of marriage and the traditional family structure had special meaning to the South,[51] given that region's distinctive pattern of demographic transition and continued religiosity. In the last three decades of the twentieth century, a growing gap had begun to emerge between family ideals and practices in the tradition-bound South. On one hand, the region experienced a massive increase in liberalized family and sexual practices (seen in its now high rates of divorce and teen pregnancies), and on the other hand, southerners continued to strongly cherish conservative and religious-infused family morality, a value system developed on a cherished unity of sex, marriage, and childbearing.[52] Republican governor of Oklahoma, Frank Keating, initiator of the first statewide marriage initiative, recalled his second inaugural address in which he said "to a large group of Southern Baptist pastors," "how come we can be so good and yet have so much divorce?" Governor Keating told senators that he was able to secure the funding of public monies for this marriage initiative from the Oklahoma state legislature, as they were not just a "public community" but also as a "faith community," where "about 70 percent of our people go to church twice a month or more."[53] Listing the economic and social advantages of marriage—reducing poverty and living longer and healthier—Governor Keating highlighted economic independence and self-sufficiency of married families.[54] Marriage, like religion, within the Soul family approach thus combined southerners' desire for a traditional social order with other (state and economy) ideals, such as limited federal government and privatized self-sufficiency.

The centrality of marriage, as a southern Republican value, in the late twentieth century is also evidenced by the family cases referred to by members of Congress from 1980 to 2004. Far more than northeastern family cases, only 63 percent of which were married or widowed, larger proportions of family examples from the South (73 percent) and West (78 percent) talked of being married or widowed. In comparison to southern families, family cases hailing from the Northeast were more unmarried (19 percent) and divorced (17 percent). A majority of family cases referenced by Republican legislators thus comprised two married parents (53 percent) in contrast to 44 percent of Democratic cases. Also, Democratic family examples were more often drawn from single-parent families (42 percent of Democratic cases vs. 37 percent of Republican cases); all these differences are statistically significant.[55]

Finally, Republicans' emphasis on authoritarian structures and discipline within their conservative Soul family values approach[56] also mirrored southern family ideals. Survey findings from the 1990s document southern parents' higher preference for corporal punishment as an appropriate form of discipline in contrast to parents from the Northeast. Instilling a sense of order and respect for authority among children was more important to southern parents across sociodemographic groups, surpassing all other regional parent groups.[57] Republican members in Congress, starting from 1980, similarly invoked such themes to emphasize discipline and tough love within the family, tying them to society-wide ideals of law and order. In so doing, they advocated several policies, affirming the role of strict punishment to combat, among other things, rising rates of juvenile delinquency and social disorder.[58] Family order, for Soul advocates, was both the proxy and the means to create lasting social order.

As Dan Coats (R-IN), in a hearing on youth violence, said, strong families were "developers of inner policemen," since "mothers and fathers teach the difference between right and wrong better than any police department or court system."[59] Jim DeMint, a rising conservative from South Carolina, in a hearing in 1999 on school violence, also stressed the importance of discipline, tough love, and authority as a solution for schools. Schools, he said, should have "the means and the resources to create an orderly and discipline environment," emphasizing "the need to turn more responsibility as well as the authority over to teachers and principals . . . when they implement common sense disciplinary procedures."[60]

Numerous witnesses invited to Republican-led committee hearings made similar references to the importance of strict discipline and firm authority by parents and teachers. One of them, Christopher Lyle, a sophomore at Columbine High School, Littleton, Colorado, again highlighted the role of parents as strict moral stewards. He cited a meeting between his mother and homeroom teacher on his first day of junior high as an example of an "early detection and intervention and counseling session": "[My mother] told my homeroom teacher with me sitting there with her, 'I expect Lyle to behave in school, like he does as at home. If he misbehaves . . . you have the right to punish him. And you call me, and when he comes home, I will punish him.' "[61]

The salience of strict family values on late twentieth-century family politics is especially notable insofar as it extended to Democrats as well. From 1980 to 2004, Democratic members used family cases in committee hearings to highlight some of the same values illustrated by Republicans, using many family cases to focus on "responsible parenting" and illustrating qualities of good or bad parents. Both parties invoked various valuational messages of parenting when they discussed public policies. Table 14 indicates the comparable high proportions by which Democrats and Republicans used family cases to extol conservative family values such as moral parenting, work ethic, and love for family, alongside other cases depicting parental irresponsibility and absentee parenting.

However, Democrats used family cases in high proportions to also illustrate secular-humanist values, such as equality, which they inherited from the New Left. Twenty-four percent of Democratic family cases emphasized equality in contrast with 2 percent of Republican cases. Reflecting the concerns of feminist and other New Left activists, the data on family cases during committee hearings suggest that the late twentieth-century Democratic emphasis on equality significantly began to focus on *gender* equality, in addition to the party's longer-standing commitment to class equality.

Women's inclusion into the workforce was a central demographic feature of shifting familial practices, bridging public and private spheres of work and family more than ever before. From 1980 to 2004, Democratic members of

Table 14. Cultural Values Illustrated in Democratic and Republican Family Cases, 1980–2004

		Party of Active MC			
		Democratic		Republican	
		Count	Percent	Count	Percent
Secular theme	Involved parents	55	24.4	39	26.5
	Liberty[a]	1	.4	7	4.8
	Equality[a]	53	23.6	3	2.0
	Justice	7	3.1	4	2.7
	Work ethic	47	20.9	37	25.2
	Family privacy[a]	27	12.0	38	25.9
	Irresponsible parent	35	15.6	19	12.9
	Total	225	100.0	147	100.0
Moral theme	Thrift/savings	8	7.3	13	10.5
	Charity	3	2.7	6	4.8
	Sexual abstinence	0	.0	3	2.4
	Love for family	28	25.5	19	15.3
	Parenting	39	35.5	47	37.9
	Gender roles	2	1.8	8	6.5
	Promiscuity	2	1.8	5	4.0
	Absentee parent	28	25.5	23	18.5
	Total	110	100.0	124	100.0

[a] Values in the same row are significantly different for Democratic and Republican cases at $p < .05$ in the two-sided test of equality for column proportions. Tests assume equal variances.

Congress repeatedly highlighted this, advocating public policy proposals that created an equal playing field for mothers and fathers pursuing both work and family. They called for an enhanced role of the state to provide services, such as childcare, gender pay equity, and family leave measures, to allow for dual-earner families, supporting women to be both effective workers and nurturing mothers. Unlike many conservative Soul proponents and much like the "Blue State values" described in Cahn and Carbone, Democratic members of Congress most consistently viewed the mother's work outside of the home in neutral, economic, and not valuational terms—as an economic necessity for most families, frequently described as the result of postindustrial economic restructuring and the decline of family wages for male workers. Women's choice of career or family was thus often presented as a specious one since, for most mothers, participation in the workforce was seen as an economic decision rather than a valuational choice.

This is evident in an exchange between Chairman George Miller (D-CA) and Rebecca Rhones, a separated, single mother of four from Fairfax, Virginia. Ms. Rhones described turning down numerous promotions and pay increases so that she could keep her eligibility for subsidized daycare. She said she would have to continue to do this "until the baby is no longer eligible for day care or until I feel reasonably comfortable that she can come home by herself." She explained her rationale by saying, "It comes to a point where it is career versus children, and the raises, even though they look good, if you really add up through the year it is less than what it would actually cost if I have to find somebody to take care of the children." In addition, she described, "It is easier because you know the child is in a setting that you feel secure with and you can trust these people rather than put them with a babysitter part time that you do not know what is going on." Throughout the hearing, Congressman Miller referred to Rhones's decision to forego career advancement in favor of quality childcare as "the ultimate private subsidy," decrying the "penalty" women made "when you pick your children over your career."[62] Economics, not values, was at the core of such family decisions, and state public assistance was essential to ensuring private experiences of gender equality in workplaces and other spaces.

In addition and much in contrast to previous periods such as the postwar era, women's participation in the workforce was applauded by Democratic members as a means of personal satisfaction and individual growth for women and not merely an economic necessity.[63] In response to the growing ranks of women, feminists, and college-educated constituents within their ranks, Democrats, when discussing family cases, addressed women and gender equality far more in policy debate than did Republicans. They highlighted the impact of various policies specifically for women, in a significantly greater proportion than did Republicans, who were instead more prone to stress traditional gender roles within family units, encouraging mothers to remain in the home. Eight percent of Democratic cases expressly mentioned women's issues in their family description (versus 1 percent of Republican cases), and not one Democratic case mentioned traditional gender arrangements in the family, in contrast to 2 percent of Republican cases that did.

Democratic cultural liberals espousing Hearth principles in the late twentieth century thus began to look to public policies to create various programs and services in order to enhance individuals' choices, emphasizing the value of choice and self-determination over tradition and biology in many aspects of family life, including family formation. In addition to child care services and public assistance, when discussing federal funding of domestic violence shelters and even alternative reproductive technologies, personal choice—primarily women's choice—began to be invoked as a key valuational goal of Democratic social policies.[64] Democratic-sponsored witnesses, such as Laurie Dixon, a high school student from Bethesda, Maryland, testified to the virtues of "new" extramarital family formations, such as living with divorced parents, saying, "I am now thankful that my parents did divorce. If my parents were together, I would have a terrible home situation." She asserted the emerging liberal position by claiming, "Divorce itself is not the true problem for kids today"; instead, "bad marriages which continue or end and lack of communication pose much more substantial threats to the healthy upbringing of a child."[65]

Democrats' attention to egalitarian family values was fitted within their larger, more abiding focus on family economics. Democratic legislators often described "postmaterial," quality-of-life issues, mental and emotional, as inseparable from a family's material circumstances. For instance, numerous hearings on rising unemployment during the 1980s and early 1990s emphasized the effects of joblessness on the family's quality of life, highlighting the stress, anguish, and depression caused by long-term unemployment on the family. Family problems such as alcoholism, substance abuse, domestic violence, and child abuse were tied to economic instability and increasing hardship and not declining values. In the postwar era, Democratic Hearth advocates had newly begun to include a family's emotional needs, in addition to its material ones, then considered important in light of postwar and Cold War uncertainty. Even in the late twentieth century, Democrats, following the legacy of their party, continued to advocate for such programmatic assistance to reduce the stress, mental anguish, and other negative quality-of-life concerns that they then began to associate with a postindustrial society.[66]

At a hearing on the new unemployed, Democratic-invited witness John Morris, a former unemployed autoworker from Dearborn, Michigan, described the family circumstances of unemployed auto workers, emphasizing the mental anguish joblessness brings: "The greatest impact of job loss," he said, "is a loss of confidence and feeling of un-usefulness." He described his experiences with the families of displaced autoworkers at "UAW, local 600," recounting "the financial stress of mortgage payments that cannot be met, automobiles being repossessed, and the pressure of not being able to provide the basic necessities of life." The economic insecurity and "loss of economic freedom," he said, often "brings on the pressures that many times result in alcohol or substance abuse," and "personality changes and violent behavior are not uncommon."[67] In another hearing on alcohol abuse, Democratic Representative Lindy Boggs (D-LA) reiterated the economic origins of family ailments, acknowledging the "tragic progression of events" illustrated by families of witnesses from Detroit, Michigan, and Ames, Iowa, where "problem drinking increased with unemployment" and in turn caused an "increase in spouse abuse, child abuse and in the numbers of teenagers who ran away from home or the so-called throwaway children who were thrown out by parents who could no longer cope."[68]

Whereas in the Democratic Hearth framework, family ailments, such as domestic violence and child abuse, were tied to economic instability, similar problems were approached more valuationally by Republican Soul members—as the outcome of decreasing commitments to marriage, religion, and social order and an increasing self-centeredness and sexual permissiveness.[69]

Thus, despite the parties' collective turn toward "family values" in the late twentieth century, seen through the GOP's wholehearted embrace of the Soul family approach and Democrats' references to secular-humanist and egalitarian values within their own liberal Hearth family system, both parties, now more than ever, continued to polarize over the family. Democratic and Republican legislators persisted in approaching family problems either as structural or innate, respectively, as a question of economic deprivation or as one of declining moral values.

These lasting differences in partisan family ideals remained embedded in differing sectional realities that were the focus of Democratic and Republican agendas. As the next section reveals, the Republican-Soul family values approach reflected and accommodated suburban, often small-business southern family life, and the Democratic-Hearth family economic approach was geared to reflect lower-income northern urban working family realities.

Democratic-Hearth and Republican-Soul Family Lived Realities

Several scholars attest to the intertwining of regional material shifts and sectional values as shaping the late twentieth-century culture wars. For example, political scientist Nicole Mellow attributes the Sunbelt's traditionalist family values to the timing of demographic family changes there and the region's late industrialization compared to other regions. Addressing abortion policies, she writes, "The rhetoric . . . framed the issue as a choice between tradition and modernization, and the regions responded differently." In contrast to "areas with long histories of economic development," like the Northeast, where "the changes driving the demand for abortion rights and gender equality were welcomed," those "areas newly experiencing economic development and widespread change, such as the historically rural South and West," prized tradition and social stability.[70]

Similarly, legal scholars Naomi Cahn and June Carbone point to a peculiar ongoing disjuncture between ideals and practice in the "red states" of the South, asserting that these regions' traditionalist values did not match the actual family changes that occurred with its postindustrial shift. They observe, "In [tradition-bound] communities that most revolve around marriage . . . divorce has consequences not only for individual well-being but . . . for the foundation of the shared notions or morality."[71] Cahn and Carbone, like Self and the assertion in this book, acknowledge that in the red, Republican states of the South and Southwest, the family changes that began in the late twentieth century were perceived as a "moral crisis"—a crisis of values.

In contrast, the "blue states" of the North, say Cahn and Carbone, "had greater concentrations of wealth and education a half century ago,"[72] with more opportunities for higher education and career ambitions among the nonpoor, and consequently marriage in those states was much more delayed and not a central organizing feature of these communities. These blue states, they say, viewed demographic family change neutrally, not as a moral crisis, and were able to embrace a new family culture and value system more aligned with a postindustrial economy. For Cahn and Carbone, differences in wealth, education, housing prices, and so on all contributed to materially structuring red and blue community and family life differentially, engendering sectional differences in family values and policy preferences.

Within congressional committee hearings, legislators and their witnesses acknowledged, in positive and negative ways, enduring southern cultural distinctiveness. Witnesses such as Polly Porter, from Metter, Georgia, described her family's pursuit of "the good way of life in rural Georgia" as "life out of the fast lane where we could spend time together with God, with nature and on our own land,"[73] and lamented on its loss due to economic restructuring of the southern hinterland. Others, such as Dr. Ted Holloway from the Southeast Public Health Unit, spoke of intensely local identities in small southern communities and animosity to outsiders, recounting, "I grew up in a small, rural place in South Carolina named Ware Shoals and [even] today as I drive through Honea Path, which is 8 miles away, I get this terrible feeling because I hate those people so much . . . [these] rural areas have a great deal of conflict between towns."[74]

Timothy Vann, whose family was previously discussed, attributed "successes and achievements made by my family" to "my parents, my grandparents, and my friends" and to the fact that "we inherited the good southern tradition of discipline, work, respect for parents and elderly, and all people . . . the teachings of love and honor for God, respect for my parents, respect and consideration of all people, honesty, industriousness, self-reliance and self-worth were passed to me and then, on to my children."[75] Congressman Clyde Holloway (R-LA) spoke of his own childhood, growing up in Louisiana and its close family networks, saying, "I grew up in a home in a very rural area (in Louisiana) and where my mother cared for my grandparents, and my wife grew up in a home in New York City." His childhood taught him what "love is all about," and "in this world today" policies should be "encouraging . . . who cares for who[m]."[76]

In the last few decades of the twentieth century, in the face of increasing family demographic transition and upheaval, Republican legislators highlighted embedded social networks, strong social ties, and robust community and civic life, which they illustrated through (mostly) southern family examples. Democrats instead often used family examples more to highlight families' increasing social isolation or thinning social bonds and diminishing community networks. Of the family cases that discussed family's social connectedness, 58 percent of Republican cases stressed this by discussing civic participation in voluntary organizations versus 36 percent of Democratic family cases. Many more Democratic family cases (17 percent) mentioned isolation and lack of connectedness to neighbors, communities, and extended families than did Republican (7 percent). Two sides of the late twentieth-century demographic transition—family's growing anonymity and individualism versus family's continued localism and community networks—were thus alternatively highlighted in Democratic and Republican family cases.

Importantly, southern distinctiveness disappeared from partisan discourse when policy discussions turned to family economic conditions.

Legislators, mostly Democratic, stressed economic hardships of *all* families, including those in the South "as elsewhere," pointing to "poverty as the one common denominator" uniting disadvantaged communities across the country. William Lehman, a Democrat from Florida, observed common family problems in "the backwoods and the decaying farms in Appalachia, to the poor whites there," also the "migratory farm laborers, such as we have in Belle Glade, FL," and "the homeless in our big cities, where people are sleeping under bridges in Miami, and on top of grates in Washington," to "inner city public housing minorities where families are abandoned frequently by one of their parents."[77] Whereas a significant statistical difference existed between Republican and Democratic family cases from non-South regions on the basis of whether the family received or did not receive welfare (Democrats consistently cited more families on welfare in the Northeast, Midwest, and West as compared to Republicans), both Republican and Democratic legislators comparably drew high proportions of their southern family examples from those on welfare.[78]

In fact, in contrast to the postwar period but again resembling the Progressive Era, Republican and Democratic family cases in the late twentieth century varied most evidently by class/income. As seen in Table 15B, Democratic members from 1980 to 2004 disproportionately cited lower-income family cases in significantly greater proportions than Republicans (54 percent of Democratic versus 32 percent of Republican cases cited families from lower-income groups). Unlike certain ascriptive or social factors such as race or parent's country of origin, economic status was a key dividing line between the parties' family examples (Table 15A and Table 15B).

Significant differences also existed in other economic characteristics of the family examples referenced by Republican and Democratic members, including differences in income status and the employment statuses of fathers and mothers.[79] Democratic members used more unemployed and part-time employed fathers to illustrate their policy concerns, whereas Republicans drew more on self-employed fathers and mothers. Twenty-two percent of Democratic cases that mentioned father's employment status described cases of unemployed fathers and 5 percent that of part-time employed fathers; this is in contrast to 9 percent of Republicans who mentioned unemployed fathers and less than 1 percent who discussed fathers who were only partially employed.

Sectional variations are very evident in policy debate among Republicans and Democrats, demonstrating the Republican Soul reliance on smaller

Table 15A. Ascriptive Characteristics of Family Cases by Party of Active MC, Committee Hearings, 1980–2004

| | | Party Sponsor of Family | | | |
| | | Democratic | | Republican | |
		Count	Percent	Count	Percent
Parents' nativity	Native born	652	96.7	419	97.4
	Foreign born	22	3.3	11	2.6
	Total	674	100.0	430	100.0
Number of children	One	260	44.6	185	51.0
	Two	141	24.2	72	19.8
	Three	182	31.2	106	29.2
	Total	583	100.0	363	100.0
Family race	White	60	32.8	51	42.1
	African American	72	39.3	47	38.8
	Other	51	27.9	23	19.0
	Total	183	100.0	121	100.0

towns in the South and the Democratic Hearth focus on the more urban North. The largest proportions of family cases invoked by Republican members resided in the South. In contrast, the largest proportion of Democratic family cases hailed from northern states (east of the Mississippi) (Table 16), with the differences in proportions being statistically significant.[80] Forty-one percent of Republican family cases resided in the South, whereas an almost equivalently large 42 percent of Democratic family cases were from the North.

The overall southernization of family politics in the late twentieth century is starkly illustrated by the increasing count of southern family stories referenced by members of *both* parties in recent congresses. In contrast, the number of family stories from the postindustrial regions of the North, stressing mainly the declining economic condition of families, has declined precipitously since the 1990s. This is especially noticeable after the 104th Congress and its Contract with America (Figure 19).

Figure 19 suggests that the trends in the regional distribution of family examples match the shifting locus of power between the two parties. Reagan Republicans, such as Senator Denton from Alabama or Representative Clyde Holloway from Louisiana, approached social policies through the cultural

Table 15B. Economic Characteristics of Family Cases by Party of Active MC, Committee Hearings, 1980–2004

| | | Party Sponsor of Family | | | |
| | | Democratic | | Republican | |
		Count	Percent	Count	Percent
Income status*	Lower income[a]	285	54.1	124	37.2
	Middle income[a]	187	35.5	154	46.2
	Upper income[a]	55	10.4	55	16.5
	Total	527	100.0	333	100.0
Father's employment*	Unemployed[a]	47	21.8	13	9.2
	Part-time employed[a]	11	5.1	1	7
	Employed	132	61.1	96	67.6
	Self-employed[a]	26	12.0	32	22.5
	Total	216	100.0	142	100.0
Mother's employment*	Unemployed	57	19.0	33	19.0
	Part-time employed	34	11.3	11	6.3
	Employed	196	65.3	101	58.0
	Self-employed[a]	13	4.3	29	16.7
	Total	300	100.0	174	100.0
Housing status	Public housing	82	38.5	28	27.5
	Private assistance	24	11.3	18	17.6
	Rent	24	11.3	7	6.9
	Homeowners	83	39.0	49	48.0
	Total	213	100.0	102	100.0

[a]Values in the same row are significantly different for Democratic and Republican cases at $p < .05$ in the two-sided test of equality for column proportions. Tests assume equal variances.
*Variable with significant partisan differences.

and economic ideals most prevalent among southern families; this is reflected in the large count of southern family examples in the early 1980s (97th–99th Congresses). Again, at the height of Republican strength, when Republicans dominated both houses in Congress (104th–106th Congresses, 1996–2002), families from the South and the Mountain West (i.e., the so-called red states) were again increasingly referenced in policy debates, indicating their enhanced political value to the Republican coalition. In contrast, in the mid-1980s to early 1990s, when Democrats and Republicans battled for control over the two branches in Congress, family examples from the

Table 16. Region of Democratic and Republican Family Case Examples, 1980–2005

| | | Party of Active MC | | | |
| | | Democratic | | Republican | |
		Count	Percent	Count	Percent
Region of family	North[a]	284	42.2	142	35.7
residence*	South[a]	215	31.9	177	41.3
	West	84	12.5	62	14.5
	Pacific	90	13.4	48	11.2
	Total	673	100.0	429	100.0

[a]Values in the same row are significantly different for Democratic and Republican cases at $p < .05$ in the two-sided test of equality for column proportions. Tests assume equal variances.
*Chi-square statistic is significant at the .05 level.

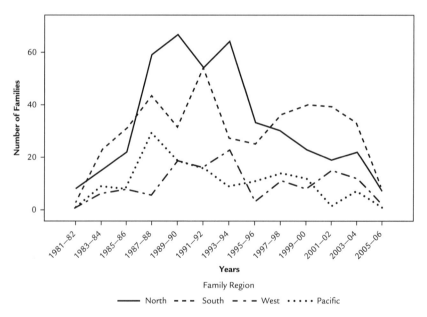

Figure 19. Region of families referenced in hearings, 97th–109th Congresses (1980–2005).

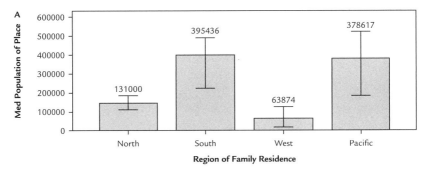

Figure 20A. Median population distribution of family case example by region, committee hearings, 1980–2005: Democratic sponsor of family.

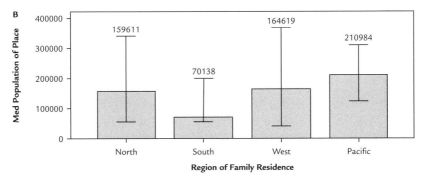

Figure 20B. Median population distribution of family case examples by region, committee hearings, 1980–2005: Republican sponsor of family.

blue states of the North and Pacific Coast were evenly referenced alongside those from the red, southern, and mountain states.

In addition to region, there are also differences in each party's family examples based on the size of the towns in which they reside. As seen in Figures 20A and Figure 20B, there is no statistical difference between Republicans and Democrats in the median population size of towns for northern and Pacific family cases. However, among their southern family examples, Republicans relied on families from significantly smaller-sized towns than did Democrats. A larger proportion of Democratic family cases hailed from southern metropolises such as Atlanta (Georgia), Baltimore

(Maryland), and New Orleans (Louisiana), while Republican southern family cases were more scattered across smaller cities such as Mobile (Alabama), Charlottesville (Virginia), and Plano (Texas). In contrast, a large proportion of Republican family cases from the West were drawn from higher population cities such as Salt Lake City (Utah) and Phoenix (Arizona) than were Democratic ones.

In sum, there were significant sectional differences in the two partisan family ideals shaping Democratic-Hearth and Republican-Soul family approaches at this time. The economics-centered Hearth family approach, with its increasing liberal individualist family values of gender equality, individual choice, and self-determination, began to be pursued actively by Democratic members and was constructed around the concerns and practices of more urban, postindustrial, often harder-hit, low-income, northern families. And the Soul family approach, stressing conservative moral and neoliberal values of self-reliance, personal responsibility, marriage, and moral discipline, was illustrated more extensively by smaller-town/suburban, self-employed, southern families. Collectively, the turn to an enhanced "value-ization" of family policy discourse is observable in members' increasing reliance on red state families mostly from the South to illustrate their policy concerns and preferences, indicating both the region's rising political value to both parties as well as its impact on the shifting ideational character and normative goals of late twentieth-century family policy.

Conclusion

The findings of the chapter revise and/or modify two important stories in American politics, one regarding the development of the welfare state and the other related to party polarization. First, this examination finds the increased salience of "family values" in policy discourse, catapulting a previously subterranean cultural politics into current prominence. However, unlike the usual depiction in well-known scholarly and popular works where cultural politics competes and, to some extent, replaces economics as the central framework (McCarty et al., Stonecash et al., Miller and Schofield, Thomas Frank, etc.), the chapter shows how both parties now fit their concern with cultural issues *onto* persisting differences over economy and redistribution; the amalgamation produced new family ideologies that resembled but were in many ways distinct from their antecedents. Whereas the two approaches (Hearth and Soul) have continued to remain divided over the relative political value ascribed to family economic conditions over its culture/values or vice versa, the chapter's discursive investigation into policy debates has assembled how the two dimensions of values and economics became more deeply conjoined and started to coexist in partisan agendas in a deeply entwined, imbricated way. The extent of this ideological melding of values to economics and the deployment of family as a common partisan cause is distinctive of the late twentieth-century period, marking also the start of the current character of the American welfare state.

As critical literature on the welfare state has rightly noted, progressives' engagement with the family during previous periods (such as the Progressive Era or postwar era) was by no means acultural; instead, family economic assistance often also implied the accompanying imposition of a racist, classist, and gendered social-cultural system on immigrant, ethnic, and other minority families.[81] Similarly in the postwar era, the ideological battle over social welfare by Hearth and Soul proponents also contained ideational contests over different sets of cultural ideals. Nevertheless, up until the 1970s, the liberal family approach of the Hearth framework had legitimated national state expansion into families' lives by stressing the economic aspects of family need, its values remaining deliberated muted. Traditionalists, such as southern Democrats, advocating Soul ideologies were previously content with the mechanism of localistic control of federal economic programs to mollify their own concern with family values. However, to counter the New Politics, late twentieth-century Democratic-Hearth advocates and their emergent secular-humanism traditionalists altered the previous conservative Republican approach, now enlisting the national state in active pursuit of traditionalist, Soul family values. Whether a companionable Big Brother or a sterner Strong Father, the (federal) state began to play a far more central role in engineering family values. One important goal of the last two chapters has been to document this recently enhanced relationship between national state and family values and to demonstrate how the two party systems, through their preferred policies, first began to accommodate this development.

Second, the picture of intersectionality of the two frames, values and economics, also has implications for how to approach and understand party polarization. Relying on committee hearings as sources, the chapter finds that the picture gleaned from roll call analysis is incomplete. Partisan divisions starting with Reagan have not occurred along the economic redistributionist dimension alone, but partisan ideation continued to be divided over *how* the two economic or valuational dimensions intersect and connect, if at all. This also revises the conventional understanding of American politics as a whole. Instead of viewing politics as comprising separate, competing dimensions such as values/culture or economics, the data on the family suggest a more complex conception of party politics as a layered tapestry of interweaving frames in which polarization and convergence can occur simultaneously and that both economy and cultural concerns can blend into a single policy focus, such as the family. The task is not to determine "which one" but "how" the intersection of the two axes has developed over time. Focusing on the family allows one to do this. Taking such a family-centered approach thus opens the door to uncovering new ways to conceptualize and understand late twentieth-century developments in party politics.

Conclusion

The story of family political development is a deeply human and sectional one—grounded in the lives and realities of everyday American families. Family demographic transformations have occurred disparately across the United States, and this phenomenon, coupled with regional historical and cultural legacies, has ensured that families interpret (and thus experience) their changing lives in diverse ways, displaying a sectional pattern that differentiates southern (and southwestern) families from those in the Northeast. In the wake of such demographic overhaul, by the end of the twentieth century, Republican legislators presented and idealized family as still inherently private, morally steadfast, self-sufficient, and embedded in thick social networks and robust community life, and Democrats highlighted the emerging isolation and anonymity felt by families in northern (often urban) sections, idealizing instead family as increasingly interdependent on government to adapt to a brave new world of thinning familial resources. Lived family differences contextualize and thus operate as both opportunities and constraints upon political actors seeking to formulate successful policy and electoral strategies, whereby diverse actors can pick and choose distinct aspects of family life to emphasize over others, to fit into their policies and overarching ideologies. In this regard, massive family demographic transition has played a transformative role on party politics, shaping conservative Republican ascendance and southern realignment as much as the more familiar story of race and the civil rights movement.

The tale of family reframes the narrative on race and gender in American politics. Rather than as direct points of contention between the two parties, race and gender in this account play important but indirect roles in partisan divisions over family, surfacing more clearly in some periods than others. Racial ideologies, for instance, played a prominent, formative role in the Democratic Soul family approach of the Progressive Era but less so in the Republican free enterprise Soul family ideology of the post–World War II period, only to regain relevance in the late twentieth-century moralistic Republican Soul family iteration. Competing ideologies of gender and womanhood also played decisive roles in family party development, as seen in the Progressive and late twentieth-century periods, and were less prominent as points of division in the 1950s. The Progressive Era and the late twentieth century thus resemble each other in the polarizing, gendered, and racial ways by which the parties invoked family, despite the fact that the two parties had switched their allegiances to Hearth and Soul family ideologies by then.

The family-centered story of party competition complements and parallels the periodization found in works on race. For instance, building on the work of others such as Joseph Lowndes, Desmond King and Rogers Smith point to a durable shift in racial ideologies since the 1970s, from race-conscious approaches to colorblind ones, as marking a "critical ideational development" that produced advantages for conservative coalition building and contributed to the Reagan Revolution and polarization.[1] In their account, the "critical-ness" of this political development lay in the fact that its impact extended beyond explicitly racial policies but also encompassed GOP advantage in setting taxes, social spending, and criminal law agendas. As they write, "Color-blind principles have thereby helped conservatives build elite and mass coalitions that cooperate on many issues, not just racial ones." They assert that a central aspect in building the conservative colorblind alliance was the "politics of character" and "personal responsibility," by which "modern conservative leaders have persuaded their supporters that they share a common ground . . . [for] all conservatives favor policies that reward good individual character and responsible economic, moral, and civic behavior, while discouraging and punishing bad character and conduct."[2] Conservative colorblind politics of character, as constructed by King and Smith and in a related way by Lowndes, in no small way reflects the late-century turn to Republican Soul family values as discussed and assembled in this book, in their overlapping timing of emergence and focus on moral and character traits as opposed to material conditions.

However, a more important implication of the book to the story of race in political development is that the politics of family shapes the politics of race. Thus, the conservative embrace of the colorblind approach can be seen as *part* of the late-century Republican adoption of a Soul family values approach. As southern conservatives came to dominate the Republican Party (and as GOP elites made southernization an electoral strategy), the policy turn to family as a valuational, self-regulating unit unmoored from its economic conditions also enabled its separation from *racial* economic inequality that was the mainstay of the liberal race-conscious alliance. Whereas values such as responsibility and moral character in the Hearth family approach were long grounded (at least since the Progressive Era) in economic conditions, values in the Soul approach have persistently been upheld as universal, natural, and timeless—*transcending* economic structure and historically contingent conditions. In this way, the late twentieth-century GOP's revival of Soul family values also accommodated and facilitated a universal color-blindness that could be differentiated from race-conscious efforts focused on economic disadvantages. The racial undertones within the late-century Soul family values framework become clear from the finding that legislators and partisans disproportionately directed the (universalist colorblind) "family values" or "character" policy frames to target families of African American and racial minorities in policy discussions.[3] In conjunction with King and Smith's claim that "race still matters," this book thus makes the claim that family matters and that the story of family in many ways shapes the story of race in political development, an intertwining narrative that is one feature of this book but could be a valuable object of inquiry on its own in future work.

Attention to family's political story also unearths evolving patterns in policy configurations used by legislators and parties. These patterns too underscore the similarity between the Progressive and late twentieth-century periods. Throughout the twentieth century, legislators addressed family through four types of policies. These policy configurations are historically contingent insofar as they are shaped by the causes and conditions of each historical period, yet distinct patterns also emerge across the three eras. Welfare and regulation policies have, by and large, formed the mainstay of advocates advancing a Hearth family economics approach, although there was much greater reliance on regulation policies, particularly parental regulation, among proponents of the late twentieth century compared to previous times. Soul family values advocates expressed greater preoccupation with ascriptive policies in the Progressive Era and with autonomy policies in the late twentieth century, although ascriptive policies were also resurgent in the more recent congresses investigated.

The resemblance of the Progressive Era to the late twentieth century is thus unmistakable. In both political times, the family ideals invoked were polarized, racial, and gendered, generating higher levels of policy differences between the two parties. The resemblance of the two eras in the story of family political development is tied to the prominence of southern legislators to party politics in those times. For the most part, southern legislators were the central, recurrent characters, whose most consistent concern was the preservation of conservative family values through a moralistic, racial/parochial, now also nationalistic, Soul family frame. Whether in the Democratic Party or in the Republican Party, the presence of a strong southern delegation, as in the Progressive Era and late twentieth century, consistently pushed the party toward viewing (and advocating for) family through a moralistic valuational lens. Yet southern support for the Hearth family economics approach is evidenced in both the Progressive and post–World War II periods, during which southern Democratic legislators also supported economics-based welfare policies for families. By the late twentieth century, however, southern legislators now in the Republican Party were much more strongly tied to Soul family values than any other delegation and eschewed more completely the Hearth economics approach, in part perhaps because of the growing economic prosperity of the region. Southern legislators most consistently thus viewed families as valuational moral units—transmitting, reproducing, or potentially upending shared legacies and traditional values. This suggests that southern accommodation in either of the two parties invariably shifts the party to advocate more concertedly for Soul family values. And the southernization of American politics hence portends the increasing acceptance of ascriptive and autonomy valuational policies as legitimate, prized agendas instead of plainly welfare policies.

Used as two poles to chart and organize how legislators and parties have approached family in policy, Hearth family economics and Soul family values must also be viewed as inextricably intertwined. This becomes far more evident in the late twentieth century, although such imbrication is also found in the Progressive Era. In both periods, family material assistance through policy was predicated on distinct values that were constructed to regulate very particular groups of families, such as those of immigrants, racial minorities, and the poor, all of whom were perceived as deficient in these values. Yet it is only in the late twentieth century that preserving or, in some cases, engineering family values became a prominent, *independent* policy focus, whereby even material policies came to be cast in terms of values. Hearth and Soul family approaches thus became more intertwined than ever. No longer, as this author argues elsewhere, was (economic) "need" alone sufficient for policy intervention; instead, the focus turned to which pro-grammatic assistance could generate and/or uphold liberal or conservative family values (women's independence, for example, or preservation of family integrity and/or strength).[4] Divergent family values have thus come to be more deeply intertwined than ever with party competition over economic redistribution, shaping current polarization on a host of issues and not just those directly related to family social welfare.

The late twentieth-century turn to the Soul values approach has gener-ated clear policy winners and losers. Income has consistently and sharply divided the parties' family political ideals through the twentieth century, with some legislators invoking the Hearth family economics approach to ad-dress lower-income families and other legislators using more upper-income families as the basis of their Soul family values approach. Thus, the emer-gence of the Soul family framework in the last two decades of the twentieth century and its eclipsing of the Hearth ideal suggests that poor families (par-ticularly in urban areas without extended families) were now the clearest losers. Insofar as economic deprivation engenders non–nuclear family for-mations among the urban poor, and parties can increasingly view such fam-ilies as deficient in universal family values, they are disqualified from policy support. Alternative families, such as gay/lesbian/transgendered families, to the extent that they have been able to portray self-sufficiency as a family value, have been able to make successful cases for inclusion into partisan agendas. Perhaps the greatest legacy of the "culture wars" of the 1990s has thus been to elevate universalist family "autonomy" and "self-sufficiency" as the most widely accepted political family value across both political par-ties. From this reading, neoliberals have been able to score the greatest victory over cultural liberals as well as over more moralistic, paleo-conservatives, and they have done so at the expense of the (urban) poor.

The story of family political development thus suggests a distinct dark side to the Soul family values approach and the way the parties have deployed it. For one, conservative racial ideologies, including those extolling white su-premacy, the self-sufficiency of yeoman farm families, and the virtues of (often Christian and white) moral families, have historically been expressed more consistently by family values advocates. When legislators deployed family values as the predominant approach to public policy, the values they invariably advocated were the values of native-born white middle-income families, whose racial appeal is either expressly acknowledged or still identi-fiable even if more muted. Racialized values have played less of a role in the construction and use of the Hearth economics approach, despite the fact that in the recent past, its advocates have veered away from race neutrality toward harnessing race-conscious values such as inclusion, personal dignity, and equity. The historical periods when the Soul family values approach gains the most policy traction and more actively competes with the Hearth family economics approach are thus customarily periods of racial upheaval, as in the Progressive and late twentieth-century periods and continuing into today.

Also notable is the brand of antistatism that Soul family values advocates have come to espouse. Far from resisting *all* forms of national state, as did conservative Republicans of the midcentury, only programs and initiatives directed at family economic conditions are the target of Soul family values legislators, enabling the retrenchment of the more traditional, economic aspects associated with the welfare state while engaging national state machinery to preserve traditional social arrangements and attendant values. This kind of Soul state need not be only a laissez-faire state, as in the tradition of the antebellum southern state, but also an activist national state that seeks to positively engineer social and, in some cases, ascriptive values. In their calls for intermarriage bans, prohibition of women's suffrage, and regulatory control of deficient mothers and later of poor families, as well as in marriage and faith-based initiatives, historically strong family values advocates have for the most part been comfortable with the idea of an active national state when harnessed in the pursuit of their values. Thus, the interplay between values *and* economics, much more than a story of big or small government, has shaped the political evolution of Hearth and Soul family political ideals in party politics.

Although their particulars change, family economics and family values are thus two grand scripts that compete or align with one another in different historical periods, informing the parties' electoral strategies and policy proposals. The attention to family and the enduring appeal of Hearth and Soul approaches suggest the presence of two, not one, interlocking dimensions—economics and values—that structure current American politics as well as more longitudinal political developments. An important implication of this study therefore is that economics and values in American party politics are codependent and cannot exist in isolation of the other. Even in periods of one-party dominance and seeming universal appeal of one focus, the other endures even if in subterranean form, continuing to remain available when conditions are right for utilization and manipulation by parties as a means to modify or even counter the prevailing script and the partisan coalition supporting it. This dynamic is especially evident in the development of family from the postwar period into the late twentieth century. In the period following World War II, despite the seeming convergence of the two parties in favor of services targeting family economic conditions, sizable factions in both Republican and Democratic Parties continued to challenge the statist ideology of the dominant political order on the basis of values, then solely private, free enterprise values. This valuational policy approach became central to late twentieth-century party politics, when the New Right capitalized on social unease following massive family demographic change and seized upon preexisting conservative social values, combining them with religious and moral values to craft an electoral and policy strategy that then successfully challenged the existing policy discourse and the electoral dominance of the liberal Democratic coalition.

Family political development of the late twentieth century now shapes current American politics in the age of Donald Trump in several ways. The nostalgic impulse channeled in the GOP's late-century southernization strategy, harkening to a lost social and political order predating the Democratic welfare state and embodied in the independent heterosexual two-parent male-centered family, continues in current political narratives. The cultural imagery of the "Forgotten Man" in Trump's campaign, for instance, deployed to bring attention to the declining economic fortunes of blue-collar workers ostensibly of both genders, draws on historic familial understandings of that image. First popularized by FDR in the New Deal, the "Forgotten Man" was a male breadwinner whose inability to provide for his family underscored his political significance. Forgotten Men were thus first and foremost the heads of traditionalist families that were white, with two parents, and centered on a single male earner,[5] and his unemployed economic status was politically valued only in relation to his idealized familial role as a breadwinner. Trump's deployment of such imagery in his campaign and policy narratives explicitly demonstrates the ongoing nostalgic cast of Republican policy ideology wherein traditional social, familial, gendered, and racial orders continue to underpin appeals to populism *and* economic deregulation. This endurance is also seen in the composition of Trump's appointees. Several Republican culture warriors of the late century, such as Jeff Sessions (R-AL) and Dan Coats (R-IN), who find extensive mention in this book as strong advocates for family values revivalism, were selected to serve in prominent roles in the Trump administration.

Furthermore, the legacy of both parties' late twentieth-century policy configurations, as well as their intertwined economic and valuational agendas, continues into contemporary politics. Similar to the GOP's juxtaposition of autonomy with more ascriptive family policy ideals, Trump's 2016 campaign presented an economic message that also relied on racially ascriptive values and cultural imagery, evident in the centrality of "radical Islamists," "Mexicans," and "Syrian refugees" in his proposals for closed borders and the promotion of domestic wealth and economic prosperity. Within the Democratic Party, Hillary Clinton, in conjunction with previous Democratic candidates, notably Barack Obama, tied redistributionist economic policies to other, more secular values of inclusion and diversity. These partisan appeals to intertwined ideals of economics *and* values, as well as to ideals of society and culture intermixed with those of economic regulation and redistribution, are unlikely to diminish in the next many election cycles, given that they are now firmly rooted in partisan discourse and have come to discursively tie to and reflect alternate—increasingly polar—sectional family conditions.

Hearth and Soul family approaches thus continue to conjure up "Two Americas." One is a more northern cosmopolitan America, where changes in demographic conditions are viewed neutrally and an urban social ideal is privileged, in which discrete, gender-egalitarian families of all races and sexualities, with two working parents and comfortable incomes, nurture children in values of personal fulfillment and tolerance. The other is more southern and communitarian, where demographic changes are resisted and a more small-town nostalgic social vision is adopted, in which interdependent family units, modeled on white heterosexual families, preferably with a stay-at-home mother, are committed to preserving timeless moral and religious values, nurture children in values of self-regulation and preservation. Given the increasing embedment of these two ideals in increasingly distinct sectional realities *and* the deepening material divide between these two, Hearth and Soul are likely to continue to pull the parties apart rather than allow them to come together. Family ideational feuds have thus come to fuel more than policy battles over marginal policy issues; they now guide and channel the parties much more fundamentally, embodying polarized interlocking normative visions of American society, economy, and state and reifying the increasingly divergent worldviews of the very partisans they rely on and hope to enlist.

Research Notes and Methodology

PLATFORM ANALYSIS: METHODOLOGY

A party platform is a statement of policy positions on a wide range of issues, representing the collective beliefs of all the members of the party.[1] Because it is presented and approved in each party's nominating convention, the final party platform is the product of much negotiation and compromise between the presidential candidate's own views and the bargains that he has made to win the support of party factions.[2] On one hand, platforms are thus campaign documents, designed to help the party's candidates win electoral success; on the other hand, however, party platforms are also ideological statements, revealing the "thinking of President and Party";[3] it is the outcome of an ideological exercise by which the party justifies its policy proposals and fits them into its overarching philosophy. Through the platform, parties combine their ideological and electoral agendas, providing, in some detail, the rationale behind their policy thinking in order to persuade voters to align with their agenda. Presented every four years to the American public, the party platform is therefore a valuable source to determine the evolution of how a party imagines and approaches any policy issue, such as the family, and what ideological rationale it offers over time to justify that vision.[4] In my analysis of the parties' platforms across the twentieth and twenty-first centuries (1900–2012), I examine (a) the extent of attention paid to the family and (b) the policy rationale that the platform provides for its family-related pledges. The platform paragraph is my unit of analysis, and I isolate, code, and analyze 1,458 family paragraphs across fifty-eight platforms.

Platform paragraphs can be as short as one to two sentences or as long as numerous sentences. In each case, however, I coded one paragraph as a single case if it addressed the family through a coherent, single, and discernable policy issue. To qualify as a "family paragraph," the policy discussed must have clearly related to the family *as a family or as a series of familial relationships* (i.e., pertained to either the family as a unit or to parents, children, or spouses *as members of a family*). Thus, all planks that address women or children as individuals and not in their familial capacity, relation, or role were not included. For example, paragraphs involving youth and adolescent drug use or job training were excluded if the youth/children/adolescents addressed were not connected directly to their families, parents, or siblings. Similarly, paragraphs that addressed women as women (e.g., as wage earners, their [nonreproductive] health, employment, discrimination) and did not address women in their capacity/role as parents or spouses were also not included or coded. The purpose behind this conservative coding scheme was to focus the measurement on family as a unit or as a set of dependent/familial relationships and not on individuals who only incidentally belong to a family.

BILL SPONSORSHIP AND COSPONSORSHIP: METHODOLOGY

The analysis of bills sponsored and cosponsored utilized the periodization revealed from platform analysis, wherein three significant periods of partisan ideological competition over the family were identified: two periods (the earliest [Progressive] and latest [1980s, 1990s] decades) in which the Hearth family ideal was comparatively less dominant and partisan ideology was more polarized and the post–World War II period, when it was by far the most dominant and the parties appeared to be less polarized in their (family) policy ideologies. Samples of family-related bills from congresses in each of these three periods were thus examined, the distribution of which is summarized in Table 17.

The bills were identified by examining each year's Congressional Record Index by searching under index family-related headings meaningful to each historical period. The headings chosen corresponded to keywords found in that era's platform paragraphs addressing the family. For instance, both parties' platforms discussed the family in the early twentieth century in pledges on veterans' pensions and homestead policies, and thus "pensions" and "public lands" headings were consulted in the Congressional Record Indexes for the relevant periods. Table 18 lists the index headings examined for each of the three periods.

All bills listed under the aforementioned headings were not selected. Instead, using the same definition of "family" used to code platform paragraphs, only those bills were included whose titles invoked a family relation (spouse, parents, dependents) or an aspect of family life (such as marriage, pregnancy, family property). For instance, bills whose titles and synopses referred to "women" or "children" only generally and without mention of their family role/ context were also excluded. Thus, many more bills related to or impinged on the family than were selected. It also should be noted that in the vast majority of the bills, the actual text of the bill was not consulted, only its title (and available synopsis in the case of contemporary bills). For the most part, however, the titles were explanatory of the main object of the bill and revealed an underlying Hearth or Soul family ideology (see Table 19 for examples of bill titles).[5] Thus, the purpose behind this coding scheme was to limit the sample to those bills in which the family is addressed more or less directly *as a family* and not merely as an indirect or implied context. Further, the objective was not to be exhaustive but to generate a represen-

Table 17. Distribution of Family Bills Examined

Era	Congresses	Years	Average Number of Bills per Congress	Total Number of Bills
Progressive	56th–66th	1899–1920	49	538
Postwar	79th–83rd	1945–1954	91	457
Contemporary	101st–108th	1989–2004	125	1,009

Table 18. Headings Examined in Congressional Record Indexes by Era

Period	Headings Examined
Progressive Era (1899–1920)	Aliens, Child/Children, Dependents, District of Columbia,[a] Domestic, Father, Housewife/ves, Infant, Marriage, Maternity, Mother, Negro, Pensions, Public lands (homesteads), Widows, and Women
Postwar era (1945–1954)	Aliens/Immigration, Child/Children, Crime, District of Columbia,[a] Family, Father, Housing, Juvenile Delinquency, Marriage and Divorce, Mother, Negro, Public Health, School, Social Security, States, Taxation, Veterans, Women
Contemporary era (1989–2004)	Family[b]

[a] The District of Columbia was administered directly by Congress during these periods; thus, its heading yielded national bills pertaining to what would have otherwise been solely state police powers, such as miscegenation, juvenile institutions, and child support, not all of which appeared under the other headings examined.

[b] The contemporary era is unlike the others insofar as "family" is now a separate heading in the annual Congressional Record Index listings, yielding family-related numerous bills and supporting my overarching contention that family policy has become a much moral salient, independent issue in recent decades than before.

tative sample of family bills for each era, which then could be analyzed for partisanship and family ideology.

In coding the family ideology of bills as Hearth or Soul, the definitions of the two family ideological frameworks were the same as those developed from party platforms: "Hearth bills" were coded as those that supported direct, material, (national) state programs and intervention into a family's material circumstances, such as providing for a family's economic welfare (such as through relief, housing, child care); providing patronage resources such as birth/marriage registrations, immigration admissions, or parental educational resources; or regulating family behavior (such as in cases of domestic violence, child abuse, child abandonment, child support enforcement). "Soul" bills were those that were "anti-Hearth," instead supporting values of family self-regulation, parental autonomy/choice, or traditional family morality and structure.

CONGRESSIONAL COMMITTEE HEARINGS: METHODOLOGY

I analyzed congressional committee, subcommittee, and select committee hearings for three periods: (1) the Progressive Era (1900–1920), (2) the post–World War II period (1945–1955), and (3) the late twentieth-century era (1980–2005). To generate a sample of family-related hearings for each of the three periods examined, I used the same period-specific family and

Table 19. Samples of Application of Coding Criteria in Family Bills

Index Heading/ Subheading	Title/Abstract	Category
Progressive Era		
Pensions, Orphans	A bill to pension orphans of soldiers and sailors of the Civil War	Hearth
Marriage and Divorce	A joint resolution for amendment to the Constitution prohibiting intermarriage of whites and negroes	Soul
DC, Abandonment of Wife and Minor	A bill to make the abandonment of wife and minor a misdemeanor	Hearth
Postwar era		
Aliens	Bills to admit spouses and children of members of the Armed Forces	Hearth
Housing	A bill to authorize a program for moderate-income families	Hearth
Veterans, Dependents	A bill to limit the eligibility of a stepchild and a stepparent for servicemen's indemnity awards	Soul
Contemporary era		
Family	A bill to amend Title X of the Public Health Service Act to establish in the program for family planning projects a requirement relating to parental notifications	Soul
Family	A bill to amend the Family and Medical Leave Act of 1993 to apply the act to a greater percentage of the U.S. workforce and to allow employees to take parental involvement leave to participate in or attend their children's educational activities and for other purposes	Hearth
Family	A bill to amend the Internal Revenue Code of 1986 to revise the estate and gift tax in order to preserve American family enterprises and for other purposes	Soul

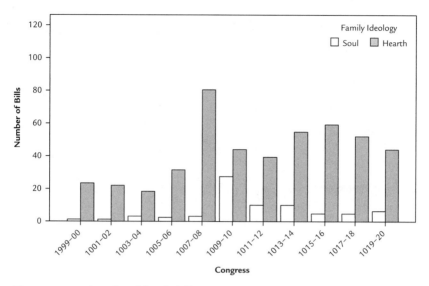

Figure 21. Hearth and Soul family bills introduced in Congress, Progressive Era, 1899–1920.

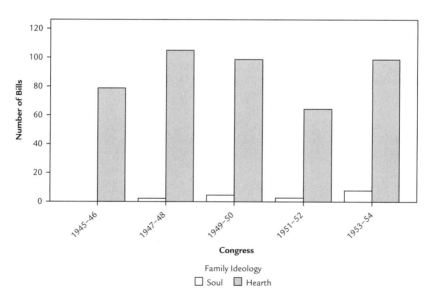

Figure 22. Hearth and Soul family bills introduced in Congress, postwar era, 1946–1954.

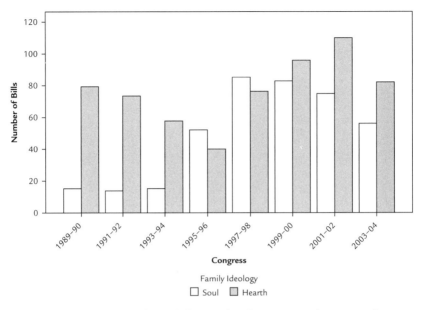

Figure 23. Hearth and Soul family bills introduced in Congress, late twentieth century, 1989–2004.

domestic relations keywords and headings used in party platforms and bill analysis (see Table 18 to search committee hearings in the Government Publishing Office database (in OCLC First-Search). These titles were cross-referenced for completeness with those generated by Lexis/Nexis Congressional Universe, another comprehensive database on congressional reference materials. Given that congressional hearing titles are extremely long and extend to the name of the committee or subcommittee that conducts the hearing, this method captured hearings that (1) have family as their legislative, oversight, or investigative subject as well as (2) those conducted by full committees, subcommittees, or select committees whose committee *names* contain the word "family" and are therefore formed around the object of "family" policy issues. Using this method, I read in entirety the transcripts of the hearings, identifying real-life family cases, as recounted by either members of Congress themselves or witnesses or entered in the statement of record. Only those family cases that satisfied the following criteria were selected for examination: (a) the case contained mention/information on *caretaker(s)*, (b) there was at least one *child* mentioned in the description of the family, (c) the *geographic location* of the family was noted, and (d) at least one *pathology* or *virtue* was described/referenced or alluded to by a member of Congress, thus enabling the case to be classified as either a legislator's "positive" or a "negative" family ideal. Because the object was to study the ideology/activity of legislators (as expressed through family cases) and not the family cases per se, the same family case in which different legislators make reference to (the same and/or different) policy issues was coded as a different case in the data set, yielding the following number of family cases (Table 20).

A positive family case could be as short as the one found in Senator Michael Enzi's (R-WY) statement in the hearing on "Healthy Marriage: What Is It and Why Should We Promote It?"[6]

Table 20. Number of Congressional Committee Hearings Examined per Period

Period	Number of Hearings	Number of Family Cases
Progressive Era (1900–1921)	246	421
Post–World War II era (1945–1956)	210	524
Late twentieth century (1980–2005)	554	1,104

that was held before the Senate Subcommittee on Children and Families (of the Committee on Health, Education, Labor, and Pensions):

> Speaking from my own experience, I have often noted the Enzi tradition of "overmarriage."
>
> Simply put, my son and I, along with many other male Enzis in the past, have been blessed to find that special someone in our lives who helped us to set goals in our lives and worked with us to achieve them.
>
> One of the most important of those goals has been the care and nurturing of our children our next generation of leaders. I have often heard it said that the most important job we have as a society is raising our children and if we don't do a good job of that, nothing else we do will matter very much. It's a philosophy I support and promote in my household and in my life. It's also the philosophy behind a healthy marriage. I have recently become a grandfather, so that has added another dimension to my belief about healthy marriages and the fruits that continue to be produced by the shared commitment of a man and woman to their future together.
>
> Yes, you can put me down as a strong believer in the importance of a healthy marriage to our society because I have been the beneficiary of it, so I may be biased.[7]

Alternatively, portraits of families were sometimes much longer, as is typically the case when found in the testimony of witnesses who are invited by legislators to tell their own personal stories:

> *Mr. Graham:* Hello, my name is Winston Graham and this is my fiancée, Saundra Corley. We live with our four children in the Benning Terrace public housing complex in Ward 7 [in Washington, D.C.]. My fiancée will begin by telling you a little more about who we are and why we intend to get married on November 26, 2005. Then I will finish our testimony. . . .
>
> *Ms. Corley:* Winston and I have been together for 20 years and we have four children together. We live in the Benning Terrace community located in Ward 7. For many of these years, drinking and drugs were a part of our lives. . . . Things changed for us when we started going to our church, Peace Fellowship, and accepted help from organizations like East of the River Clergy Police Community Partnership and East Capitol Center for Change. Like a lot of my neighbors, I used to be suspicious of anyone trying to help the community, but that changed when a mentor came to befriend my daughter in the winter of

2005. I saw that she really wanted to help us, and it made a difference. I then started to ask for help for myself and my whole family. I started working and getting involved in my community, and our family started going to church regularly. . . . Winston and I want to get married because we want to continue to make progress in our lives. We love each other dearly and we love the Lord. We want the basics, the norm in life—the whole family coming to the dinner table at the same time to eat. Neither of us had stable families growing up, but we've seen it so much at our church and we want it for ourselves now. Also, our kids are asking questions such as "Why are you and Daddy not married?" I have no answers to those questions. I want to show them something better.

   Our neighbors who have known us for years do not understand our wanting to get married. Just the other day, a neighbor asked me, "Why do you want to get married? Why now after 20 years?" I told her that we want the norm and that we want to progress in life together. She asked, "Are you forcing him to get married?" I said "No, he wants to get married as well." Then she again asked me why we were getting married, and I told her that we love each other. . . . Now that the date is coming and we're saying, "I've got the dress and we're inviting you," our neighbors are starting to adjust to what is out of the norm for them, but they still can't believe it. I know in their minds they are saying that we are risking welfare money. Many have been on the system so long that they just can't see another way. Just like we could not see another way until we were introduced to new friends, a new reality, and new possibilities.

Mr. Graham: . . . We are a close knit family. People in our community rarely see our children without Sandy or me. A lot of kids don't have father figures, so they watch me closely. As Sandy told you, some of our neighbors see our decision to get married as a terrible mistake. We definitely have their attention. . . . They tell Sandy how lucky she is that I am such a good father, but I know that that is what I am supposed to do for my children.

   I know that if one person steps up, then others will step up. I don't mind being the first to do it. . . .

   . . . We would like to continue our progress as a family by getting a house in our neighborhood. We love our community and want to stay in the area, but we want our own place with a backyard and less chaos. We think this will be good for our children and us as a family. . . .

   Up to now, we've been traveling on a very hard road, but the road we are on now is so much better. It's little things that are different, like experiencing new things together. But mostly it's about being around people who want the best for us. The pressure is off from everyday confusion.

Ms. Corley: Yes, we have such peace now. God bless you for wanting to help us and other people find and keep that peace. Thank you for hearing our testimony.[8]

Every instance when a member of Congress approvingly or disapprovingly referenced such family cases (whether described in detail in witness testimony or his or her own) and/or their characteristics was coded separately. To analyze the family ideals of legislators, I coded the following variables for each family case so referenced (these were tweaked for each period). Legislator's variables:

1. Party of active (interacting) member
2. Family policy issue raised by active member (living conditions/education/housing/public assistance/morality or reproduction/marriage or fatherhood/jobs/property or wealth/aging/veteran affairs/child care/child support/juvenile delinquency/parental rights/race/immigration/limiting government)
3. Policy category raised by active member (ascriptive/autonomy/welfare/regulation)
4. Family frame (Hearth/Soul)
5. Family ideal (positive/negative)
6. Region of active member (census categories: Northeast/South/Midwest/West)

Family's variables:

1. Family state of residence—fifty states by letter code or by Federal Information Processing Standards (FIPS) numeric code
2. Family residence population
3. Family region (FIPS numeric code: Northeast/Midwest/West/South)
4. Marital status of caregiver/parent (married, unmarried, widowed, divorced)
5. Parent's nativity (native/foreign born)
6. Number of dependents
7. Family structure (nuclear/nonnuclear)
8. Family race (white/African American/other nonwhite or mixed)
9. Family income (lower/middle/upper income)
10. Mother's employment (unemployed/part-time/full-time/self-employed)
11. Father's employment (unemployment/part-time/full-time/self-employed)
12. Mother criminal record mentioned (yes/no)
13. Father criminal record mentioned (yes/no)
14. Family religiosity mentioned (yes/no)
15. Gendered nature of caregivers (traditional roles/equal roles/reversed roles)
16. Family community involvement (isolated/family or friends/active [voluntary civic groups])
17. Addiction of caregiver/parent mentioned (yes/no)
18. Family ever on welfare (yes/no)
19. Values mentioned (yes/no)
20. Types of family values (secular/patriotic/moral/religious)
21. Types of secular values (liberty/equality/justice/work ethic/family privacy/irresponsibility)
22. Types of moral values mentioned (thrift/charity/sexual abstinence/love for parents/parenting/gender roles/promiscuity)
23. Family participation in government-funded programs (yes/no)
24. Family participation in privately funded programs (yes/no)
25. Mention of abuse (yes/no)
26. Mention of abortion (yes/no)

Notes

Introduction

Note to epigraph: Aristotle, *Politics*, trans. C. D. C. Reeve (Indianapolis, IN: Hackett, 1998), 5.

1. On the importance of "culture wars" and cultural conflict to late twentieth-century party politics, see Thomas Frank, *What's the Matter with Kansas? How Conservatives Won the Heart of America* (New York: Metropolitan Books, 2004); Ben Wattenberg, *Values Matter Most: How Republicans or Democrats or a Third Party Can Win and Renew the American Way of Life* (New York: Free Press, 1995); Thomas Edsall and Mary Edsall, *Chain Reaction: The Impact of Race, Rights, and Taxes on American Politics* (New York: Norton, 1992). The term "culture wars" was first used by sociologist James D. Hunter, *Culture Wars: The Struggle to Define America* (New York: Basic Books, 1991), who asserted the presence of a new cultural division between (religious) "orthodox" and "progressive" political and social elites. On the overall trend toward "postmaterialism," see Ronald Inglehart, *Culture Shift in Advanced Industrial Society* (Princeton, NJ: Princeton University Press, 1990) and Ronald Inglehart and Paul R. Abramson, "Measuring Postmaterialism," *American Political Science Review* 93 (1999): 665–677.

2. On "thematic tapestry" as a heuristic device to organize American political development, see Richard Bensel, "The Tension Between American Political Development as a Research Community and as a Disciplinary Subfield," *Studies in American Political Development* 17, no. 1 (2003): 103–106, 104.

3. See symposium on "Family, State and American Political Development," *Polity* 48, no. 2 (April 2016): 140–242; Patricia Strach, *All in the Family: The Private Roots of American Public Policy* (Stanford, CA: Stanford University Press, 2007); Priscilla Yamin, *American Marriage: A Political Institution* (Philadelphia: University of Pennsylvania Press, 2012); Melanie Heath, *One Marriage Under God: The Campaign to Promote Marriage in America* (New York: New York University Press, 2012); Gwendoline Alphonso, "Hearth and Soul: Economic and Cultural Conceptions of the Family in the Progressive Era, 1900–1920," *Studies in American Political Development* 24 (2010): 206–232 and "From Need to Hope: The American Family and Poverty in Partisan Discourse, 1900–2012," *Journal of Policy History* 27, no. 4 (2015): 592–635; Laura Lovett, *Conceiving the Future: Pronatalism, Reproduction, and the Family in the United States, 1890–1938* (Chapel Hill: University of North Carolina Press, 2007); Natasha Zaretsky, *No Direction Home: The American Family and the Fear of National Decline, 1968–1980* (Chapel

Hill: University of North Carolina Press, 2007); Elaine Tyler May, *Homeward Bound: American Families in the Cold War Era* (New York: Basic Books, 1988); Rebecca Edwards, *Angels in the Machinery: Gender in American Party Politics from the Civil War to the Progressive Era* (New York: Oxford University Press, 1997); Peter Bardaglio, *Reconstructing the Household: Families, Sex, and the Law in the Nineteenth-Century South* (Chapel Hill: University of North Carolina Press, 1995); Naomi Cahn and June Carbone, *Red Families v. Blue Families: Legal Polarization and the Creation of Culture* (New York: Oxford University Press, 2010).

4. James A. Morone, *Hellfire Nation: The Politics of Sin in American History* (New Haven, CT: Yale University Press, 2003). On family within partisan politics, see Byron Shafer, *The Two Majorities and the Puzzle of Modern American Politics* (Lawrence: University of Kansas Press, 2003); Ian Dowbiggin, "From Sander to Schiavo: Morality, Partisan Politics, and America's Culture War over Euthanasia, 1950–2010," *Journal of Policy History* 25, no. 1 (2013): 12–41, especially 13–14; Jeffrey Stonecash, Mark Brewer, and Mack Mariani, *Diverging Parties: Realignment, Social Change, and Political Polarization* (Boulder, CO: Westview, 2003); Theda Skocpol, *Protecting Soldiers and Mothers: The Political Origins of Social Policy in United States* (Cambridge, MA: Belknap Press of Harvard University Press, 1995).

5. Laurel Elder and Steven Greene, *The Politics of Parenthood: Causes and Consequences of the Politicization and Polarization of the American Family* (Albany: State University of New York Press, 2012); Robert Urbatsch, *Families' Values: How Parents, Siblings, and Children Affect Political Attitudes* (New York: Oxford University Press, 2014).

6. Melissa M. Deckman, *Tea Party Women: Mama Grizzlies, Grassroots Leaders, and the Changing Face of the American Right* (New York: New York University Press, 2016); Jill S. Greenlee, *The Political Consequences of Motherhood* (Ann Arbor: University of Michigan Press, 2014); Cynthia Stavsianos, *The Political Uses of Motherhood in America* (New York: Routledge, 2015); Kristin A. Goss, *The Paradox of Gender Equality: How American Women's Groups Gained and Lost Their Public Voice* (Ann Arbor: University of Michigan Press, 2013).

7. Strach, *All in the Family*, 40, 21–35. By so doing, she suggests that family is central to a span of nonfamily policies and its significance to public policy is not confined to more explicit "family-oriented" policy issues like welfare or family leave.

8. For (a), see Alphonso, "Hearth and Soul," and George Lakoff, *Moral Politics: How Liberals and Conservatives Think*, 2nd ed. (Chicago: University Press of Chicago, 2002). For (b), see Strach, *All in the Family*. For (c), see Robert O. Self, *All in the Family: The Realignment of American Democracy Since the 1960s* (New York: Hill and Wang, 2012) and Edwards, *Angels in the Machinery*.

9. Nolan McCarty, Keith Poole, and Howard Rosenthal, *Polarized America: The Dance of Ideology and Unequal Riches* (Cambridge, MA: MIT Press, 2006); Matthew Levendusky, *The Partisan Sort: How Liberals Became Democrats and Conservatives Became Republicans* (Chicago: University of Chicago Press, 2009); Stonecash, Brewer, and Mariani, *Diverging Parties*; Larry M. Bartels, *Unequal Democracy: The Political Economy of the New Gilded Age* (New York: Russell Sage Foundation, 2008), 64–97. For a contrary third position, asserting the absence of current partisan polarization, see Morris Fiorina, Samuel Abrams, and Jeremy Pope, *Culture War? The Myth of a Polarized America* (New York: Pearson Longman, 2005).

10. McCarty, Poole, and Rosenthal, *Polarized America*, Figs. 1.2, 1.3 on 8, 9.

11. Bartels, *Unequal Democracy*, 95.

12. Gary Miller and Norman Schofield, "The Transformation of the Republican and Democratic Party Coalitions in the U.S.," *Perspectives on Politics* 6 (2008): 433–450; Mark D.

Brewer and Jeffrey M. Stonecash, *Split: Class and Cultural Divisions in American Politics* (Washington, D.C.: CQ Press, 2006); also Geoffrey Layman, *The Great Divide: Religious and Cultural Conflict in American Party Politics* (New York: Columbia University Press, 2001) and Michael P. Young, *Bearing Witness Against Sin: The Evangelical Birth of the American Social Movement* (Chicago: University of Chicago Press, 2006).

13. George Lakoff (*Moral Politics*) has shown how differing family ideals organize cognitive ideation; thus, engendering variation in what we even imagine is possible through policy intervention. I similarly argue that alternative ideals of family and of society centrally frame partisan policy agendas and the policy ideals of members of Congress.

14. Rogers Smith and Desmond King, "'Without Regard to Race': Critical Ideational Development in Modern American Politics," *Journal of Politics* 76, no. 4 (2014): 958–971, 963; also see Joseph Lowndes, Julie Novkov, and Dorian T. Warren, *Race and Political Development* (New York: Routledge, 2008), 10–17.

15. The term "ideology" is used throughout in its conventional sense, as "a systematic scheme of ideas, usu. relating to politics or society, or to the conduct of a class or group, and regarded as justifying actions" (*Oxford English Dictionary* [1989], 2nd ed., Definition §4), with its key elements being "systematic" and "ideas." Ideals of family therefore form the units of an aggregate, systematized, family ideology. Policy ideologies are similarly an aggregation of systematic policy ideas that together cohere into a larger scheme, containing normative ideas about the state and when and how it should intervene in society and in the economy.

16. David McCandless, *The Visual Miscellaneum: A Colorful Guide to the World's Most Consequential Trivia* (New York: Collins Design, 2009).

17. On ideology as an abstract principle, see John Gerring, *Party Ideologies in America, 1828–1996* (New York: Cambridge University Press, 1998); Vernon Van Dyke, *Ideology and Political Choice: The Search for Freedom, Justice, and Virtue* (Chatham, NJ: Chatham House, 1995); Isaac Kramnick and Frederick Mundell Watkins, *The Age of Ideology: Political Thought, 1750 to Present* (Englewood Cliffs, NJ: Prentice-Hall, 1979); Louis Hartz, *The Liberal Tradition in America: An Interpretation of American Political Thought Since the Revolution* (New York: Harcourt, Brace, 1955).

18. Among political scientists, Barry Burden has come closest to this approach to the extent that situates legislators' policy preferences in their personal experiences. Barry C. Burden, *Personal Roots of Representation* (Princeton, NJ: Princeton University Press, 2007). In other disciplines, theorists have connected ideation and material experience more thoroughly, arguing for the spontaneous, organic nature of human cognition in which idea and material experience interact continually and nondeliberately to produce a constant, seemingly coherent generation of ideas and knowledge. See, for example, Pierre Bourdieu, *The Logic of Practice* (Cambridge: Polity, 1990); Friedrich Hayek, *Law, Legislation and Liberty: A New Statement of the Liberal Principles of Justice and Political Economy: Vol. 1. Rules and Order* (Chicago: University of Chicago Press, 1973); James C. Scott, *Seeing Like a State: How Certain Schemes to Improve the Human Condition Have Failed* (New Haven, CT: Yale University Press, 1998). The correlation between ideas (their timing) and material structures has also been recognized in the literature on social movements. In this literature, concepts such as "transvaluation," "cognitive liberation," and others are developed to capture cognitive or ideational shifts among social movement participants whose perception of hopelessness changes to one of hope. These cognitive shifts are shown as embedded in the changing material conditions and lives of potential participants. Cognition, ideation, and material structures are thus intertwined. See

Doug McAdam, *Political Process and the Development of Black Insurgency, 1930–1970* (Chicago: University of Chicago Press, 1982), 48–51; Frances Fox Piven and Richard A. Cloward, *Poor People's Movement: Why They Succeed and How They Fail* (New York: Vintage, 1977), chap. 1.

19. For more details on the methodology, selection, and use of family stories or family cases, see the Appendix ("Congressional Committee Hearings: Methodology").

20. On social and economic changes such as immigration and wealth disparity, as well as their cumulative effect on party polarization, see McCarty, Poole, and Rosenthal, *Polarized America*; also see Stonecash, Brewer, and Mariani, *Diverging Parties,* 51–77. This book does not focus on changes in immigration and wealth inequality patterns, although those too are certainly part of the changing landscape facing families and the elected officials who represent them. Instead, it highlights demographic family transitions (rise of single-mother families, increase in divorce and working mothers) as measures of "social and economic change." Nevertheless, like other polarization literature and unlike party ideology scholarship, party changes at the elite level here too are presented as shaped by changes in social and economic conditions on the ground.

21. See Brian Glenn and Steven Teles, eds., *Conservatism and American Political Development* (New York: Oxford University Press, 2009). In their introduction, Glenn and Teles discuss reasons for why "conservatives are almost always the bridesmaids and never the brides" in most public policy and APD literature (3–5). For other examples in APD attentive to conservatives and their formative role in political change, also see Joseph Lowndes, *From the New Deal to the New Right: Race and the Origins of Modern Conservatism* (New Haven CT: Yale University Press, 2009) and Ira Katzenelson, *Fear Itself: The New Deal and the Origins of Our Time* (New York: Liveright, 2013).

22. Stephen Skowronek, "Afterword: An Attenuated Reconstruction: The Conservative Turn in American Political Development," in *Conservatism and American Political Development,* ed. Brian Glenn and Steven Teles (New York: Oxford University Press, 2009), 350–351.

23. Skowronek outlines similar themes in conservatism when he alludes to "traditionalists" and "libertarians" as comprising modern conservatism. While I agree with this characterization of modern conservatives from the longitudinal perspective of the family in political development, conservatives are most consistently "traditionalists" while libertarians may or may not be family conservatives depending on the extent to which they align with traditionalists (as they most certainly do in the late twentieth century but are less so in the post–World War II period). See Skowronek, "Afterword," 352. For Rogers Smith "ascriptive" traditionalists, closest to my family conservatives, see Rogers Smith, "Beyond Tocqueville, Mrydal, and Hartz: The Multiple Traditions in America," *American Political Science Review* 87 (September 1993): 549–566; also Rogers Smith, *Civic Ideals: Conflicting Visions of Citizenship in U.S. History* (New Haven, CT: Yale University Press, 1997).

24. On the centrality of race and civil rights in party competition, see Lowndes, *From the New Deal to the New Right*; Dan T. Carter, *From George Wallace to Newt Gingrich: Race and the Conservative Counterrevolution, 1963–1994* (Baton Rouge: Louisiana State University Press, 1999); Earl Black and Merle Black, *The Rise of the Southern Republicans* (Cambridge, MA: Harvard University Press, 2003); Joseph A. Aistrup, *The Southern Strategy Revisited: Republican Top-Down Advancement in the South* (Lexington: University of Kentucky Press, 1996); and Thomas B. Edsall and Mary D. Edsall, *Chain Reaction: The Impact of Race, Rights, and Taxes on American Politics* (New York: Norton, 1992). The story of family and southernized

party change in this book complements this literature, insofar as both commonly highlight the role of the South in late twentieth-century party realignment. However, unlike race-centered works that emphasize the link between the South and race-based ideals to explain the rise of the New Right, this book points to an overlooked link between the South and conservative family ideals that encompass but are not limited to ideals of race. Southern racial ideals, although important, are not central to the family-centered story of conservative ascendance and party realignment, as this story is equally attentive to the formative impact of southern conservative ideals of society, economy, and gender (all long tied to family) in facilitating the rise of the New Right.

25. Self, *All in the Family*; Christina Wolbrecht, *The Politics of Women's Rights: Parties, Positions, and Change* (Princeton, NJ: Princeton University Press, 2001); Kira Sanbonmatsu, *Democrats, Republicans and the Politics of Women's Place* (Ann Arbor: University of Michigan Press, 2003); Jo Freeman, *A Room at a Time: How Women Entered Party Politics* (Lanham, MD: Rowman & Littlefield, 2002); Catherine E. Rymph, *Republican Women: Feminism and Conservatism from Suffrage Through the Rise of the New Right* (Chapel Hill: University of North Carolina Press, 2009); and Ronnee Schreiber, *Righting Feminism: Conservative Women and American Politics, with a New Epilogue* (New York: Oxford University Press, 2012).

26. Theda Skocpol, "Why I Am an Historical Institutionalist," *Polity* 28, no. 1 (1995): 103–106; Karen Orren and Stephen Skowronek, *In Search of American Political Development* (New York: Cambridge University Press, 2004).

27. Examples of idea-focused APD scholarship include Rogers Smith, *Political Peoplehood: The Roles of Values, Interests, and Identities* (Chicago: University of Chicago Press, 2015); Sidney M. Milkis, "Ideas, Institutions, and the New Deal Constitutional Order," *American Political Thought* 3, no. 1 (Spring 2014): 167–176; Stephen Skowronek, "The Reassociation of Ideas and Purposes: Racism, Liberalism, and the American Political Tradition," *American Political Science Review* 100, no. 3 (2006): 385–401; Robert Lieberman, "Ideas, Institutions, and Political Order: Explaining Political Change," *American Political Science Review* 96, no. 4 (2002): 697–712; Vivien Schmidt, "The Explanatory Power of Ideas and Discourse," *Annual Review of Political Science* 11 (2008): 303–326; Victoria Hattam and Joseph Lowndes, "The Ground Beneath Our Feet: Language, Culture, and Political Change," in *Formative Acts: American Politics in the Making*, ed. Stephen Skowronek and Matthew Glassman (Philadelphia: University of Pennsylvania Press, 2007), 199–219.

28. Hattam and Lowndes, "The Ground Beneath Our Feet," 204.

29. Smith, *Political Peoplehood*, 4–5.

30. Deborah Stone, *Policy Paradox: The Art of Political Decision Making* (New York: Norton, 1997), 138–145.

31. Ibid.

32. Ibid., 11.

33. Hattam and Lowndes, "The Ground Beneath Our Feet," 204.

34. Cognitive linguist George Lakoff (*Moral Politics*) highlights two conceptual family frameworks of "Strict Father" and "Nurturing Parent" as underpinning contemporary political discourse; in her work on gender and party in the nineteenth century, historian Rebecca Edwards also describes two (Republican and Democratic) family ideologies as prevailing from the Civil War to the Progressive Era; historian Self (*All in the Family*) points to "liberal" and conservative family ideals in the second half of the twentieth century; and legal theorists Cahn and Carbone (*Red Families v. Blue Families*) assemble current "red" and "blue" families.

35. Strach, *All in the Family,* 39–40.

36. Orren and Skowronek, *In Search of American Political Development,* 82–85.

37. For more detail on methodology and selection criteria of family cases, as well as variables examined, see the Appendix ("Congressional Committee Hearings: Methodology").

38. Morone, *Hellfire Nation,* 14–22.

39. For more detail on the policy typology assembled and used to track parties' shifting allegiances to family policy, see Alphonso, "Hearth and Soul," 212–214; see also Chapter 2, this volume.

40. Adam Sheingate, "Institutional Dynamics of American Political Development," *Annual Review of Political Science* 17 (2014): 461–477.

41. Smith refers to these prestructured environments as "human contexts," which, he aptly asserts, comprise "human institutions, understood as formal governmental and nongovernmental organizations, practices, understood as customary forms of behavior; and ideas of many sorts, including empirical beliefs and normative values." Smith, *Political Peoplehood,* 24.

Chapter 1

1. Dwight D. Eisenhower, "The President's News Conference," December 2, 1959. Gerhard Peters and John T. Woolley, *The American Presidency Project,* available at http://www .presidency.ucsb.edu/ws/?pid=11587 (hereafter *American Presidency Project*).

2. Rick Santorum, "Press Release—On Huckabee Tonight: Santorum Stands as the Consistent Full Spectrum Conservative Candidate for President," December 3, 2011, *American Presidency Project.*

3. For a good account of the polygamy debate, see Sarah Berringer Gordon, *The Mormon Question: Polygamy and Constitutional Conflict in Nineteenth-Century America* (Chapel Hill: University of North Carolina Press, 2001); on intermarriage since the Reconstruction, see Julie Novkov, *Racial Union: Law, Intimacy, and the White State in Alabama, 1865–1954* (Ann Arbor: University of Michigan Press, 2008).

4. Several works, including that of Christina Wolbrecht, point to the transformed GOP position/ideology on gender and women's rights issues—from a forty-year-long support of the Equal Rights Amendment, for example, to an ideology of motherhood and gender traditionalism. Christina Wolbrecht, *The Politics of Women's Rights: Parties, Positions, Change* (Princeton, NJ: Princeton University Press, 2000), 3–22.

5. Byron E. Shafer, *Two Majorities and the Puzzle of Modern American Politics* (Lawrence: Kansas University Press, 2003), 20. Shafer describes valuational concerns in contrast to the New Deal Democratic regime's "distributional" concerns, the latter pertaining to the "distribution of material goods, around economics and social welfare."

6. See Gerring, *Party Ideologies,* 147–148, especially Fig. 10 on 148 (showing support for family, as measured by the percentage of sentences within Whig-Republican nomination acceptance addresses devoted to the family or the home, demonstrating the spike in family-related sentences since 1980).

7. Democratic Party Platform of 2000, *American Presidency Project* (paragraph 25). See, for examples of Democratic repudiation of the Republican traditional ideal of family as a predominantly private and valuational entity, Hillary Clinton, "It Takes a Village," *Democratic National Convention Speech,* Chicago, 1996, available at http://www.pbs.org/newshour/bb /politics-july-dec96-hillary-clinton/ (last accessed June 27, 2017); see also Barack Obama,

"Press Release—Obama Campaign Launches Women for Obama Leadership Committees in Key February 5th States," November 28, 2007, *American Presidency Project*.

8. Michelle Obama, *Democratic National Convention Address*, Charlotte, 2012, available at http://www.npr.org/2012/09/04/160578836/transcript-michelle-obamas-convention-speech (last accessed June 27, 2017).

9. *Physical assets* are the "physical goods or material things that determine our present quality of life, such as housing, food, transportation"; *human resources* are "are those goods that contribute to the development of a human being, allowing participation in the market and making possible the accumulation of material resources that help bolster individuals' resilience in the face of vulnerability . . . often referred to as "human capital"; *social assets* include "social networks (such as the family) from which we gain support and strength"; *ecological resources* "can be conferred through our position in relation to the physical or natural environments in which we find ourselves"; and *existential resources* are provided by "systems of belief or aesthetics, such as religion, culture, or art, and perhaps even politics." Martha Fineman, "The Vulnerable Subject: Anchoring Equality in the Human Condition," *Yale Journal of Law & Feminism* 20 (2008): 1–23, 21; also see "The New Deal: From De-Regulation to Re-Regulation: The Vulnerable Subject and the Responsive State," *Emory Law Journal* 60 (2010): 251–271.

10. The year 1900 is used to mark the beginning of the Progressive Era, which many view as the onset of the modern American state. See, for example, Stephen Skowronek, *Building a New American State: The Expansion of National Administrative Capacities, 1877–1920* (New York: Cambridge University Press, 1991); Elizabeth Sanders, *Roots of Reform: Farmers, Workers, and the American State, 1877–1917* (Chicago: Chicago University Press, 1998). By choosing 1900 as the year to begin, I thus direct the inquiry at the modern (national) state and its changing relationship with the American family.

11. Theda Skocpol, *Protecting Soldiers and Mothers: The Political Origins of Social Policy in United States* (Cambridge, MA: Belknap Press of Harvard University Press, 1995), 265. "Social justice" or "social welfare" was one aim of a broader progressive reform agenda alongside the other aims of civil reform and direct democracy. See Sidney M. Milkis and Jerome M. Mileur, "Introduction: Progressivism, Then and Now," in *Progressivism and the New Democracy*, ed. Sidney M. Milkis and Jerome M. Mileur (Amherst: University of Massachusetts Press, 1999), 8–10; see also John Whiteclay Chambers II, *The Tyranny of Change: America in the Progressive Era, 1890–1920* (New Brunswick, NJ: Rutgers University Press, 2000), 141–142.

12. Gerring, *Party Ideologies*, chap. 3. Gerring describes the period from 1896 to 1924 as one of "national republicanism" in Republican Party ideology, when the GOP favored statism and social order over the individualism and antistatism of its later incarnation.

13. Republican Party Platform of 1908, *American Presidency Project* (paragraph 26).

14. On the salience of veterans' pensions in the formation of the early American welfare state up to the Progressive Era, see Skocpol, *Protecting Soldiers*, 102–151.

15. See, for example, Republican Party Platform of 1900, *American Presidency Project* (paragraph 23). Republicans committed to the Hearth economic family ideal in other contexts as well, pledging material help to dependent families of other employees of the federal government, such as federal judges and postal workers. See William H. Taft, Second Annual Message, December 6, 1910, *American Presidency Project*. Dependent benefits like mothers' pensions were tied to the progressive impulse of nation building. Both were seen as responsibilities of the nation (i.e., the national state) to either compensate the morally deserving

(veterans and their dependents) or alleviate the hardships of the economically deserving (widowed, poor mothers). Republican platforms also endorsed mothers' pensions in this way.

16. Republican Party Platform of 1900, *American Presidency Project* (paragraph 11); also see Democratic Party Platform of 1904, *American Presidency Project* (paragraph 36). Under the Civil War pension system, veterans and their dependents came to have enhanced political value to both political parties, and veterans' benefits expanded from a minimalist program of compensation to disabled veterans and their dependents to a generous program of disability, old age, and survivors' benefits with expansive eligibility rules. For the history of veterans' benefits as an outcome of prevailing electoral strategies and congressional and party politics, see Skocpol *Protecting Soldiers and Mothers*, 115–130.

17. Democratic Party Platform of 1908, *American Presidency Project* (paragraph 129); the same plank was renewed in Democratic Party Platform of 1912, *American Presidency Project* (paragraph 222).

18. On the importance of self-sufficient (yeoman) farmer and rancher families in the West to national development—and the centrality of the homestead family to national prosperity—see Theodore Roosevelt, Second Annual Message, December 2, 1902, *American Presidency Project* ("the sound and steady development of the West depends upon the building up of homes therein. Much of our prosperity as a nation has been due to the operation of the homestead law.").

19. Republican Party Platform of 1900, *American Presidency Project* (paragraph 33) (emphasis added).

20. Democratic Party Platform of 1904, *American Presidency Project* (paragraph 79) (emphasis added): "we call attention to . . . *reserving the lands reclaimed for homeseekers in small tracts and rigidly guarding against land monopoly,* as an evidence of the policy of domestic development contemplated by the Democratic party, should it be placed in power."

21. Democratic Party Platform of 1912, *American Presidency Project* (paragraph 77).

22. Democratic Party Platform of 1920, *American Presidency Project* (paragraphs 29, 68, 70).

23. Democratic Party Platform of 1920, *American Presidency Project* (paragraph 115). Similar acknowledgment of the "well-being" of workers and their families, as a rationale for labor policy positions, is mentioned in the Socialist Party Platform of 1916 (the Socialist Platform of 1916 is found appended to the Republican Party Platform of 1916, *American Presidency Project* [paragraphs 123–261, 243]). Democratic platforms had also previously invoked family status to justify their support for liberal labor policies but only in relation to female (federal) employees. Democratic Party Platform of 1916, *American Presidency Project* (paragraph 89).

24. Democratic Party Platform of 1924, *American Presidency Project* (paragraph 219). It need be noted that despite the increased Democratic attention to "family life" and "national interest or duty," this did not as yet indicate a whole-hearted Democratic embrace of the national state or its machinery. Instead, Democratic platforms through the 1920s continued to press for "the rights of States" as a "bulwark against the centralizing and destructive tendencies of the republican party," repeatedly promising to "oppose bureaucracy and the multiplication of offices and officeholders." "The Rights of States," Democratic Party Platform of 1924 (paragraphs 103–107), repeated in Democratic Party Platform of 1928, *American Presidency Project* (paragraphs 26–32).

25. During World War I, for instance, they called on "all Americans, whether naturalized or native-born," to be true to "the American spirit which made the country and saved the union" and "to the traditions of their common country." Republican Party Platform of 1916, *American Presidency Project* (paragraph 120). Common American values were similarly em-

phasized in planks on "immigration" and "naturalization" in which they pledged extensive support for programs to "educat[e] . . . the alien in our language, customs, ideals and standards of life," asserting the importance of assimilating an "alien" into "becom[ing] genuinely American." Republican Party Platform of 1924 (paragraph 242) and Republican Party Platform of 1920 (paragraph 92), *American Presidency Project*.

26. Republican Party Platform of 1924, *American Presidency Project* (paragraph 126) (emphasis added).

27. Republican Party Platform of 1924, *American Presidency Project* (paragraph 144).

28. Democratic Party Platform of 1908, *American Presidency Project* (paragraph 98); for other "Asiatic Immigration" planks, see Democratic Party Platform of 1920 (paragraphs 139–140) and Democratic Party Platform of 1924 (paragraphs 108–109), *American Presidency Project*.

29. "Condemnation of Polygamy" in Democratic Party Platform of 1904 (paragraphs 50–51) and Democratic Party Platform of 1916 (paragraph 111), *American Presidency Project*.

30. Brookings Institute Report, from Stephen Mintz and Susan Kellogg, *Domestic Revolutions: A Social History of American Family Life* (New York: Free Press, 1988), 135.

31. Democratic Party Platform of 1932, *American Presidency Project* (paragraphs 37, 51).

32. Democratic Party Platform of 1936, *American Presidency Project* (paragraph 13).

33. Democratic Party Platform of 1936, *American Presidency Project* (paragraphs 30–62).

34. Democratic Party Platform of 1936, *American Presidency Project* (paragraphs 133, 129) (emphasis added).

35. Democratic Party Platform of 1936, *American Presidency Project* (paragraph 19); the emphasis on family as an essential part of the human condition was also evident in earlier planks on labor pertaining to the family life of the worker and in planks on immigration that acknowledged the "comfort" and "support" provided by "close family ties" to immigrants. Democrats emphasized their "humanity" in contrast to the "cold materialism" of Republicans, illustrating what John Gerring refers to as the "Christian humanism" of Democratic ideology at this time. Gerring, *Party Ideologies*, 213–221.

36. The Republican Party ideological era from 1928 to 1991 is called the "neoliberal" epoch by John Gerring, centered on themes of antistatism, free-market capitalism, right-wing populism, and individualism. Gerring, *Party Ideologies*, Table 1, 16.

37. Republican Party Platform of 1924, *American Presidency Project* (paragraph 164); also Republican Party Platform of 1928, *American Presidency Project* (paragraphs 294–296).

38. Republican Party Platform of 1924, *American Presidency Project* (paragraph 166).

39. Republican Party Platform of 1928, *American Presidency Project* (paragraph 294).

40. Republican Party Platform of 1936, *American Presidency Project* (paragraphs 230– Conclusion).

41. Democratic Party Platform of 1940 (paragraph 216), Republican Party Platform of 1944 (paragraph 57), Democratic Party Platform of 1948 (paragraph 113), Republican Party Platform of 1948 (paragraph 129), and Democratic Party Platform of 1952 (paragraphs 512–513), *American Presidency Project*.

42. Democratic Party Platform of 1944 (paragraph 017), Republican Party Platform of 1944 (paragraph 057), Democratic Party Platform of 1952 (paragraph 447), and Democratic Party Platform of 1956 (paragraph 427), *American Presidency Project*.

43. Democratic Party Platform of 1936 (paragraph 041), Democratic Party Platform of 1940 (paragraph 226), Republican Party Platform of 1944 (paragraph 061), Democratic Party Platform of 1948 (paragraph 085), Republican Party Platform of 1948 (paragraph 127),

Democratic Party Platform of 1952 (paragraph 481), Republican Party Platform of 1952 (paragraph 151), Democratic Party Platform of 1956 (paragraphs 251, 447), and Republican Party Platform of 1956 (paragraph 024), *American Presidency Project.*

44. Republican Party Platform of 1944 (paragraphs 89–91) and Democratic Party Platform of 1952 (paragraph 521), *American Presidency Project.*

45. Republican Party Platform of 1936, *American Presidency Project* (paragraph 080).

46. Republican Party Platform of 1944, *American Presidency Project* (paragraphs 89–113); also Republican Party Platform of 1936, *American Presidency Project* (paragraphs 109–139).

47. Republican Party Platform of 1944, *American Presidency Project* (paragraphs 89–113).

48. Republican Party Platform of 1940, *American Presidency Project* (paragraph 092).

49. Republican Party Platform of 1936, *American Presidency Project* (paragraph 108).

50. Democratic Party Platform of 1940, *American Presidency Project* (paragraph 65); Democratic platforms characterized their agricultural policies, such as locally elected farmer committees, as providing "economic security to the farmer and his family, while recognizing the dignity and freedom of American farm life." Democratic Party Platform of 1944, *American Presidency Project* (paragraph 107).

51. "To ensure no needy family shall be denied an adequate and wholesome diet because of low income." Democratic Party Platform of 1956, *American Presidency Project* (paragraph 355).

52. "The future of America depends on adequate provision by Government for the needs of those of our children who cannot be cared for by their parents or private social agencies." Democratic Party Platform of 1952, *American Presidency Project* (paragraph 509).

53. Democratic Party Platform of 1956, *American Presidency Project* (paragraph 299).

54. Franklin D. Roosevelt, *State of the Union Message to Congress,* January 11, 1944, *American Presidency Project*, and the Democratic Party Platform of 1960, *American Presidency Project* (paragraph 370).

55. Democratic Party Platform of 1968, *American Presidency Project* (paragraphs 616, 618).

56. For example, see Republican Party Platform of 1960, *American Presidency Project* (paragraph 450): "Government's primary role is to help provide the environment within which the individual can seek his own goals. In some areas this requires federal action to supplement individual, local and state initiative . . . in approaching such problems as those of the aged, the infirm, the mentally ill, and the needy."

57. Republican Party Platform of 1968, *American Presidency Project* (paragraph 174).

58. Republican Party Platform of 1960, *American Presidency Project* (paragraph 252).

59. Republican Party Platform of 1968, *American Presidency Project* (paragraph 092).

60. Republican Party Platform of 1960, *American Presidency Project* (paragraphs 211, 421).

61. Republican Party Platform of 1968, *American Presidency Project* (paragraph 92): "By reducing interest rates through responsible fiscal and monetary policy we propose to lower the costs of home-ownership."

62. Republican Party Platform of 1964, *American Presidency Project* (paragraphs 163, 165).

63. Republican Party Platform of 1960, *American Presidency Project* (paragraph 644).

64. Republican Party Platform of 1960, *American Presidency Project* (paragraph 492): "The Federal Government can and should help state and local communities combat juvenile delinquency by inaugurating a grant program for research, demonstration, and training projects and *by placing greater emphasis on strengthening family life* in all welfare programs for which it shares responsibility" (emphasis added).

65. Republican Platform of 1968, *American Presidency Project* (paragraph 198); also see Republican Party Platform of 1972, *American Presidency Project* (paragraphs 617–621).

66. Republican Party Platform of 1968, *American Presidency Project* (paragraph 198).

67. Democratic Party Platform of 1964, *American Presidency Project* (paragraph 004).

68. Democratic Party Platform of 1964, *American Presidency Project* (paragraph 212).

69. Democratic Party Platform of 1968, *American Presidency Project* (paragraph 513).

70. Democratic Party Platform of 1968, *American Presidency Project* (paragraphs 616, 618, 622).

71. Democratic Party Platform of 1968, *American Presidency Project* (paragraph 319).

72. Democratic Party Platform of 1972, *American Presidency Project* (paragraphs 023–027).

73. See note 54 of this chapter and accompanying text.

74. Democratic Party Platform of 1980, *American Presidency Project* (paragraph 567).

75. Democratic Party Platform of 1984, *American Presidency Project* (paragraph 409).

76. Kevin Phillips, *The Emerging Republican Majority* (New Rochelle, NY: Arlington House, 1969). Leo P. Ribuffo, "Family Policy Past as Prologue: Jimmy Carter, the White House Conference on Families, and the Mobilization of the New Christian Right," *Review of Policy Research* 23, no. 2 (2006): 319.

77. Republican Party Platform of 1976, *American Presidency Project* (paragraphs 235–237).

78. Republican Party Platform of 1976, *American Presidency Project* (paragraph 235).

79. Republican Party Platform of 1980, *American Presidency Project* (paragraph 245).

80. Republican Party Platform of 1980, *American Presidency Project* (paragraph 245).

81. For a discussion on similar valuational differences, see Shafer, *Two Majorities*, 31.

82. The theme of "fairness" and programmatic assistance of families who "play by the rules" continues to feature prominently in the discourse of Democratic leaders in the twenty-first century. See, for example, Barack Obama, Presidential Debate in Hempstead, New York, October 16, 2012, *American Presidency Project*: "I believe in self-reliance and individual initiative and risk takers being rewarded. But I also believe that everybody should have a fair shot and everybody should do their fair share and everybody should play by the same rules, because that's how our economy is grown."

83. Democratic Party Platform of 1996, *American Presidency Project* (paragraph 168).

84. Democratic Party Platform of 2004, *American Presidency Project* (paragraph 324).

85. A striking example is the promotion of "responsible fatherhood" to reduce child poverty; Democratic Party Platform of 2000, *American Presidency Project* (paragraph 347). "Welfare reform" was one of four pledges in the "Responsibility" section of the 1992 Democratic Party platform, the other three being "Strengthening the Family," "Choice" (reproductive rights), and "Making Schools Work"; Democratic Party Platform of 2000, *American Presidency Project* (paragraph 106).

86. Democratic Party Platform of 1992, *American Presidency Project* (paragraphs 19, 106) and also paragraph 21 (emphasis added): "The Revolution of 1992 is about putting government back on the side of *working* men and women—*to help those who work hard, pay their bills, play by the rules, don't lobby for tax breaks, do their best to give their kids a good education and to keep them away from drugs*, who want a safe neighborhood for their families, the security of decent, productive jobs for themselves, and a dignified life for their parents."

87. Democratic Party Platform of 1992 (paragraph 72), Democratic Party Platform of 1996 (paragraph 89), Democratic Party Platform of 2004 (paragraph 324), Democratic Party Platform of 2008 (paragraph 22), and Democratic Party Platform of 2012 (paragraph 339), *American Presidency Project.*

88. Democratic Party Platform of 1992, *American Presidency Project* (paragraph 166).

89. Democratic Party Platform of 2012, *American Presidency Project* (paragraph 016).

90. Republican Party Platform of 2012, *American Presidency Project* (paragraph 479), part of a section entitled, "Renewing American Values to Build Healthy Families, Great Schools, and Safe Neighborhoods" (paragraphs 479–480).

91. For example, the party once again reiterated its welfare policy agenda in terms of underscoring the neoliberal goal of family self-reliance: "that low-income parents and individuals should strive to support themselves." Republican Party Platform of 2012, *American Presidency Project* (paragraphs 485–486).

92. Wolbrecht, *The Politics of Women's Rights,* 77.

93. Members of Congress who sponsor or add their names to (i.e., cosponsor) specific bills may be seen to have a greater preference for that policy issue and position than those who vote yea or nay in floor votes. Yet, members are often also willing to sign onto bills as symbolic measures of support and not expect them to pass or involve any further effort. In this sense, sponsorship and cosponsorship are much less consequential than roll call voting. Richard L. Hall, *Participation in Congress* (New Haven, CT: Yale University Press, 1996), 178; also Wendy J. Schiller, "Senators as Political Entrepreneurs: Bill Sponsorship to Shape Legislative Agendas," *American Journal of Political Science* 39 (1995): 186–203, 186–187. However, for my purposes, the difference between sincere and weak preferences is not significant; I am also not concerned with the strength of the link between (co)sponsorship data and actual policy outcome. Instead, my objective is to determine the ideology contained in the types of bills that members from the two parties choose to be associated with. Cosponsorship is found to be not unlike other forms of legislative behavior, being motivated by some of the same factors—ideology of member and his or her policy position being a prominent one. Keith Krehbiel, "Cosponsors and Wafflers from A to Z," *American Journal of Political Science* 39 (1995): 906–923.

94. For the constraints on members related to roll call voting and its unrepresentative character in terms of the members' revealed preferences, see Hall, *Participation in Congress,* 177–178.

95. On the methodology of bill selection and coding, see the Appendix (the section titled "Bill Sponsorship and Cosponsorship: Methodology").

96. See, for example, bills regarding *White slave traffic, illegal importation or interstate transportation of alien women or girls for prostitution,* S 4008, S 4009, S 4514, HR 12315, HR 14517, HR 14518, HR 15431, HR 15816, HR 20379, HR 21484, HR 21584, HR 21588, 61st Cong., 2nd sess. (1910); *Proposing an amendment to the Constitution of the United States, prohibiting intermarriage between negroes or persons of color and Caueusian [sic] or any other character of persons,* 62nd Cong., 3rd sess. H. J. Res. 368 (1912); *To prohibit the intermarriage of persons of the white and negro races within the United States of America; to declare such contracts of marriage null and void; to prescribe punishments for violations and attempts to violate its provisions,* HR 20779, 63rd Cong., 3rd sess. (1915).

97. A total of 56.5 percent and 52.8 percent of family bills introduced in the 104th and 105th Congresses, respectively, were Soul. I should note that at this juncture, it is inexpedient

to discuss the changes in the (generic) *types* of policies engendered in Hearth and Soul family bills across the three periods. For instance, the Hearth family bills of the midcentury predominantly focused on social welfare, whereas those of the contemporary era pay much greater attention to regulatory policies. Similarly, Soul family bills of the contemporary era contain much higher proportions of moral policies, and those of earlier periods were, instead, more preoccupied with policies concerning family property. While I have made this distinction (of policy type) in the coding of family bills, a full discussion and implications of changes/developments in Hearth and Soul policy *types* will occur only in the later chapters.

98. In total, 71.4 percent of all Soul bills were cosponsored, compared to 71.8 percent of all Hearth bills.

99. Cosponsorship data are available only for Senate bills of the postwar congresses and all late twentieth-century (Senate and House) bills. This is because the House allowed members to cosponsor bills only in 1967 (Rule 22) and had previously, in 1909, explicitly prohibited it. In the Senate, members have cosponsored bills since the 1930s. Gregory Koger, "Position Taking and Cosponsorship in the U.S. House," *Legislative Studies Quarterly* 28 (2003): 225–246, 227; Rick K. Wilson and Cheryl D. Young, "Cosponsorship in the U.S. Congress," *Legislative Studies Quarterly* 22 (1997): 25–43, 26. Note: Postwar cosponsorship data are not illuminative in that only seventeen of the family bills examined ($N = 547$) were cosponsored.

100. The party switch in family bill ideology can be seen from the altered directionality of their correlation in the two periods (Table 2). Partisan affiliation is coded as a nominal dummy variable, taking the value of 0 or 1 for Democratic or Republican, respectively. "Family ideology" (of bill) is similarly coded as a dummy: 0 for Hearth and 1 for Soul. In the Progressive Era, the correlation coefficient has a positive sign, indicating a positive correlation between partisan affiliation on the introducing member and the bill's family ideology, meaning a move in partisanship from Democratic (0) to Republican (1), and is correlated with an increasing likelihood of sponsorship of a Hearth (1) over a Soul (0) bill (Table 2). Thus, Republican members and the introduction of Hearth family bills are correlated, as are Democratic affiliation and Soul bills in the Progressive Era, supporting evidence from platforms that had showed Republican platforms as being slightly more Hearth oriented in their family policy planks than Democrats for this period. (In the Progressive Era, for the sake of simplicity, the rare third-party sponsoring members were conflated into the closest major party. Thus, Populists were coded as Democrats, and Silver-Republicans, Prohibitionists, and Progressives were coded as Republicans. Despite possible contention over the classification of "Progressives" as Republicans, I have followed those scholars who have identified "Progressivism" as more aligned with the Republican rather than Democratic Party up until 1912, that is, the majority of the Progressive Era examined; Milkis and Mileur, *Progressivism and the New Democracy*, 1–39.) Partisanship of bill sponsor and the bill's family ideology are once again statistically correlated in the late twentieth-century era (Table 2). However, in this period, in contrast to the Progressive Era, the *sign* of the correlation coefficient is now *reversed*, and the two are no longer positively but *negatively correlated*. In other words, an *increase* in partisan affiliation toward the Republican Party is likely to result in a *decrease* of family ideology of the bill introduced (i.e., now toward a Soul ideology).

101. Chi-square tests of independence/correlation as well as z tests of column proportions at the .01 and .05 levels identify the 60th (1907–1908), 61st (1909–1910), 64th (1915–1916), and 66th (1919–1920) Congresses as the four congresses in this period when partisan affiliation of the bill sponsor and ideology of family were significantly correlated with each other. Thus,

the mid-Progressive Era, the height of the white slave and child labor debates, and the late Progressive period, prior to and leading up to the Nineteenth Amendment and women's suffrage, had the most significant relationships between partisan affiliation and bill family ideology.

102. Of the 1,009 family bills examined, 723 were cosponsored.

103. By running *t* tests of column means for two pairs of variables per Congress—(1) "percentage of Republicans cosponsoring" and "ideology of family bills" cosponsored and (2) "percentage of Democratic cosponsoring" and "ideology of family bills"—I tested the significance of the relationship between partisan affiliation of cosponsors and ideology of cosponsored family bills for each of the eight congresses.

Chapter 2

1. Interview with Flossie Moore Durham by Mary Frederickson, September 2, 1976, interview H-0066, in the *Southern Oral History Program Collection #4007,* Southern Historical Collection, Wilson Library, University of North Carolina at Chapel Hill, 2.

2. Gwendoline Alphonso, "Of Families or Individuals? Southern Child Workers & the Progressive Crusade for Child Labor Regulation, 1899–1920," in *Children and Youth During the Gilded Age and Progressive Era*, ed. James Marten (New York: New York University Press, 2014), 59–80, 59.

3. Ibid. Also see Stephen Mintz and Susan Kellogg, *Domestic Revolutions: A Social History of American Family Life* (New York: Free Press, 1988), 109–113.

4. Mintz and Kellogg, *Domestic Revolutions*, 109–113.

5. Carl N. Degler, *At Odds: Women and the Family in America from the Revolution to the Present* (Oxford: Oxford University Press, 1980), 376–377.

6. Mintz and Kellogg, *Domestic Revolutions*, 84–85, 89–90; Susan Householder Van Horn, *Women, Work, and Fertility, 1900–1986* (New York: New York University Press, 1988), 21–22, 24–25; Robyn Muncy, *Creating a Female Dominion in American Reform, 1890–1935* (New York: Oxford University Press, 1991), 4–5.

7. Mintz and Kellogg, *Domestic Revolutions*, 110–111; Van Horn, *Women, Work and Fertility*, 10–11.

8. Marten, *Children and Youth During the Gilded Age and Progressive Era*, 5–6.

9. Mintz and Kellogg, *Domestic Revolutions*, 117–118, 120–121; Van Horn, *Women, Work and Fertility*, 11–12.

10. Polarization scholars such as McCarty, Poole, and Rosenthal, as well as Stonecash, Brewer, and Mariani, have measured high levels of polarization at the start and end of the twentieth century. Party polarization takes the form of a U-shaped curve, with high polarization at the two poles and decreased polarization levels during the postwar midcentury decades. Nolan McCarty, Keith Poole, and Howard Rosenthal, *Polarized America: The Dance of Ideology and Unequal Riches* (Cambridge: MIT Press, 2006), 3–10; Jeffrey M. Stonecash, Mark D. Brewer, and Mack D. Mariani, *Diverging Parties: Social Change, Realignment, and Party Polarization* (Boulder, CO: Westview, 2003), 1–11.

11. Theda Skocpol, *Protecting Soldiers and Mothers: The Political Origins of Social Policy in United States* (Cambridge, MA: Belknap Press of Harvard University Press, 1995), 263; also Elizabeth Sanders, *Roots of Reform: Farmers, Workers, and the American State* (Chicago: University of Chicago Press, 1999), 160–161; Mark D. Brewer and Jeffrey M. Stonecash, *Dynamics of American Political Parties* (New York: Cambridge University Press, 2009), 58–59.

12. Skocpol, *Protecting Soldiers*, 263–264.

13. Stephen Skowronek, *Building a New American State: The Expansion of National Administrative Capacities 1877–1920* (New York: Cambridge University Press, 1991), 39. On electoral partisan politics leading up to the Progressive Era, see John Whiteclay Chambers II, *The Tyranny of Change: America in the Progressive Era 1890–1920* (New Brunswick, NJ: Rutgers University Press, 2000), 41–44.

14. Robert Harrison, *Congress, Progressive Reform, and the New American State* (Cambridge: Cambridge University Press, 2004), 13–49.

15. Skocpol, *Protecting Soldiers*, 265. Eileen L. McDonagh similarly describes what she calls the "institutional axis" of progressivism as "a reform orientation that seeks to implement the power of state authority and government institutions—in contradistinction to dependence upon private, philanthropic institutions—to solve social and economic inequalities viewed as the source of societal ills." Eileen L. McDonagh, "Race, Class, and Gender in the Progressive Era," in *Progressivism and the New Democracy*, ed. Sidney M. Milkis and Jerome M. Mileur (Amherst: University of Massachusetts Press, 1999), 147. See also Chambers, *The Tyranny of Change* 133–171. This book follows such an intervention-focused definition of progressivism (lowercase). For description of various reform groups and the progressive impulse, see also Robert H. Wiebe, *The Search for Order 1877–1920* (New York: Hill and Wang, 1967); Richard Hofstadter, *Age of Reform: From Bryan to F.D.R.* (New York: Knopf, 1955); Robyn Muncy, *Creating a Female Dominion in American Reform 1890–1935* (New York: Oxford University Press, 1991); also see Sanders, *Roots of Reform*, 164–165, as a farmer-based refutation of the Hofstadter-Wiebe elite-based interpretation of progressive reform actors.

16. The strain of mobilization that combined public protest with specialized sins has been traced back to the antebellum period; see Michael P. Young, *Bearing Witness Against Sin: The Evangelical Birth of the American Social Movement* (Chicago: University of Chicago Press, 2006).

17. "Social progressivism" refers to social movements and ideologies in the Progressive Era "that worked not primarily for structural reforms in civil service and the parties but mainly for new public measures to improve working conditions, to help families and children, and to ensure better products, services, and environmental conditions for consumers." Skocpol, *Protecting Soldiers*, 265. As an effective specification of the concept of "social progressivism," Skocpol cites Irwin Yellowitz, *Labor and the Progressive Movement in New York State, 1897–1916* (Ithaca, NY: Cornell University Press, 1965). In this chapter, progressivism is used in the context of *social* progressive ideology and not civil reform ideology. Typically, "social justice" or "social welfare" is mentioned as one distinct aim of the progressive reform agenda alongside civil reform and direct democracy—see Milkis and Mileur, *Progressivism*, 8–10; also Chambers, *The Tyranny of Change*, 141–42. A more detailed definitional outline of the progressive ideology of the family, specifically, follows later in the chapter (see Figure 11 in this chapter).

18. Chambers, *The Tyranny of Change*, 138–139.

19. Divisions in family ideologies were apparent in the party system as early as the 1840s; for this, see Rebecca Edwards, *Angels in the Machinery: Gender in American Party Politics from the Civil War to the Progressive Era* (New York: Oxford University Press, 1997), 17–35. The question of which one, region or party, was more influential (or coequal) in accounting for ideational differences is not one that space constraints allow me to address; instead, I merely restrict my focus to aggregate party differences, paying attention to regional anomalies within and across parties.

20. The conceptualization of "family party systems" or "family party alignments" is akin to the concept of "political orders" found in the literature on American political development and can be defined as constellations of partisan structures, family practices, ideals, and policies that hang together, exhibiting a coherence and predictability, analogous to constitutional orders, party regimes, and such. Adapted from definition of "political order" taken from Karen Orren and Stephen Skowronek, *Search for American Political Development* (New York: Cambridge University Press, 2004), 14–15.

21. Separate sphere literature is vast; some of the more influential works on this are Barbara Welter, "The Cult of True Womanhood: 1820–1860," *American Quarterly* 18 (1966): 151–174; Nancy Cott, *The Bonds of Womanhood: "Women's Sphere" in New England 1780–1835* (Ithaca, NY: Cornell University Press, 1977); Mary P. Ryan, *Womanhood in American: From Colonial Times to the Present*, 3rd ed. (New York: F. Watts, 1983).

22. Senator Owen (D-OK), 63rd Cong., 2nd sess., *Congressional Record* (March 4, 1914), 4275.

23. Senator Bryan (D-FL), 63rd Cong., 2nd sess., *Congressional Record* (March 3, 1914), 4207.

24. Ibid., 4209.

25. Senator Bryan (D-FL), 63rd Cong., 2nd sess., *Congressional Record* (March 3, 1914), 4203.

26. 63rd Cong., 2nd sess., *Congressional Record* (March 3, 1914), 4214.

27. Ibid., 4211 (Bryan [D-FL]).

28. Senator Bryan, 63rd Cong., 2nd sess., *Congressional Record* (March 3, 1914), 4214.

29. Senator Chamberlain (D-OR), 63rd Cong., 2nd sess., *Congressional Record* (March 4, 1914), 4276.

30. Extension of Remarks of Representative Everis Hayes (R-CA) in the speech of Representative William Kent (I-CA), 63rd Cong., 1st sess., *Congressional Record* (September 3, 1913), 263; also Senator Wesley L. Jones (R-WA), 63rd Cong., 1st sess., *Congressional Record* (September 13, 1913), 5121: "Another objection [to suffrage] is that it will break up the home. . . . As a matter of fact it strengthens home ties and makes more of a community of interest between the mother and son, brother and sister, and husband and wife, and develops . . . a sweeter companionship in both."

31. See Patricia M. Fields, "Democracy and the Social Feminist Ethics of Jane Addams: A Vision for Public Administration," *Administrative Theory & Praxis* 28 (2006): 418–443, 423; also, more generally on female participation in reform in the Progressive Era, see Muncy, *Creating a Female Dominion*, 3–37.

32. On poverty in the Progressive Era and the influence of maternalist ideology, see Michael B. Katz, *Poverty and Policy in American History* (New York: Academic Press, 1983); for maternalist ideology and the changes to ideals of citizenship, see Gwendolyn Mink, *Wages of Motherhood: Inequality in the Welfare State, 1917–1942* (Ithaca, NY: Cornell University Press, 1995); on maternalist-influenced child welfare policies, see Molly Ladd-Taylor, "'My Work Came Out of Agony and Grief': Mothers and the Making of the Sheppard-Towner Act," in *Mothers of a New World: Maternalist Politics and the Origins of the Welfare States*, ed. Seth Koven and Sonya Michel (New York: Routledge, 1993), 321–342; and on the relationship between maternalism and workplace and public health reform, see Skocpol, *Protecting Soldiers*, 302–304, also 509–511.

33. House Committee on Education, *Federal Aid for Home Economics*, 66th Cong., 3rd sess., 1921, 28–29.

34. 63rd Cong., 2nd sess., *Congressional Record* (March 3, 1914), 4203.

35. Ibid. See also Senator Williams (D-MS), 63rd Cong., 2nd sess., *Congressional Record* (March 3, 1914), 4214.

36. Statements of William G. Sullivan, Esq. and G. O. Nations, Esq., Senate Subcommittee of the Committee on District of Columbia, *Juvenile Court in D.C.*, 64th Cong., 1st sess., 1916, 61 and 35–36, respectively. Soul advocates claimed that parental autonomy was essential to the independence and self-sufficiency of a family, failing which a family would be thrown on public relief and/or charity. For example, Edward J. Maginnis, an open letter to the legislators of Pennsylvania, material submitted in Senate Committee on Interstate Commerce, *Interstate Commerce in Products of Child Labor, Part 1,* 64th Cong., 1st sess., 1916, 82; also Statement of Mr. S. F. Patterson, Treasurer and General Manager of Roanoke Mills, Roanoke, North Carolina, House Committee on Labor, *Child-Labor Bill,* 64th Cong., 1st sess., 1916, 62.

37. Statement of John D. Bradley, president of the Washington, D.C. Secular League, Federal Motion Picture Commission, Hearing Before the Committee on Education, House of Representatives, 64th Cong., 1916, 209. Also for position of managers of cotton mills of the South, as representing the Soul position in favor of parental autonomy, see Gwendoline Alphonso, "Hearth and Soul: Economic and Cultural Conceptions of the Family in the Progressive Era, 1900–1920," *Studies in American Political Development* 24 (2010): 206–232, 19–21.

38. Senator Lawrence Sherman (R-IL), Senate Subcommittee of the Committee on the District of Columbia, *Juvenile Court in D.C.*, 64th Cong., 1st sess., 1916, 36; also Statement of Julia C. Lathrop, Children's Bureau, Chief, Department of Labor, in House Committee on the District of Columbia, *School and Home for Feeble-Minded Persons*, 64th Cong., 1st sess., 1916, 7: "We are in this country past the time when we need to argue as to whether the public should take care of those who can neither take care of themselves or remain uncared for, without a fearful menace to society as a whole." On this point, as on others, Hearth advocates often used structural changes in the family and modern socioeconomic change as the primary rationale for the increased role of the government in the family: "We are getting away from the old family life, where other members of the family took care of those who were not so well able to take care of themselves." Statement of Thomas Crago (R-PA), in Senate Committee on Pensions, *Widows of Soldiers of War with Spain*, 62nd Cong., 3rd sess., 1913, 5.

39. Hearth members turned to lower-income family examples far more often than Soul, citing them in 68 percent of all their family cases where income was suggested compared to 51 percent of families cited by Soul. Hearth legislators also addressed widowed family examples far more frequently than their Soul colleagues: in 13.5 percent of those family cases where marital status was mentioned or implied, compared to 7.5 percent of Soul family cases.

40. See, for instance, House Committee on Interstate and Foreign Commerce, *Public Protection of Maternity*, 67th Cong., 1st sess., 1921, 12. The use of scientific, systematic approaches to social problems is especially evident in the hearings concerning the Children's Bureau. See, for instance, Julia Lathrop, Children's Bureau, Chief in House Committee on Appropriations, *Legislative, Executive, and Judicial Appropriation Bill, 1917*, 64th Cong., 1st sess., 1916, 1053–1056, 1053; House Committee on Expenditures in Interior Department, *Hearings on H.R. 24148, Establishment of Children's Bureau in the Interior Department*, 60th Cong., 2nd sess., 1909, especially 32–35 (statement of the National Child Labor Committee regarding the need for a standardized, systematic approach to children's welfare); and remarks of Andrew Peters (D-MA) in support of the Children's Bureau, 60th Cong., 2nd sess., *Congressional Record* (February 19, 1909), 2705. See also Senate Committee on Education and Labor, *Study of the*

Criminal, Pauper and Defective Classes, 60th Cong., 1st sess., 1908 (supporting bill S. 3066, whose purpose was "to study crime, pauperism and other social evils . . . by the best methods known to science and sociology, with the idea of preventing or lessening such evils." Ibid., 5).

41. Senator Williams (D-MS), 63rd Cong., 2nd sess., *Congressional Record* (March 3, 1914), 4214.

42. Ibid., 4214 ("The line of cleavage, moral and mental, in society is not a sex [gender] line at all. . . . When you get into a bad population the women are bad with the men—and when you get into a good population the women are good with the men . . . it depends on the family, the population, and not the sex.").

43. Peter Bardaglio, *Reconstructing the Household: Families, Sex, and the Law in the Nineteenth-Century South* (Chapel Hill: University of North Carolina Press, 1995), xi.

44. Laura F. Edwards, *The People and Their Peace: Legal Culture and the Transformation of Inequality in the Post-Revolutionary South* (Chapel Hill: University of North Carolina Press, 2009), 169–201; also see Ariela Gross, *What Blood Won't Tell: A History of Race on Trial in America* (Cambridge, MA: Harvard University Press, 2008).

45. Edwards, *People and Their Peace*, 95.

46. Bardaglio, *Reconstructing the Household*, 79–80.

47. Senator Bryan (D-FL), 63rd Cong., 2nd sess., *Congressional Record* (March 3, 1914), 4200.

48. For example, alternative marriage practices among *non*white families were used as illustrations of their defective moral character, threatening to American society. See positions by Senator James D. Phelan (D-CA) and Representative Raker (D-CA): "Japanese are an immoral people . . . [they have] no home life," in House Committee on Immigration and Naturalization, *Japanese Immigration*, 66th Cong., 2nd sess., 1920, 20, 198; on picture brides, see 228–229; on Japanese family (defective) gender relations, see 472–473.

49. Senator Milton (D-FL), 60th Cong., 2nd sess., *Congressional Record* (March 1, 1909), 3481.

50. Mintz and Kellogg, *Domestic Revolutions*, 108.

51. See, for instance, remarks by Thomas Sisson (D-MS), House Subcommittee on D.C. Appropriations of Committee on Appropriations, *D.C. Appropriation Bill, 1922*, 66th Cong., 3rd sess., 1920, 315.

52. See remarks by Senator Milton (D-FL), 60th Cong., 2nd sess., *Congressional Record* (March 1, 1909), 3482.

53. For example, *Proposing an amendment to the Constitution of the United States, prohibiting intermarriage between negroes or persons of color and Caueusian [sic] or any other character of persons*, 62nd Cong., 3rd sess., H. J. Res. 368 (1912); *To prohibit the intermarriage of persons of the white and negro races within the United States of America; to declare such contracts of marriage null and void; to prescribe punishments for violations and attempts to violate its provisions*, HR 20779, 63rd Cong., 3rd sess., 1915.

54. Emphasis added. Seaborn Roddenbery (D-GA) remarks when introducing H. J. Res. 368 "Marr & Divorce—joint resolution for amendment to Constitution prohibiting intermarriage of whites and negroes." 62nd Cong., 3rd sess., *Congressional Record* (December 11, 1912), 503.

55. Roddenbery (D-GA), 62nd Cong., 3rd sess., *Congressional Record* (January 30, 1913), 2312. On the case of Jack Johnson and Lucille Cameron and the impact of race relations and

ideologies in Progressive Era society, see Al-Tony Gilmore, "Jack Johnson and White Women: The National Impact," *Journal of Negro History* 58 (1973): 18–38; also Randy Roberts, *Papa Jack: Jack Johnson and the Era of White Hopes* (New York: Free Press, 1983).

56. Roddenbery (D-GA), 62nd Cong., 3rd sess., 2312.

57. Bardaglio, *Reconstructing the Household*. However, there was almost no regulation of interracial sexual activity, seen as contrary to the power of the slaveholder, since the products of these liaisons were legally "black" and, if the mother were a slave, also the slave property of their fathers.

58. Senator Milton (D-FL), 60th Cong., 2nd sess., *Congressional Record* (March 1, 1909), 3483.

59. Ibid., 3482–3483.

60. Progressive Era reformers extensively engaged in a nationalist, pronatalist project through a series of reforms and programs (such as eugenic "fitter families" campaigns and the maternalist policy agenda) that promoted selective human reproduction, idealized agrarian motherhood, and promoted scientific racism and eugenics; this was the product of their modernist conviction that reproduction could be regulated in the national interest. Laura Lovett, *Conceiving the Future: Pronatalism, Reproduction, and the Family in the United States, 1890–1938* (Chapel Hill: University of North Carolina Press, 2007).

61. On the cultural hegemony of middle-class, native-born, white ideals of family in Progressive Era social policy, see Mink, *Wages of Motherhood*, 5–13.

62. Statement of Senator Arthur Capper (R-KS), Senate Committee on Education and Labor, *Federal Aid for Physical Education*, 66th Cong., 2nd sess., 1920, 10–11.

63. Lovett, *Conceiving the Future*, 134–139.

64. The four coding categories were created and classified (as cultural and/or economic) from the Clausen and Peltzman issue coding schemes as described in Keith Poole and Howard Rosenthal, *Congress: A Political Economic History of Roll-Call Voting* (New York: Oxford University Press, 1997), 259–260.

65. Alston and Ferrie have shown that welfare benefits in the South were long used to maintain a system of paternalism, wherein benefits (such as medical care and protection from violence) were used instrumentally by white planter elites to maintain control over black and poor white agricultural workers. See Lee J. Alston and Joseph P. Ferrie, *Southern Paternalism and the American Welfare State: Economics, Politics, and Institutions in the South, 1865–1965* (New York: Cambridge University Press, 1999). Historians and legal scholars have also demonstrated that ideals of households and families among the political elite of the South (white planters), stressing the importance of harmony, dependency, and hierarchy, were at odds with the more egalitarian family ideals of the increasingly bourgeois northern elite. Bardaglio, *Reconstructing the Household*; also see Edwards, *Angels in the Machinery*.

66. Pearson's chi-square statistic (137.05) is significant at the .05 level for "party of active MC" and "policy category." Results of a comparison of column proportions (z tests) for the same two variables show significant differences in the proportion of family cases used to discuss ascription and autonomy issues by Democratic members, as well as welfare and regulation issues by Republicans. Results are based on two-sided tests with a significance level of .05 (Tables 4A and 4B). Democratic members disproportionately focused on the specific ascription and autonomy policy issues of sexuality and reproduction, family lineage and "blood" affiliation in Native American and also foreign families, and parental rights and limited

government intervention into the family. They also disproportionately raised race-based issues and intermarriage concerns and espoused the maintenance of traditional gender roles. Republican members, on their part, focused on the particular regulation and social welfare issues of child labor, juvenile institutions, family property and wealth, immigration/Americanization of foreign families, gender equality, and uniformity in marriage registration and divorce laws across the country.

67. For the following analysis, I control for party and use "active MC" as the unit of analysis, in contrast to other tables, where the unit of analysis is the family case referenced by the MC.

68. This distribution broadly matches Sanders's distribution of overall delegations in the House for the 63rd and 64th Congresses (see Table 5.1: Regions and Parties in the Progressive Era in the House of Representatives, in Sanders, *Roots of Reform*, 162–163); in so doing, the regional distribution of members who were active in family cases reflects the broader sectional distributional clusters in Congress at the time.

69. See, for example, House Committee on Foreign Affairs, *Relating to Expatriation of Citizens*, 62nd Cong., 2nd sess., 1912, 22–23; House Committee on District of Columbia, *Intermarriage of Whites and Negroes in D.C. and Separate Accommodations in Street Cars for Whites and Negroes in D.C.*, 64th Cong., 1st sess., 1916; see also remarks by Seaborn Roddenberry (D-GA), 62nd Cong., 2nd sess., *Congressional Record* (December 11, 1912), H 502–504; on Native Americans and blood rules, House Committee on Indian Affairs, *Treaty of Dancing Rabbit Creek*, 62nd Cong., 2nd sess., 1912, 3–13, 106.

Also, from the party splits in the roll call votes on an antimiscegenation bill (*To Prohibit the Intermarriage of Persons of the White and Negro Races within the District of Columbia*, HR 1710, 63rd Cong., 3rd sess., *Congressional Record* (January 11, 1915), H 1362), we see that of the 239 yeas, 103 came from southern Democrats (100 percent of that delegation), while the 60 nays were distributed between northern Republicans (who voted 50 nays to 36 yeas) and a few northern Democrats (who voted 7 nays to 95 yeas) (data for Roll Call No. 236, 63rd Cong., available at http://www.voteview.com/partycount.htm).

70. See House Committee on District of Columbia, *School and Home for Feeble-Minded Persons*, 64th Cong., 4th sess., 1916, 16–17, 25.

71. Column proportions (*z* tests) at a significance level of .05 confirm that among the regional Democratic delegations, midwestern Democrats alone referred to economic family issues in a significantly greater proportion than cultural ones.

72. Significant differences (at the .05 level) are found between midwestern and northeastern Republicans versus western Republicans in the high proportion of welfare issues they raised, whereas western Republicans are significantly different from other factions in the high proportion of regulation issues they raised.

73. Unlike in its transformed position in the forthcoming New Deal, the congressional Democratic Party in the Progressive Era was still the party of individual autonomy, states' rights, and limited national government; see Sidney Milkis, "Presidency and Political Parties," in *Presidency and the Political System*, ed. Michael Nelson, 8th ed. (Washington, DC: CQ Press, 2006), 304–348.

74. For example, the following committee hearings: House Committee on Military Affairs, U.S. House of Representatives, *To Restore the Canteen in the Army,* 62nd Cong., 3rd sess., 1913; Senate Committee on District of Columbia, *Regulation of Sale of Intoxicating Liquors in D.C.*, 60th Cong., 1st sess., 1908; Prohibition Hearings: House Committee on Judiciary, *En-*

forcement of Prohibition, Part 2, 66th Cong., 1st sess., 1919; and Senate Committee on Judiciary, *Prohibiting Intoxicating Beverages, Part 1,* 66th Cong., 1st sess., 1919.

75. For example, the organic statute establishing the Children's Bureau, a landmark Hearth bureaucracy, outlined the mission of the bureau in terms of data gathering, underscoring the importance of reliable demographic data as a basis for policy formulation; see HR 24148, 60th Cong., 2nd sess. (introduced by Herbert Parsons [R-NY]), cited in *Congressional Record,* 60th Cong., 2nd sess., 1909, 2897.

76. See, for example, remarks of Chairman Warren Gard (D-OH). House Committee on Judiciary, *Uniform Laws as to Marriage and Divorce,* 64th Cong., 1st sess., 1916, 27–28. Also see Statement of Rev. Harry Adams Hersey, Chairman of the Commission of Public Morals of the Universalist General Convention, Foxboro, Massachusetts, House Committee on Judiciary, *Uniform Marriage and Divorce Laws,* 66th Cong., 2nd sess., 1920, 24.

77. Statement of Mr. Francis Miner Moody, M.A., Chicago, Executive Sec'y of the International Committee on Marriage and Divorce, House Committee on Judiciary, *Uniform Laws as to Marriage and Divorce,* 65th Cong., 2nd sess., 1918, 3.

78. Ibid.

79. For infant mortality statistics as marking the importance of the work of the Children's Bureau, see House Committee on Interstate and Foreign Commerce, *Public Protection of Maternity,* 1920, 22–23; regarding statistics relating to the Sheppard-Towner Maternity and infant programs, see Senate Committee on Public Health and National Quarantine, *Protection of Maternity and Infancy,* 66th Cong., 2nd sess., 1920, 11; for the use of birth and death rates and the impact of prenatal healthcare, see House Committee on Labor, *Hygiene of Maternity and Infancy,* 65th Cong., 3rd sess., 1919, 29, 35. The Sheppard-Towner Infancy and Protection Act in 1921 established the first federal social welfare program. It provided for the dissemination of health care information to mothers by the federally subsidized pre- and postnatal clinics, conceived as a public health entitlement of all women, not just the poor. The Sheppard-Towner maternity health program ultimately lost favor with powerful political interests and succumbed to demise only to be resurrected, in a modified form, by the Social Security Act of 1935. Muncy, *Creating a Female Dominion,* 93–101; Ladd Taylor, *Mothers of a New World,* 322.

80. For statistics on women's employment and increased burden of wage labor in addition to homemaking, as justifying home economics programs, see House Committee on Education, *Federal Aid for Home Economics,* 66th Cong., 3rd sess., 1921, 7; on immigration statistics and reform of naturalization laws for immigrant families, see House Committee on Immigration and Naturalization, *Proposed Changes in Naturalization Laws,* 66th Cong., 1st sess., 1919, 21; immigrant family literacy data and need for Americanization programs, see ibid., 15; on patterns of living arrangements, tenement house laws, and associated death rates among poor, urban families as a rationale for housing policy reform, see Senate Select Committee on Reconstruction and Production, *Reconstruction and Production: Vol. 1,* 66th Cong., 3rd sess., 1921, 111, 456–457, 917 (Chicago as prime example).

81. See, for example, Representative Whaley (D-SC), House Committee on the Judiciary, *Uniform Laws as to Marriage and Divorce,* 1916, 19–20.

82. Table 8, Percent Distribution of Martial Condition of the Population by Sex, by Divisions, and States, 1920, 1910, 1920 in "Chapter IV: Marital Condition," *1920 Census Report,* U.S. Bureau of Census, 358.

83. Ibid.

84. Ibid., 322. The link between fertility and nuptiality trends is not surprising since, during this period, conception of children predominantly occurred during marriage. For the link between fertility and nuptiality (as well as the increasing practice of contraception), see Michael Haines, "Long Term Marriage Patterns in the United States from Colonial Times to the Present," *History of the Family: An International Quarterly* 1 (1996): 15–39; also Michael Haines, "White Population, 1790–1920," in *Population History of North America*, ed. Michael R. Haines and Richard H. Steckel (New York: Cambrige University Press, 2000), 317–323.

85. Senator Bryan (D-FL), 63rd Cong., 2nd sess., *Congressional Record* (March 3, 1914), 4199.

86. Extension of remarks of Edwin Y. Webb (D-NC), 63rd Cong., 3rd sess., *Congressional Record* (January 23, 1915), 170.

87. Methodological note: In the Progressive Era, Congress undertook the task of direct city management of the District of Columbia. Thus, among the numbers of committee hearings pertaining to the family, several were by the Committee of the District of Columbia and discussed (state-like) police power policies in that city. A considerable percentage (roughly 35 percent) of total family cases referenced by members of Congress during this period hailed from the nation's capital. In order to analyze more effectively the partisan dimensions of the kinds of families used as policy examples, I therefore split the data set of family cases into "D.C." and "non-D.C." families. I then analyzed the "non-D.C." family cases. While this method reduced the total number of family case examples, the aim was to study a more representative sample of cases from around the country without skewing the results (particularly in terms of region) by including the 146 D.C. family cases. Among "non-D.C." family examples, clear partisan divisions in family region are observed.

88. I coded family case examples by the size of town in which they resided. A town with fewer than 5,000 people was coded as a "village," that with a population between 5,000 and 10,000 as a "small town," between 10,000 and 25,000 as a "city," 25,000 to 100,000 as a "large city," and over 100,000 as a "metropolis."

Chapter 3

1. Current Population Reports, "Income of Families and Persons in the United States: 1961," Series P=60, No. 39, available at http://www2.census.gov/prod2/popscan/p60-039.pdf.

2. Gallup Poll (AIPO), March 1952, USGALLUP.52–488. Q03A. Data obtained from the Roper Center for Public Opinion Research, University of Connecticut.

3. Gallup Poll (AIPO), August 1954, USGALLUP.54–535. QK02A. Data obtained from the Roper Center for Public Opinion Research, University of Connecticut.

4. Elaine Tyler May, *Homeward Bound: American Families in the Cold War Era* (New York: Basic Books, 1988), 11.

5. It is interesting to note that social dislocations in previous periods, such as during the Great Depression or after World War I, did not result in such a policy development. While Congress then did consider and enact several pieces of prominent legislation to assist stricken families, the goal of family stability or rather "containing" family disruption was not actively pursued through a concerted, national policy effort.

6. Steven Mintz and Susan Kellogg, *Domestic Revolutions: A Social History of American Family Life* (New York: Free Press, 1988), 170–171; Patricia H. Shiono and Linda Sandham Quinn, "Epidemiology of Divorce," *Children and Divorce* 4, no. 1 (1994): 18.

7. Between 1941 and 1944, 6.5 million women entered the workforce, more than 50 percent of whom had previously been unpaid homemakers. By the end of the war in Europe, in May 1945, women workers comprised 57 percent of all employed persons, and almost half of all working women at that time were married, a dramatic increase in just five years from the previous low proportion (36 percent) of married women among female workers. The phenomenal increase in married women's participation in the labor force during World War II was in marked contrast to previous female labor patterns where married women would by and large eschew paid labor, outside of the home, with single women constituting the vast majority of working women. Carl N. Degler, *At Odds: Women and the Family in America from the Revolution to the Present* (New York: Oxford University Press, 1980), 420–421; also see Karen Anderson, *Wartime Women: Sex Roles, Family Relations and the Status of Women During World War II* (Westport, CT: Greenwood, 1981), 25–29; Mintz and Kellogg, *Domestic Revolutions*, 172. Moreover, the war widened the occupational opportunities for women enormously, and millions of women moved out of low-wage work into good-paying jobs, war related and otherwise, that had previously been out of their reach.

8. In the first year after the end of the war, 2.25 million women workers gave up their jobs voluntarily, and another million were laid off in anticipation of returning male workers. Degler, *At Odds*, 422.

9. Women's Bureau Bulletin #297, *Handbook on Women Workers, 1975* (Washington, DC: n.d.). In fact, at about the same time (in 1946), when women were leaving the workforce, 2.75 million women workers newly entered paid labor. Degler, *At Odds*, 422.

10. Anderson, *Wartime Women*, 7.

11. Ibid., 111.

12. In the decades between 1940 and 1960, increases in birth rates and in women's employment occurred in tandem with each other, throughout the social and economic spectrum, in contrast to the conventional inverse relationship between fertility and female work patterns in the periods prior and since. See Susan Householder Van Horn, *Women, Work, and Fertility, 1900–1986* (New York: New York University Press, 1988), 5–7, especially Figure 1.2, and 83.

13. Anderson, *Wartime Women*, 9–10.

14. Ibid., 10, 111; also Richard Polenberg, *War and Society: The U.S., 1941–1945* (Philadelphia: Lippincott, 1972).

15. May, *Homeward Bound*, 16–22.

16. Statement of Mrs. B. H. Dillard, East Knoxville County Democratic Women's Club, Senate Subcommittee to Investigate Juvenile Delinquency of the Committee of the Judiciary, *Juvenile Delinquency (Education)*, 84th Cong., 1st sess., 1955, 108.

17. Postwar veterans' policies were a continuation of the American conscription system, which, as Dorit Geva has demonstrated, were shaped by political and military leaders' concerns about family, particularly the effects of men's service on their family lives, as breadwinners and figures of paternal authority. Dorit Geva, *Conscription, Family, and the Modern State: A Comparative Study of France and the United States* (New York: Cambridge University Press, 2013), chaps. 4 and 5. For primary evidence on the centrality of men's intertwined family and service lives in policy, see House Subcommittee No. 10, Pay and Administration, of the Committee on Armed Services, *Subcommittee Hearing on H.R. 1363*, 80th Cong., 1st sess., 1947; House Committee on Pensions, *Increase in Service Pensions for Certain Veterans and Widows of Veterans of Spanish-American War*, 79th Cong., 2nd sess., 1946, 13–14 (describing the concern of Mr. William Gallagher [D-MN] and Mr. Leonard Allen [D-LA] over the liberality of

pension laws that include young women marrying "old goats" solely for their pensions versus Mr. Alvin Weichel [R-OH] and Mr. William Stevenson [R-OH], who stressed eligibility of the widow regardless of her motivation for marriage); also House Subcommittee on Spanish War Veterans of the Committee on Veterans' Affairs, *Increasing Service Pensions for Veterans of the Spanish-American War and Their Dependents*, 80th Cong., 1st sess., 1947 (same set of debates).

18. Senate Committee on Armed Services, *Dependents Assistance Act of 1950 (Family Allowances), Part 1*, 81st Cong., 2nd sess., 1950, 7; Senate Committee on Armed Services, *Dependents Assistance Act of 1950 (Family Allowances), Part 2*, 81st Cong., 2nd sess., 1950, 17–20 (note that bill sponsors of the Senate and House version of 81 S. 3986, bill to provide family allowances for the dependents of enlisted members of the Armed Forces of the United States and for other purposes, were Senators Millard Tydings [D-GA] and Carl Vinson [D-GA]). For a similar assertion that draft policy in World War II (in contrast to World War I) emphasized avoiding family disruptions conceived primarily in terms of preserving the moral quality of parenting, rather than family economic maintenance, see Geva, *Conscription, Family, and the Modern State*, 164–165, chap. 5 more generally.

19. The hearings in which this issue is raised are too numerous to list exhaustively. Representative examples may be found in House Committee on Ways and Means, *Social Security Act Amendments of 1949. Part 1: Public Assistance and Welfare*, 81st Cong., 1st sess., 1949, 421, 547–548; Senate Committee on Finance, *Social Security Revision, Part 1*, 81st Cong., 2nd sess., 1950, 138–139; Senate Committee on Finance, *Social Security Revision, Part 2*, 81st Cong., 2nd sess., 1950, 286–287, 295, 574; House Subcommittee on Social Security of the Committee on Ways and Means, *Analysis of the Social Security System Part 4: OASI: Coverage, Eligibility, Benefits; and Public Assistance*, 83rd Cong., 1st sess., 1953, 632–633; House Subcommittee on Social Security of the Committee on Ways and Means, *Analysis of the Social Security System Part 3: Economic Status of the Aged and Public Assistance*, 83rd Cong., 1st sess., 1953, 301–305; Senate Subcommittee on Housing of the Committee on Banking and Currency, *Housing Act of 1955*, 84th Cong., 1st sess., 1955, 366–378; House Committee on Ways and Means, *Public Assistance Titles of the Social Security Act*, 84th Cong., 2nd sess., 1956, 59–61.

20. "Senators to Hold Teen Age Hearings," *New York Times*, September 19, 1953.

21. On working mothers as the cause of juvenile delinquency and other social problems, see Senate Subcommittee to Investigate Juvenile Delinquency in the U.S. of the Committee on Judiciary, *Juvenile Delinquency (Television Programs)*, 83rd Cong., 2nd sess., 1954, 82, 112; Senate Subcommittee to Investigate Juvenile Delinquency in the U.S. of the Committee on Judiciary, *Juvenile Delinquency (Obscene and Pornographic Materials)*, 84th Cong., 1st sess., 1955, 5–6; also see Senate Committee on Appropriations, *Labor-Health, Education, and Welfare Appropriations for 1955*, 1954, 465–466. For a contrary position, refuting the significance of the negative role of the "much-blamed mother," see Statement of Dr. Frederick Wertham, Senate Subcommittee to Investigate Juvenile Delinquency in the U.S. of the Committee on Judiciary, *Juvenile Delinquency (Comic Books)*, 83rd Cong., 2nd sess., 1954, 86; Senate Subcommittee to Investigate Juvenile Delinquency in the U.S. of the Committee on Judiciary, *Juvenile Delinquency (Philadelphia, Pa)*, 83rd Cong., 2nd sess., 1954, 170. On strong, responsible fathers as curative of juvenile delinquency among other ills, see Senate Subcommittee to Investigate Juvenile Delinquency in the U.S., *Juvenile Delinquency (Television Programs)*, 40; Senate Subcommittee to Investigate Juvenile Delinquency in the U.S, *Juvenile Delinquency (Education)*, 358, 360.

22. Priscilla Yamin, *American Marriage: A Political Institution* (Philadelphia: University of Pennsylvania Press, 2012).

23. See, as an example of the Progressive Era Hearth focus on conditions of deprivation, Address of Judge Ben B. Lindsey, Judge of the Juvenile Court, Denver, Colorado, *Proceedings of the Conference on the Care of Dependent Children*, 1909 S.Doc. 721, 60th Cong., 2nd sess., 1909 Serial Set, 218–219.

24. In the 1950s, parenting became increasingly reliant on the advice and expertise of child development and relationship professionals. Suburbanization and serial migration facilitated this turn, most widespread among middle-class families. Faced with new technologies and the uncertainties of an atomic age, unmoored from kinship networks and ever on the move, postwar suburban families came to rely on professional advice in books, magazines, and child care manuals. Dr. Benjamin Spock, for instance, became a household name. Mintz and Kellogg, *Domestic Revolutions*, 184–185.

25. Mintz and Kellogg, *Domestic Revolutions*, 185.

26. Minority Report of the Annual Meeting of the Children's Bureau and Advisory Committees on Maternal and Child Health Services and on Services for Crippled Children, Children's Bureau, United States Department of Labor, November 8 and 9, 1945, cited in House Committee on Labor, *Aid to Physically Handicapped, Part 25*, 79th Cong., 2nd sess., 1946, 2765; for other witnesses opposing the "revolutionary" character of the Pepper bill and the lack of a means test, mostly individual physicians and physician groups, see House Committee on Labor, *Aid to Physically Handicapped, Part 25*, 2918–2919 (representative of the American Academy of Pediatrics); also Statement of Charles J. Chandler, Chairman of the Kansas Crippled Children's Commission, submitted by Edward Rees (R-KS): "such a move would seriously undermine the individual responsibility of our citizens which we believe to be a basic requirement of the successful continuance of our form of government" (House Committee on Labor, *Aid to Physically Handicapped, Part 25*).

27. Senate Special Subcommittee to Investigate Juvenile Delinquency in the United States of the Committee on Labor and Public Welfare, *Juvenile Delinquency, Part 1*, 84th Cong., 1st sess., 1955, 181–182.

28. Theodore Lowi, *End of Liberalism: The Second Republic of the United States*, 2nd ed. (New York: Norton, 1979).

29. Mark D. Brewer and Jeffrey M. Stonecash, *Dynamics of American Political Parties* (New York: Cambridge University Press, 2009), 81.

30. James L. Sundquist, *Dynamics of the Party System: Alignment and Realignment of Political Parties in the United States* (Washington, DC: Brookings Institution, 1973), 183–217.

31. John Gerring, *Party Ideologies in America, 1828–1996* (New York: Cambridge University Press, 1998), chap. 4.

32. See, for example, Richard Hofstader, *The American Political Tradition and the Men Who Made It* (New York: Knopf, 1948); also Louis Hartz, *The Liberal Tradition in America* (New York: Harcourt Brace, 1955); Nicole Mellow, *The State of Disunion: Regional Sources of Modern American Partisanship* (Baltimore: Johns Hopkins University Press, 2008), 29.

33. Brewer and Stonecash, *Dynamics of American Political Parties*, 105. Although Brewer and Stonecash indicate the increasing rifts within the Democratic Party at this time, between more conservative southerners and increasingly liberal nonsoutherners, they also assert that "Democrats were in a reasonably good situation" (84) and that "committed conservatives" within the Republican Party were marginalized and "could not persuade the rest

of their party that a sustained attack on the size and scope of the federal government would pay off" (83).

34. Byron E. Shafer, *Two Majorities and the Puzzle of Modern American Politics* (Lawrence: Kansas University Press, 2003), 8.

35. Ibid., 9.

36. Byron E. Shafer, *Partisan Approaches to Postwar American Politics* (Chatham, NJ: Chatham House, 1998), chap. 3.

37. Brewer and Stonecash, *Dynamics of American Political Parties*, 83.

38. For example, see Daniel DiSalvo, *Engines of Change: Party Factions in American Politics, 1868–2010* (New York: Oxford University Press, 2012) and Geoffrey Kabaservice, *Rule and Ruin: The Downfall of Moderation and the Destruction of the Republican Party* (New York: Oxford University Press, 2012).

39. Shafer, *Two Majorities*, 10; Shafer argues that "because president and Congress were separately elected, there had to be, in effect, *four* institutional parties within the American two-party system: a presidential and a congressional Democratic and Republican Party" (4–5). He notes that this institutional differentiation in incentive structures between Congress and the presidency rendered the prospects for Republican control of government dire in the postwar era but presented no difficulties for the majority Democrats.

40. Ibid., 10.

41. Thirty-nine percent of Republican cases illustrated Soul ideals versus 14 percent of Democratic cases (chi-square = 35.5, p = .000). The 1950s saw what many refer to as the founding of the modern conservative movement. Influential conservative intellectuals such as Friedrich Hayek, William F. Buckley Jr., and Russell Kirk began to widely disseminate their ideas, urging limited government as essential to the American democratic order. Although these ideas would grow in significance through the following decades, affecting a whole-scale party realignment only in 1980 with Ronald Reagan, as we see here, the political environment of the early postwar period was not bereft of such ideas either, as usually claimed. For an overview of postwar conservative thinking, see Donald Critchlow, *The Conservative Ascendancy* (Cambridge, MA: Harvard University Press, 2007), 6–40 and Leo R. Ribuffo, "The Discovery and Rediscovery of American Conservatism Broadly Defined," *OAH: Magazine of History* 17, no. 2 (2003): 5–10. Also see George H. Nash, *The Conservative Intellectual Movement in America* (New York: Basic Books, 1976) as the classic treatment of conservatism during the period.

42. The proportion of Hearth cases offered by Democratic MCs was significantly different from those by Republicans through the congresses (79th–84th) (chi-square [Hearth/Party * Congress] = 236.2, p = .000), and similarly, the number of Soul cases offered by Democratic and Republican MCs was also significantly different (chi-square = 25.6, p [exact] = .000).

43. See, for example, William E. Leuchtenberg, *Franklin D. Roosevelt and the New Deal, 1932–1940* (New York: Harper & Row, 1963); also Sidney M. Milkis, *President and the Parties: Transformation of the American Party System Since the New Deal* (New York: Oxford University Press, 1993).

44. Lowi, *End of Liberalism*.

45. See, for instance, the central role of civic narratives regarding familial figures such as the "nagging wife" and "white male, breadwinner" in structuring New Deal programs. Holly Allen, *Forgotten Men and Fallen Women: The Cultural Politics of New Deal Narratives* (Ithaca, NY: Cornell University Press, 2015).

46. Democratic Party Platform of 1936, *American Presidency Project* (paragraph 13).

47. In comparison, seven Soul bills were introduced per Progressive Congress in contrast to three in the postwar period.

48. On the Fair Deal, see, for example, Alonzo Hamby, *Harry S. Truman and the Fair Deal* (Lexington, MA: D. C. Heath, 1974) and *Beyond the New Deal: Harry S. Truman and American Liberalism* (New York: Columbia University Press, 1973).

49. Harry S. Truman, "Special Message to the Congress Recommending a Comprehensive Health Program," November 19, 1945, *American Presidency Project* (emphasis added), available at http://www.presidency.ucsb.edu/ws/?pid=12288 (last accessed July 2, 2017).

50. Claude Pepper (D-FL), Statement, House Committee on Labor, *Aid to Physically Handicapped, Part 25*, 2710.

51. Ibid.

52. Major General Lewis B. Hershey, Director, Selective Services System, Statement, House Committee on Interstate and Foreign Commerce, *Health of School Children*, 80th Cong., 1st sess., 1947, 26–27.

53. See William M. Tuttle, *"Daddy's Gone to War": The Second World War in the Lives of America's Children* (New York: Oxford University Press, 1993).

54. Elizabeth R. Rose, *A Mother's Job: The History of Day Care, 1890–1960* (New York: Oxford University Press, 1999), 169.

55. Claude Pepper (D-FL), Statement, House Committee on Labor, *Aid to Physically Handicapped, Part 25*, 2708.

56. Anderson, *Wartime Women*, 103–104.

57. Marilyn E. Hegarty, *Victory Girls, Khaki-Wackies, and Patriotutes: The Regulation of Female Sexuality During World War II* (New York: New York University Press, 2008).

58. Public Law 381 (May Act), 79th Congress.

59. Thomas H. Sternberg, Ernest B. Howard, Leonard A. Dewey, and Paul Padget, "Chapter X. Venereal Disease," in *Preventive Medicine in World War II: Vol. 5, Communicable Diseases Transmitted Through Contact or Through Unknown Means*, ed. Leonard D. Heaton, John B. Coates Jr., Ebbe C. Hoff, Phebe M. Hoff, and Office of Surgeon General (Army) (Ft. Belvoir, VA: Ft. Belvoir Defense Technical Information Center, 1960).

60. Anderson, *Wartime Women*, 104 (also see 103–110).

61. S. Rept. No. 1332, 79th Cong., 2nd sess., 1946: "Experience has revealed that, but for the existence of the [May] act, women of ill repute would assemble in communities adjacent to practically every military and naval post for the purpose of engaging in immoral and illicit conduct." Cited in Senate Subcommittee of the Committee on Appropriations, *Federal-Labor Security Appropriation Bill for 194*, 79th Cong., 2nd sess., 1946, 131.

62. Statement of Russell W. Ballard, Director, Hull House Settlement, Chicago, Illinois, Senate Committee on Education and Labor, *Maternal and Child Welfare*, 79th Cong., 2nd sess., 1946, 31.

63. House Committee on Public Buildings and Grounds, *Housing for Distressed Families of Servicemen and Veterans with Families (No. 1)*, 79th Cong., 1st sess., 1945, 20.

64. Ibid., 22–23.

65. House Committee on Public Buildings and Grounds, *Housing for Distressed Families*, 29 (emphasis added).

66. Senate Subcommittee of the Committee on Labor and Public Welfare, *National Health Program, Part 1*, 80th Cong., 1st sess. 1947, 565–566 (see also 550–551).

67. On the preoccupation with centralization as engendering a tyrannical state, see Senator Robert A. Taft, speech in Syracuse, New York, quoted in statement submitted by Dr. J. P. Sanders, Louisiana State Medical Society, Dr. Guy R. Jones, and Dr. W. P. D. Tilly. Ibid., 609.

68. See, for instance, Taft's (R-OH) debate with Hearth advocate Claude Pepper (D-FL), in Senate Subcommittee of the Committee on Labor and Public Welfare, *National Health Program, Part 1*, 55–61; Homer Capehart (R-IN) in Senate Committee on Banking and Currency, *Housing Act of 1955*, Senate, 84th Cong., 1st sess., 1955. Capehart, along with Senator Kenneth Wheery, was a strong proponent for military housing (the Capehart Act passed in 1955 to authorize construction of housing units for military families). Yet his support for national housing projects was limited to the military, while he staunchly opposed public housing projects. In the hearing, he supports witness Henry G. Waltemade, President, National Association of Real Estate Boards, who submits material by Judge Roy F. Campbell, 80th District Judge, on the immoral practices, promiscuity, crime, and juvenile delinquency in the San Felipe Courts projects in Houston, Texas. Ibid., 339, 366–368.

69. Nelson Polsby, *How Congress Evolves: Social Bases of Institutional Change* (New York: Oxford University Press, 2004), 13–15.

70. Dewey Grantham, "The South and Congressional Politics," in *Remaking Dixie: The Impact of World War II on the American South*, ed. Neil R. McMillen (Jackson: University Press of Mississippi, 1997), 21–22. Also Polsby, *How Congress Evolves*, 14.

71. Brewer and Stonecash, *Dynamics of American Political Parties*, 80; also Ira Katznelson, *Fear Itself: The New Deal and the Origins of Our Time* (New York: Liveright, 2013), 131–157.

72. Alan Ware, *The Democratic Party Heads North, 1877–1962* (New York: Cambridge University Press, 2006).

73. Earl Black and Merle Black, *The Rise of Southern Republicans* (Cambridge, MA: Belknap Press of Harvard University Press, 2002). Nelson Polsby referred to this period (1940s and 1950s) in the House of Representatives as a period of "stalemate" between the increasingly urban liberal and moderate Democratic and Republican factions and the conservative coalition of conservative Republicans and southern Democrats. Polsby, *How Congress Evolves*, 6.

74. House Committee on Ways and Means, *Social Security Act Amendments of 1949, Part 1*, 471.

75. Senate Committee on Finance, *Social Security Revision, Part 2*, 165.

76. Joseph Lowndes, *From the New Deal to the New Right: Race and the Origins of Modern Conservatism* (New Haven, CT: Yale University Press, 2009); Dan T. Carter, *From George Wallace to Newt Gingrich: Race and the Conservative Counterrevolution, 1963–1994* (Baton Rouge: Louisiana State University Press, 1999); Mathew Lassiter, *The Silent Majority: Suburban Politics in the Sunbelt South* (Princeton, NJ: Princeton University Press, 2007); Ira Katznelson, *Fear Itself: The New Deal and the Origins of Our Time* (New York: Liveright, 2013).

77. Lee J. Alston and Joseph P. Ferrie, *Southern Paternalism and the American Welfare State: Economics, Politics, and Institutions in the South, 1865–1965* (New York: Cambridge University Press, 1999).

78. See on this especially Katznelson, *Fear Itself*; William E. Leuchtenberg, *The White House Looks South: Franklin D. Roosevelt, Harry S. Truman, and Lyndon B. Johnson* (Baton Rouge: Louisiana State University Press, 2005).

79. Ibid.; also Brewer and Stonecash, *Dynamics of American Political Parties*, 84–87.

80. $N = 524$, correlation $= -0.421$, $p = .000$.

81. Mintz and Kellogg, *Domestic Revolutions*, 186.

82. Ibid.

83. Ibid., 187.

84. House Committee on Ways and Means, *Social Security Act Amendments of 1949, Part 2: Old-Age, Survivors and Disability Insurance*, 81st Cong., 1st sess., 1949, 1515.

85. House Committee on Ways and Means, *Social Security Act Amendments of 1949, Part 1*, 11–12. On Altmeyer, see David Brian Robertson, "Policy Entrepreneurs and Policy Divergence: John R. Commons and William Beveridge," *Social Service Review* 62, no. 3 (1988): 504–531, 513 and Arthur J. Altmeyer, *The Formative Years of Social Security* (Madison: University of Wisconsin Press, 1968).

86. House Committee on Ways and Means, *Social Security Act Amendments of 1949, Part 1*, 878.

87. Dean W. Roberts, "Highlights of the Midcentury White House Conference on Children and Youth," *American Journal of Public Health and the Nation's Health* 41, no. 1 (1951): 96–99.

88. Harry S. Truman, "Address Before the Midcentury White House Conference on Children and Youth," December 5, 1950, *American Presidency Project*. The conference was held in Washington, DC, December 3–7, 1950, and the address was broadcast.

89. Statement of Jane M. Hoey, Director, Bureau of Public Assistance, Social Security Administration, Federal Security Agency in House Committee on Ways and Means, *Social Security Act Amendments of 1949, Part 1*, 402.

90. On the "whole child approach," as well as its origins and development in the postwar era, see Kriste Lindenmeyer, "The Child, the State, and the American Dream," in *Reinventing Childhood After World War II*, ed. Paula S. Fass and Michael Grossberg (Philadelphia: University of Pennsylvania Press, 2011), 85–109, 87–89.

91. Statement of Katharine Lenroot, Chief, Children's Bureau in House Committee on Labor, *Aid to Physically Handicapped, Part 25*, 2717.

92. Statement of Katharine Lenroot, Chief, Children's Bureau in House Committee on Labor, *Aid to Physically Handicapped, Part 25*, 2717. Also, Claude Pepper (D-FL), a primary Hearth proponent, when justifying the combined inclusion of health and child welfare services in the proposed Maternal and Child Welfare Act of 1946, referred to the "common knowledge" among child specialists who acknowledge that the "roots" of children's "medical problems" lie in the "social problems of their families." House Committee on Labor, *Aid to Physically Handicapped, Part 25*, 2708. Also see House Committee on Interstate and Foreign Commerce, *Health of School Children*, 47, 48 on provisions of the proposed bill, providing for prevention, diagnosis, and treatment of physical defects in schoolchildren along with similar "mental hygiene" services for them.

93. May, *Homeward Bound*, 26.

94. Ibid..

95. See William J. Brockelbank and Felix Infausto, *Interstate Enforcement of Family Support (The Runaway Pappy Act)* (Indianapolis: Bobbs-Merrill, 1971).

96. Statement of Louis C. Rabuat (D-MI), House Subcommittee No. 2 of the Committee on the Judiciary, *Making Abandonment of Dependents a Federal Crime*, 81st Cong., 1st and 2nd sess., 1949, 1950, 46.

97. Ibid., 99, 100.

98. In 1935, the federal government first got involved with family support through the creation of the first national welfare program: Aid to Dependent Children, as part of Title IV-A of the Social Security Act. The program involved the disbursement of federal money to the states in support of children whose fathers had died, become disabled, or otherwise deserted the family. Its original purpose was to "encourag[e] the care of dependent children in their own homes on in the homes of relatives by enabling each state to furnish financial assistance" (Act of August 24, 1935, Ch, 531, § 1, 49 Stat. 620). Through the postwar period, there were several proposals to expand this program by providing greater sums for assistance and including even those families where the father was unemployed rather than dead, disabled, or deserting. See, for example, House Committee on Ways and Means, *Social Security Act Amendments of 1949, Part 1*; also Senate Committee on Finance, *Social Security Revision, Parts 1, 2, 3*, 81st Cong., 2nd sess., 1950.

99. Tom Steed (D-OK), House Subcommittee No. 2 of the Committee on the Judiciary, *Making Abandonment of Dependents a Federal Crime*, 57.

100. Ibid., Andrew Jacobs (D-MI), 114.

101. Ibid.

102. For example, in the Progressive Era, progressive settlement workers and maternalist bureaucrats would target mothers in their attempt to change nutritional and health practices that had been discovered to be unhealthy. Mothers were also seen as crucial in progressives' quest to Americanize children and families of immigrants. See Gwendolyn Mink, *Wages of Motherhood: Inequality in the Welfare State, 1917–1942* (Ithaca, NY: Cornell University Press, 1995) and Chapter 2, this volume.

103. Mintz and Kellogg, *Domestic Revolutions*. 189.

104. Anderson, *Wartime Women*, 10.

105. Mintz and Kellogg, *Domestic Revolutions*, 190.

106. In the companionate ideal of family life, "the American housewife was now respected as full and 'active' partner in her marriage. In fact, partnership did not mean equality. A wife's primary role was to serve as her husband's ego massager, sounding board—and housekeeper. . . . The fifties ideal of a marital partnership was based on the assumption of a wife's role as hostess and consort." Mintz and Kellogg, *Domestic Revolutions*, 186–187.

107. Anderson, *Wartime Women*, 111.

108. See note 112 of this chapter.

109. On the need for mothers to provide "moral guidance" to delinquent girls, see Senate Subcommittee to Investigate Juvenile Delinquency in the U.S., *Juvenile Delinquency (Philadelphia PA)*, 37 (Statement of Norma B. Carson, Former Chief Policewoman, Juvenile Bureau, Police Department, Philadelphia, Pennsylvania); on maternal authority as being resented by boys and the need, instead, for fathers to instill discipline and responsibility, see Senate Subcommittee to Investigate Juvenile Delinquency in the U.S., *Juvenile Delinquency (Education)*, 358, 360 (Statement of Reverend Nicholas W. Wegner, Director, Boy's Town, Omaha, Nebraska).

110. Indeed, widowed mothers were central to policies regarding veterans' dependent benefits, Social Security, and Aid to Dependent Children.

111. See testimony of Msgr. John O'Grady, Secretary, National Conference of Catholic Charities, Senate Committee on Finance, *Social Security Revision, Part 2*, 589–602 (and general agreement by Chairman Walter F. George [D-GA] and Owen Brewster [R-ME]).

112. Thomas A. Van Sant, Director, Division of Adult Education, Baltimore, Maryland, Statement, Senate Subcommittee to Investigate Juvenile Delinquency in the U.S., *Juvenile Delinquency (Education)*, 276.

113. Ibid., 277.

114. Senate Subcommittee to Investigate Juvenile Delinquency in the U.S., *Juvenile Delinquency (Education)*, 4–7. Also Senator William Purtell (R-CT), Senate Subcommittee to Investigate Juvenile Delinquency in the U.S., *Juvenile Delinquency*, 84th Congress, 1st sess., July 6–8, 1955, 158.

115. Statement of Dr. J. B. Bittinger, Pastor, Second Presbyterian Church, Nashville, Tennessee, and Mrs. J. B. Bittinger, Director of Social Services, Monroe Harding Home, Nashville, Tennessee, Senate Subcommittee to Investigate Juvenile Delinquency in the U.S., *Juvenile Delinquency (Education)*, 57–58.

116. By running column proportions tests (z tests), these proportions are found to be (statistically) significant ($p \leq .05$), indicating a significant difference between Hearth and Soul cases on these issues.

117. On the clash between "big city" values and "the values of the countryside" in late twentieth-century culture wars, as well as more enduringly throughout American history, see E. J. Dionne Jr., *Souled Out: Reclaiming Faith and Politics After the Religious Right* (Princeton, NJ: Princeton University Press, 2008), 46, 55–56.

118. Within party competition, for the new centrality of small business to the postwar Republican agenda, in contrast to its previous corporate business base, see Shafer, *Two Majorities*, 186. Also, Gerring documents the Republican Party's new ideological shift (since 1928) "from economic nationalism to economic liberalism . . . identifying themselves with *small* business." Gerring, *Party Ideologies*, 136.

119. Senate Committee on Finance, *Social Security Revision, Part 2*, 164–165.

120. Ibid., 285.

121. Testimony of Dr. Isadore Lubin, New York, appearing on Behalf of Americans for Democratic Action, in House Subcommittee No. 4 of the Committee on Education and Labor, *Minimum Wage Standards and Other Parts of the Fair Labor Standards Act of 1938, Vol. 3*, 80th Cong., 1st sess., 1947, 1715; also Senator Douglas (D-IL), Senate Subcommittee on Labor of the Committee on Labor and Public Welfare, *Amending the Fair Labor Standards Act of 1938, Part 1*, 84th Cong. 1st sess., 1955, 54–55.

122. Statement of Solomon Barkin, Director of Research, Textile Workers Union of America, on Behalf of the Congress of Industrial Organizations, in House Subcommittee No. 4 of the Committee on Education and Labor, *Minimum Wage Standards, Vol. 3*, 1807–1808.

123. Edwin L. Douglass, on Behalf of Southern Hardwood Producers Inc., Augusta, Georgia, in House Subcommittee No. 4 of the Committee on Education and Labor, *Minimum Wage Standards, Vol. 3*, 1464.

124. Testimony of Harry J. Broomhall, President, Hoffman Auto Body Service Inc., Columbus, Ohio, in House Subcommittee No. 4 of the Committee on Education and Labor, *Minimum Wage Standards, Vol. 3*, 1489–1490.

125. House Subcommittee No. 4 of the Committee on Education and Labor, *Minimum Wage Standards, Vol. 3*, 2099–2100.

126. Nicholas Lemann, *The Promised Land: The Great Black Migration and How It Changed America* (New York: Vintage, 1992), chap. 1; Gavin Wright, *Old South, New South:*

Revolutions in the Southern Economy Since the Civil War (New York: Basic Books, 1986), 230–257.

127. Lee J. Alston and Joseph P. Ferrie, *Southern Paternalism and the American Welfare State: Economics, Politics, and Institutions in the South, 1865–1965* (New York: Cambridge University Press, 1999).

128. Chi-square = 49.1, $p = .000$.

Chapter 4

1. Karen Bogenschnieder, *Family Policy Matters: How Policymaking Affects Families and What Professionals Can Do*, 2nd ed. (Mahwah, NJ: Lawrence Erlbaum, 2003), 55.

2. G. Steiner, "The Family as a Public Issue: Many Causes with Many Votaries," *Carnegie Quarterly* 28, no. 4 (1980): 1–5, cited in Bogenschneider, *Family Policy Matters*, 5.

3. Clinton, also like Reagan, issued an executive order requiring family impact statements (much like environment impact statements) on policies affecting families; this was, however, more limited in scope than Reagan's executive order, which required agencies to review *all* policy proposals for their potential impact on families.

4. The impact of economic/structural disadvantage on disintegrating family life was first systematically highlighted in the 1964 Moynihan Report. The report, entitled *The Negro Family: The Case for National Action*, was the work of sociologist and Assistant Secretary of Labor Daniel Patrick Moynihan. Moynihan presented research on the black family to demonstrate a "tangle of pathology" among urban, state-dependent African American families, evidenced through their unconventional family behavior (mainly high rates of extramarital fertility and absentee fathers). The Moynihan Report influenced the commitment of the federal government to antipoverty programs (e.g., Johnson's War on Poverty in 1964). Family restoration came to be seen as vital to the long-term success of antipoverty and welfare programs. See William Graebner, "The End of Liberalism: Narrating Welfare's Decline, from the Moynihan Report (1965) to the Personal Responsibility and Work Opportunity Act (1996)," *Journal of Policy History* 14, no. 2 (2002): 170–190; Shirley L. Zimmerman, *Family Policy: Constructed Solutions to Family Problems* (Thousand Oaks, CA: Sage, 2001), 13; Steven Mintz and Susan Kellogg, *Domestic Revolutions: A Social History of American Family Life* (New York: Free Press, 1988), 213.

5. "Family Delegates Rank Issues," *Minneapolis Sunday Tribune*, July 14, 1980, A8, cited in Zimmerman, *Family Policy*, 21.

6. Zimmerman, *Family Policy*, 21.

7. Ibid., 21.

8. Jacob Hacker, "Privatizing Risk Without Privatizing the Welfare State: The Hidden Politics of Social Policy Retrenchment in the United States," *American Political Science Review* 98 (2004): 243–260.

9. For example, Deadbeat Parents Punishment Act, 1997; Child Support Recovery Act, 1992; Personal Responsibility and Work Opportunity Reconciliation Act, 1996; Fathers Count Bill, 1997; and Child Support Distribution Bills of 2000, 2001. On policies focused on strengthening marriage and family, see Zimmerman, *Family Policy*, 140–161; also Bogenschneider, *Family Policy Matters*, 104–107.

10. Family Preservation and Support Act, 1992; Adoption and Safe Family Act, 1997.

11. Flex time employment opportunities; Health Security Bill, 1993; and Daycare for Working Families Bill, 1987, respectively.

12. Robert Self, *All in the Family: The Realignment of American Democracy* (New York: Hill and Wang, 2012), 5–6.

13. For example, on race, see Dan T. Carter, *From George Wallace to Newt Gingrich: Race and the Conservative Counterrevolution, 1963–1994* (Baton Rouge: Louisiana State University Press, 1999); Joseph E. Lowndes, *From the New Deal to the New Right: Race and the Origins of Modern Conservatism* (New Haven, CT: Yale University Press, 2008); Earl Black and Merle Black, *The Rise of the Southern Republicans* (Cambridge, MA: Harvard University Press, 2003); Joseph A. Aistrup, *The Southern Strategy Revisited: Republican Top-Down Advancement in the South* (Lexington: University of Kentucky Press, 1996).

On women's rights and party realignment, see, for example, Christina Wolbrecht, *The Politics of Women's Rights: Parties, Positions, and Change* (Princeton, NJ: Princeton University Press, 2001); Kira Sanbonmatsu, *Democrats, Republicans and the Politics of Women's Place* (Ann Arbor: University of Michigan Press, 2003); Jo Freeman, *A Room at a Time: How Women Entered Party Politics* (Lanham, MD: Rowman & Littlefield, 2002); Catherine E. Rymph, *Republican Women: Feminism and Conservatism from Suffrage Through the Rise of the New Right* (Chapel Hill: University of North Carolina Press, 2009); Ronnee Schreiber, *Righting Feminism: Conservative Women and American Politics, with a New Epilogue* (New York: Oxford University Press, 2012).

Generally, see David Karol, *Party Position Change in American Politics: Coalition Management* (Cambridge: Cambridge University Press, 2009); Daniel DiSalvo, *Engines of Change: Party Factions in American Politics, 1868–2010* (New York: Oxford University Press, 2012).

14. Stephanie Coontz, *Marriage, a History: From Obedience to Intimacy or How Love Conquered Marriage* (New York: Viking, 2005).

15. Steven Mintz and Susan Kellogg, *Domestic Revolutions: A Social History of American Family Life* (New York: Free Press, 1988), 203.

16. Ibid.

17. Ron Lesthaeghe and Lisa Niedert, *The Second Demographic Transition in the U.S.: Spatial Patterns and Correlates* (March 2006), available at http://www.psc.isr.umich.edu/pubs /pdf/rr06-592.pdf. See also Naomi Cahn and June Carbone, *Red v. Blue Families: Legal Polarization and the Creation of Culture* (New York: Oxford University Press, 2010), 34–35.

18. See generally Andrew J. Cherlin, *The Marriage-Go-Round: The State of Marriage and the Family in America Today* (New York: Knopf, 2009).

19. Lesthaeghe and Niedert, *Second Demographic Transition*, 3.

20. Judith Stacey, "Virtual Social Science and the Politics of Family Values in the United States," in *Changing Family Values*, ed. Gill Jagger and Caroline Wright (London: Routledge, 1999), 187–199.

21. Andrew J. Cherlin, *Marriage Divorce Remarriage* (Cambridge, MA: Harvard University Press, 1981), 73; see diagrammatic representation of the complex relationship between contemporary kinship/familial structures and households, Figure 3–2, on 86.

22. According to the census, a *household* contains one or more people—everyone living in a housing unit makes up a household. One of the people who own or rent the residence is designated as the *householder*. For the purposes of examining family and household composition, two types of households are defined: *family* and *nonfamily*. A *family household* has at least two members related by birth, marriage, or adoption, one of whom is the householder. Family households are maintained by married couples or by a man or woman living with other relatives—children may or may not be present. Family units that do not include the

householder are called *subfamilies*. A *nonfamily household* is either one person living alone or a householder who shares the housing unit only with his or her nonrelatives—for example, boarders or roommates. *Children* include sons and daughters by birth, stepchildren, and adopted children of the householder regardless of the child's age or marital status. *Own children* are a subset of all children—they identify the householder or a family reference person as a parent in a household, family, or family group. In this report, own children are limited to those children who are never-married and under age eighteen. Jason Fields, "America's Families and Living Arrangements, 2003: Population Characteristics," *Current Population Reports*, Series 20–553 (Washington, DC: Department of Commerce, 2004), 2.

23. On the growth of households that do not contain a marriage couple as outpacing the growth of husband-wife households, see Cherlin, *Marriage Divorce*, 73–74.

24. Marilyn Coleman, Lawrence H. Ganong, and Kelly Warzinik, *Family Life in 20th-Century America* (Westport, CT: Greenwood, 2007), 26.

25. Ibid., 24.

26. Ibid., 24.

27. Mintz and Kellogg, *Domestic Revolutions*, xix.

28. Ibid., xix.

29. Coleman, Ganong, and Warzinik, *Family Life*, 230. It has also been found that in this past decade, the labor force participation of married mothers has leveled off and even decreased; this is especially so in the case of mothers of infants under twelve months old. Coleman, Ganong, and Warzinik, *Family Life*.

30. Women continue to be primarily responsible for household management and childrearing; by some estimates, working mothers in 2000 spent an average of eighty hours a week engaged in parenting and paid employment. In fact, the hours white married mothers spent doing primary care tasks (feeding, cooking, cleaning, etc.) for individual children nearly doubled between the 1920s and 1980s. When families were larger earlier in the century, mothers had less time to interact with children individually than do mothers more recently, who are in the labor force but have fewer children. Paid employment thus has not diminished; instead, in many cases, it has added to married mothers' responsibilities. Coleman, Ganong, and Warzinik, *Family Life*, 148.

31. For the consistent prominence of work-and-family issues in family policy debates, see Bogenschneider, *Family Policy Matters*, 102–104.

32. Frank Hobbs and Nicole Stoops, *Demographic Trends in the 20th Century: Census 2000 Special Reports* (November 2002), 7, available at https://www.census.gov/prod/2002pubs/censr-4.pdf (last accessed July 21, 2017).

33. Lesthaeghe and Niebert, *Second Demographic Transition*; also Cahn and Carbone, *Red v. Blue Families*, 20–32.

34. Regional categories used (South, West, Northeast, Midwest) follow census regional divisions. See http://www.census.gov/geo/www/us_regdiv.pdf (last accessed July 21, 2017).

35. On marriage cycles, see Alexander A. Plateris, "100 Years of Marriage and Divorce Statistics, 1867–1967," *Vital and Health Statistics* series 21, no. 24 (Washington, DC: Government Printing Office, 1973).

36. Robert H. Freymeyer and Barbara Johnson, "Southern Families," in *Families with Futures: A Survey of Family Studies for the 21st Century*, ed. Meg Wilkes Karakker and Janet R. Grochowski (New York: Taylor & Francis, 2006), 8–9.

37. Scott J. South, "Historical Changes and Life Course Variation in the Determinants of Premarital Childbearing," *Journal of Marriage and Family* 61 (1999): 753–763; Scott South and K. M. Lloyd, "Marriage Markets and Nonmarital Fertility in the United States," *Demography* 29 (1992): 247–264; R. Plotnick, "The Effects of Attitudes on Teenage Premarital Pregnancy and Its Resolution," *American Sociological Review* 57 (1992): 800–811; Cahn and Carbone, *Red v. Blue Families*, 20–29.

38. Cahn and Carbone, *Red v. Blue Families*, chaps. 1 and 2.

39. House Select Committee on Children, Youth, and Families, *Children, Youth, and Families: Beginning the Assessment*, 98th Cong., 1st sess., 1983, 1–2.

40. House Select Committee on Children, Youth, and Families, *Supporting a Family: Providing the Basics*, 98th Cong., 1st sess., 1983, 1–2.

41. House Select Committee on Children, Youth, Families, *Diversity and Strength of American Families*, 99th Cong., 2nd sess., 1986, 80.

42. Julie Matthaei, Associate Professor and Chair, Department of Economics, Wellesley College, Statement in House Select Committee on Children, Youth, and Families, *Working in America: Implications for Families*, 99th Cong., 2nd sess., 1986, 62.

43. For example, see Senate Subcommittee on Social Security and Family Policy of the Committee on Finance, *Benefits of a Healthy Marriage*, 108th Cong., 2nd sess., 2004. On the cost-effectiveness (and therefore desirability) of long-term home care by families of elderly relatives rather than impersonal institutional care, see Senate Special Committee on Aging, *Families Helping Families: Tax Relief Strategies for Elder Care*, 108th Cong., 2nd sess., 2004, 2–8 (case of Trudy Elliott, Family Caregiver and Home Health Nurse, Coeur d'Alene, Idaho, introduced by Larry Craig [R-ID]).

44. Senate Subcommittee on Children and Families of the Committee on Health, Education, Labor, and Pensions, *Healthy Marriage: Why We Should Promote It? Examining How to Promote a Healthy Marriage, Focusing on the Healthy Marriage Initiative, the Temporary Assistance to Needy Families Program, and Discouraging Teen Pregnancy*, 108th Cong., 2nd sess., 2004, 1–2; also see Senate Subcommittee on Social Security and Family Policy of the Committee on Finance, *Benefits of a Healthy Marriage*, 108th Cong., 2nd sess., 2004.

45. House Select Committee on Children, Youth, and Families, *Children, Youth, and Families*, 39.

46. House Select Committee on Children, Youth, and Families, *Diversity and Strength of American Families*, 99th Cong., 2nd sess., 1986, 72.

47. House Committee on Small Business, *Estate Tax Reform and the Family Business*, 104th Cong., 1st sess., 1995, 34.

48. House Select Committee on Children, Youth, and Families, *Reclaiming the Tax Code for American Families*, 102nd Cong., 1st sess., 1991, 8. Also see statement of Representative Scott Klug (R-WI) also echoing "family values" transmission as the rationale for tax reform, House Select Committee on Children, Youth, and Families, *Reclaiming the Tax Code for American Families*, 11–12.

49. For methodology on collection and coding of Bill Sponsorship and Committee Hearings, see the Appendix. Tests of independence reveal significant differences between the two parties in their use of Hearth or Soul principles when (a) sponsoring bills (Pearson's chi-square $= 229.6$, $p = .000$) and (b) referring to family examples in committee hearings (Pearson's chi-square $= 382.1$, $p = .000$).

50. Barbara Bennett Woodhouse, *Hidden in Plain Sight: The Tragedy of Children's Rights from Ben Franklin to Lionel Tate* (Princeton, NJ: Princeton University Press, 2008). Also see "A Public Role in the Private Family: The Parental Rights and Responsibilities Act and the Politics of Child Protection and Education," *Ohio State Law Journal* 57 (1996): 393.

51. I coded Congress members' references during committee hearings dually for policy issues and policy goals when referring to real-life family examples. The assumption is that members will reference issues that are of concern to them and use family cases as examples of those policy concerns. As mentioned, these references are coded twice. First, they are coded as referencing a Hearth or Soul family ideology (Soul references are those that stress changes in family attitudes and morals as desirable policy goals, and Hearth references are those that emphasize a family's economic capacity as policy end). Second, references are also coded separately on the basis of the policy issue addressed: issues of family's morality and biology are coded as ascriptive (or morality) policy issues, those pertaining to family's autonomy are coded as autonomy issues, those relating to family's economic well-being are coded as welfare, and those addressing behavioral aspects of family seen as vital to public/national interest are coded as regulation.

52. For description of criteria and method used for bill sample selection, see Table 19 and accompanying text in the Appendix (section entitled "Bill Sponsorship and Cosponsorship: Methodology").

53. Senate Subcommittee on Social Security and Family Policy, Committee on Finance, *Building Assets for Low-Income Families*, 109th Cong., 1st sess., 2005, 5–6.

54. As Senator Santorum asserted, "Families where assets are owned, children do better in school, voting participation increases, and family stability improves." Ibid., 157.

Chapter 5

1. On the rightward turn in late twentieth-century politics and the emergence and significance of the New Right, see Dan T. Carter, *The Politics of Rage: George Wallace, the Origins of New Conservatism, and the Transformation of American Politics* (Baton Rouge: Louisiana State University Press, 1995); Donald T. Critchlow, *The Conservative Ascendency: How the GOP Right Made Political History* (Cambridge, MA: Harvard University Press, 2007); Mathew D. Lassiter, *The Silent Majority: Suburban Politics in the Sunbelt South* (Princeton, NJ: Princeton University Press, 2006); Kim Phillips-Fein, *Invisible Hands: The Making of the Conservative Movement from the New Deal to Ronald Reagan* (New York: Norton, 2009); Daniel J. Galvin, *Presidential Party Building: Dwight D. Eisenhower to George W. Bush* (Princeton, NJ: Princeton University Press, 2010); Barbara Sinclair, *Party Wars: Polarization and the Politics of National Policy Making* (Norman: University of Oklahoma Press, 2006); Dan Balz and Ronald Brownstein, *Storming the Gates: Protest Politics and the Republican Revival* (Boston: Little, Brown, 1996); Andrew E. Busch, *Reagan's Victory: The Presidential Election of 1980 and the Rise of the Right* (Lawrence: University of Kansas Press, 2005); William F. Connelly Jr. and John J. Pitney Jr., *Congress' Permanent Minority? Republicans in the U.S. House* (Lanham, MD: Rowman & Littlefield, 1994); Lisa McGirr, *Suburban Warriors: The Origins of the New American Right* (Princeton, NJ: Princeton University Press, 2001).

2. See Geoffrey Kabaservice, *Rule and Ruin: The Downfall of Moderation and the Destruction of the Republican Party* (New York: Oxford University Press, 2012).

3. Daniel DiSalvo, *Engines of Change: Party Factions in American Politics, 1868–2010* (New York: Oxford University Press, 2012), 16, 104–105, 136–140.

4. Ibid., 104–105.

5. On the impact of suburbs on late twentieth-century Democratic Party realignment, see Lily Geismer, *Don't Blame Us: Suburban Liberals and the Transformation of the Democratic Party* (Princeton, NJ: Princeton University Press, 2014).

6. Byron E. Shafer, *Two Majorities and the Puzzle of Modern American Politics* (Lawrence: Kansas University Press, 2003), 161.

7. Ibid., 161.

8. James T. Patterson, *Grand Expectations: The United States, 1945–1974* (New York: Oxford University Press, 1996).

9. Ibid., 15.

10. Shafer, *Two Majorities*, 162, 176–178; also Robert Self, *All in the Family: The Realignment of American Democracy* (New York: Hill and Wang, 2012), chap. 11.

11. DiSalvo, *Engines of Change*, 16, 82–84. On reforms in Congress in the 1970s instituted by the more liberal, New Politics Democrats, see John H. Aldrich and David Rhode, "The Logic of Conditional Party Government," in *Congress Reconsidered*, ed. Lawrence C. Dodd and Bruce I. Oppenheimer, 7th ed. (Washington, DC: Congressional Quarterly Press, 2000), 275–277.

12. Shafer, *Two Majorities*, 87; Nolan McCarty, Keith Poole, and Howard Rosenthal, *Polarized America: The Dance of Ideology and Unequal Riches* (Cambridge, MA: MIT Press, 2006), figs. 1.2, 1.3 on 8, 9.

13. On the introduction of "value-based issues" into late twentieth-century party politics, see Geoffrey Layman, *The Great Divide: Religious and Cultural Conflict in American Party Politics* (New York: Columbia University Press, 2001); Ted G. Jelen, "Religion and Public Opinion in the 1990s: An Empirical Overview," in *Understanding Public Opinion*, ed. Barbara Norrander and Clyde Wilcox (Washington, DC: CQ Press, 1997).

14. DiSalvo, *Engines of Change*, 14, 50–51. The support of Democratic welfare policies by southerners in Congress was qualified. Southern support long depended on local control of welfare benefits. Local control over welfare benefits allowed them to be used to maintain a system of racial and (class) hierarchical paternalism, allowing white planter elite control over black and poor white agricultural workers. See Lee J. Alston and Joseph P. Ferrie, *Southern Paternalism and the American Welfare State: Economics, Politics, and Institutions in the South, 1865–1965* (New York: Cambridge University Press, 1999), chap. 1; also Nicole Mellow, *The State of Disunion* (Baltimore: Johns Hopkins University Press, 2008), 107–109.

15. Layman, *The Great Divide*, 43.

16. Shafer, *Two Majorities*, 176; ending prayer in schools: *Engel v. Vitale*, 370 U.S. 421 (1962); *Abington School District v. Schempp* and *Murray v. Curlett*, 374 U.S. 203 (1963) and legalizing abortion: *Roe v. Wade*, 410 U.S. 113 (1973). See James Guth, John C. Green, Corwin Smidt, Lyman Kellstedt, and Margaret Poloma, "American Politics—The Bully Pulpit: The Politics of Protestant Clergy," *American Political Science Review* 92, no. 3 (1998): 707.

17. Shafer, *Two Majorities*, 176.

18. Jerome L. Himmelstein, "The New Right," in *The New Christian Right: Mobilization and Legitimation*, ed. Robert C. Liebman, Robert Wuthnow, James L. Guth, et al. (Hawthorne, NY: Aldine, 1983); Duane M. Oldfield, *The Right and the Righteous: The Christian Right Confronts the Republican Party* (Lanham, MD: Rowman & Littlefield, 1997).

19. Scholars have pointed to multiple events in the 1980s and 1990s to signal the increasing southernization of the late twentieth-century Republican Party and of American politics

in general. During the Reagan administration, for instance, despite widespread cutbacks to welfare programs serving the Northeast and Northwest, Boll Weevil southerners in Congress won several concessions such as preserving large public works in the South. Moreover, the landslide defeat of Democratic presidential candidate Walter Mondale in 1984 led to the rightward shift even within the Democratic Party, away from the New Left and closer to the South-dominated (political) center, as seen in the subsequent formation of (southern) Blue Dog Democrats into the Democratic Leadership Council. In the mid-term elections of 1994, the Democratic Party for the first time lost their southern majority in Congress, and after a fifty-year gap, Republicans were finally able to capture the House of Representatives, now under southern Republican leadership. Party changes (from Democratic to Republican) in southern presidential voting patterns that had begun in 1980 with the election of Reagan now finally translated into southern support for the GOP also in congressional elections, transforming the South into the most reliable Republican region thereafter. This ensured that the "distinctive form" of "southern conservatism" increasingly "would come to dominate the GOP." See, for example, Kabaservice, *Rule and Ruin*, 379–380.

20. Shafer, *Two Majorities*, 31.

21. House Select Committee on Children, Youth, and Families, *AIDS and Teenagers: Emerging Issues*, 100th Cong., 1st sess., 1987, 128–130.

22. Statement of Representative Frank Wolf, House Select Committee on Children, Youth, and Families, *Children, Youth, and Families: Beginning the Assessment*, 98th Cong., 1st sess., 1983, 8.

23. Opening Statement of Representative Thomas J. Bliley Jr., House Select Committee on Children, Youth, and Families, *Divorce: The Impact on Children and Families*, 99th Cong., 2nd sess., 1986, 6.

24. Republican Party Platform of 1980, *American Presidency Project* (paragraph 14).

25. Republican Party Platform of 1980, *American Presidency Project* (paragraph 245).

26. Self, *All in the Family*, 309–310.

27. Within prevailing scholarship, there is debate over the cultural distinctiveness of the modern South. For interpretations stressing the regional convergence of the South in the late twentieth century, see, for example, Bruce Schulman, *From Cotton Belt to Sunbelt: Federal Policy, Economic Development, and the Transformation of the South, 1938–1980* (New York: Oxford University Press, 1991); John Egerton, *The Americanization of Dixie: The Southernization of America* (New York: Harper's Magazine Press, 1974). See, in opposition to this interpretation, Byron Shafer and Richard Johnston, *The End of Southern Exceptionalism: Class, Race, and Partisan Change in the Postwar South* (Cambridge, MA: Harvard University Press, 2009).

28. Ann Markusen, *Regions: The Economics and Politics of Territory* (Totowa, NJ: Rowman & Littlefield, 1987); J. S. Hurlbert, "The Southern Region: A Test of the Hypothesis of Cultural Distinctiveness," *Sociological Quarterly* 30 (1989): 245–266.

29. Alan Abramowitz, "Ideological Realignment and the Nationalization of Southern Politics," in *Perspectives on the American South: An Annual Review of Society, Politics and Culture*, vol. 1, ed. Merle Black and John Shelton Reed (New York: Gordon & Breach, 1981), 83–106.

30. Richard Gray, *Writing the South: Ideas of an American Region* (New York: Cambridge University Press, 1986), 230–231, cited in Gratham, *The South in Modern America*, 312.

31. John Shelton Reed, "The South: What Is It? Where Is It?" in *The South for New Southerners*, ed. Paul D. Escott and David R. Goldfield (Chapel Hill: University of North Carolina Press, 1991), 18–41; see also John Shelton Reed, *Southerners: The Social Psychology of Sectionalism* (Chapel Hill: University of North Carolina Press, 1983); also Grantham, *The South in Modern America*, 313; Earl Black and Merle Black, *Politics and Society in the South* (Cambridge, MA: Harvard University Press, 1987), 219–229. Charles P. Roland uses southern literary works to identify aspects of southern culture that remain distinctive to the region. He writes, "Southern writers place an unusual emphasis on the very points emphasized in southern life. These are family, history, race, religion, a sense of place, of concreteness and the imperfectability of man. One would never say of Faulkner what C. Vann Woodward has said of the work of (non-southerner) Ernest Hemingway: that is, 'a Hemingway hero with a grandfather is inconceivable'"; "The Ever-Vanishing South," *Journal of Southern History* 48 (1982): 12.

32. Sean P. Cunningham, *American Politics in the Postwar Sunbelt: Conservative Growth in a Battleground Region* (New York: Cambridge University Press, 2014), 162–174; Grantham, *The South in Modern America*, 315. Also see Samuel S. Hill, "Religion," in *Encyclopedia of Southern Culture*, ed. Charles Reagan and William Ferris (Chapel Hill: University of North Carolina Press, 1989), 1269–1331. It need be noted that the (evangelical-leaning) religious beliefs and practices of southerners were not much varied from other Americans in previous periods in history. For instance, in the first half of the nineteenth century, through a period described as "The Second Awakening," revivalism and evangelical Protestantism flourished in the North, in places such as upstate New York, the so-called burned-over district. See Whitney Cross, *The Burned-Over District: The Social and Intellectual History of Enthusiastic Religion in Western New York, 1800–1850* (Ithaca, NY: Cornell University Press, 1982). During the second half of the century, however, the North moved toward a more pluralistic culture in the wake of massive influxes of immigrants and attendant secularization, while the continuing pervasiveness and intensity of religion in the South now distinguishes it from the North.

33. Samuel S. Hill, "The South's Culture-Protestantism," *Christian Century* 79 (1962): 1094–1096.

34. Roland, *Ever-Vanishing South*, 10.

35. See Black and Black, *Politics and Society*, 213–231, as suggesting this; more generally on the link between southern-based evangelicalism and support for conservative cultural policies, see Jeffrey M. Stonecash and Mark D. Brewer, *Split: Class and Cultural Divides in American Politics* (Washington, DC: CQ Press, 2007), 153–154. For a discussion of the continuing strain of anti-institutionalism and individualism within the culture of the Sunbelt, despite its otherwise predicted cultural convergence with the non-South, see John S. Reed, "Social Orientations: New South or No South? Regional Culture in 2036," in *The South Moves into Its Future: Studies in the Analysis and Prediction of Social Change*, ed. Joseph S. Himes (Tuscaloosa: University of Alabama Press, 1991).

36. Human misery and depravity within evangelical theology are based on the classical Christian doctrine of original sin, wherein sin is a more fundamental human condition than social conditioning or even ignorance. Sin is viewed as second nature to all humans, their first nature being the image of God. The doctrine of sin and inherited depravity is the foundation of evangelical teaching about salvation—requiring God's mercy and grace, which is received by personal effort, through repentance and faith. See Roger E. Olson, *The Westminster*

Handbook to Evangelical Theology (Louisville, KY: Westminster John Knox Press, 2004), 267–268.

37. Chairman Jeremiah Denton (R-AL), Senate Subcommittee on Family and Human Services of the Committee on Labor and Human Resources, *Forum for Families: Quality of American Family Life*, 98th Cong., 1st sess., 1983, 1.

38. Senate Subcommittee on Family and Human Services, *Forum for Families*, 61–63.

39. Fifty percent of family examples that mentioned religion were from the South, 31 percent were referred to by southern legislators (more than any other regional delegation), and almost 50 percent of Republican-sponsored family cases made reference to religion compared to 61 percent of Democratic family cases that did not. Chi-square for Party of Sponsoring Legislator * Religion Mentioned = 4.12 ($p = .042^*$), chi-square of Family's Region of Residence * Religion Mentioned = 9.14 ($p = .027^*$). Column proportions tests are positive for the three pairs of variables. Results are based on two-sided tests with a significance level of .05.

40. Many evangelical-minded Republicans presented poverty and social inequality, for example, as natural, if unfortunate, aspects of society, as Senator Denton (R-AL) claimed, "The Bible tells us that the poor will always be with us." Hence, social policies toward the poor, while justified by compassion for one's fellow humans, were viewed skeptically in terms of their possible successful outcome. Senate Subcommittee on Aging, Family, and Human Services of the Committee on Labor and Human Resources, *Fighting Poverty: Private Initiatives and Public Assistance,* 97th Cong., 1st sess., 1981, 2.

41. Carter, *Politics of Rage*; Lowndes, *From New Deal to New Right.*

42. Republican leaders did not renounce Jerry Falwell in 1985, for instance, when he publicly defended the apartheid system of South Africa's racist white regime. See Kabaservice, *Rule and Ruin*, 369.

43. For example, Lowndes, *From the New Deal to the New Right*; Carter, *From George Wallace to Newt Gingrich*; Earl Black and Merle Black, *The Rise of the Southern Republicans* (Cambridge, MA: Harvard University Press, 2003); Joseph A. Aistrup, *The Southern Strategy Revisited: Republican Top-Down Advancement in the South* (Lexington: University of Kentucky Press, 1996); Thomas B. Edsall and Mary D. Edsall, *Chain Reaction: The Impact of Race, Rights, and Taxes on American Politics* (New York: Norton, 1992).

44. Gwendoline Alphonso, "From Need to Hope: The American Family and Poverty in Partisan Discourse," *Journal of Policy History* 27, no. 4 (2015): 592–635.

45. House Select Committee on Children, Youth, and Families, *The Diversity and Strength of American Families*, 99th Cong., 2nd sess., 1986, 39.

46. John McAdoo, PhD, Associate Professor, School of Social Work and Community Planning, University of Maryland, Baltimore, Maryland, House Select Committee on Children, Youth, and Families, *Paternal Absence and Fathers' Roles*, 98th Cong., 1st sess., 1983, 91–93.

47. Dan Coats, House Select Committee on Children, Youth, and Families, *Diversity and Strength of American Families*, 118.

48. House Committee on Government Reform, *Black Men and Boys in the District of Columbia and Their Impact on the Future of the Black Family*, 108th Cong., 1st sess., 2003, 80.

49. Statement of William P. Wilson, MD, Professor of Psychiatry, Duke University Medical Center, Durham, North Carolina, House Select Committee on Children, Youth, and Families, *Paternal Absence and Fathers' Roles*, 98th Cong., 1st sess., 1983, 14.

50. Statement of William P. Wilson, MD, Professor of Psychiatry, Duke University Medical Center, Durham, North Carolina, House Select Committee on Children, Youth, and Families, *Paternal Absence*, 14.

51. Carter, *Politics of Rage*, 455–456.

52. Naomi Cahn and June Carbone, *Red v. Blue Families: Legal Polarization and the Creation of Culture* (New York: Oxford University Press, 2010).

53. Frank Keating, Statement, Senate Subcommittee on Children and Families of the Committee on Health, Education, Labor, and Pensions, *Healthy Marriage: Why We Should Promote It? Examining How to Promote a Healthy Marriage, Focusing on the Healthy Marriage Initiative, the Temporary Assistance to Needy Families Program, and Discouraging Teen Pregnancy*, 108th Cong., 2nd sess., 2004, 35–36.

54. Ibid., 38.

55. Chi-square statistic for "religiosity mentioned" was 4.21, $p = .042$; chi-square for "values mentioned" $= 22.8$, $p = .000$; chi-square for "values imparted" $= 61.1$, $p = .000$; chi-square for "mention of abortion" $= 15.9$, $p = .000$.

56. See previous discussion on traditional family practices and tough love as valued in Soul family approaches, Figures 8 and 1 (and accompanying text) in Chapter 1 and Introduction respectively.

57. Clifton P. Flynn, "Regional Differences in Attitudes Towards Corporal Punishment," *Journal of Marriage and the Family* 56 (1994): 314–324.

58. See Jim DeMint's (R-SC) statement in the text that accompanies note 60 of this chapter.

59. Senate Subcommittee on Children and Families of the Committee on Labor and Human Resources, *Youth Violence: On Examining the Role of the Federal Government and Non-Government Organizations in Establishing Solutions for Combating Juvenile Crime*, 104th Cong., 2nd sess., 1996, 3.

60. House Subcommittee on Early Childhood, Youth, and Families of the Committee on Education and Workforce, *School Safety, Discipline, and IDEA*, 106th Cong., 1st sess., 1999, 4.

61. House Subcommittee on Early Childhood, Youth, and Families of the Committee on Education and Workforce, *School Violence: Views of Students and The Community*, 106th Cong., 1st sess., 1999, 76.

62. House Select Committee on Children, Youth, and Families, *Child Care: Beginning a National Initiative*, 98th Cong., 2nd sess., 1984, 65.

63. See statement of Julie Matthaei, Democratic witness, note 42 in Chapter 4 and accompanying text.

64. For example, on reproductive choice, in vitro fertilization, blurred parental boundaries, and the falsity of a distinction between biological and nurturing parenthood, see Bruce Morrison's (D-CT) remarks while questioning witness Richard Doreflinger, Assistant Director, Office for Pro-Life Activities, National Conference of Catholic Bishops: "I happen to be adopted myself so I speak with some experience on this question—isn't it the same circumstance, the separation of biological parenthood from nurturing parenthood? . . . Isn't that a false issue that you're raising . . . that having different biological parenthood is an insurmountable barrier?"; House Select Committee on Children, Youth, and Families, *Alternative Reproductive Technologies: Implications for Children and Families*, 100th Cong., 1st sess., 1987, 50. Also see the example of Herb and Ginger Davis, Silver Spring, Maryland, as a successful blended (step) family also devoted to the "idea of a family," illustrating that marital choice

leading to nontraditional arrangements can be just as successful for childrearing than tradi-tional choices; House Select Committee on Children, Youth, and Families, *Diversity and Strength of American Families*, 6–11.

65. House Select Committee on Children, Youth, and Families, *Divorce*, 6.

66. On postmaterial psychological values privileging choice and self-expression as replac-ing previous materialist concerns over purely economic and material security in advanced industrial Western democracies, see Ronald Inglehart, *The Silent Revolution: Changing Val-ues and Political Styles Among Western Publics* (Princeton, NJ: Princeton University Press, 1997).

67. House Select Committee on Children, Youth, and Families, *The New Unemployed: Long-Term Consequences for Their Families*, 98th Cong., 2nd sess., 1984, 10; on the importance of parent-child open communication and crises management services in the face of the cur-rent "success-oriented" society where "a lot of children . . . struggl[e] to deal with th[e] striv-ing for success," see the testimony of Elaine DiFigilia, from Plano, Texas, describing the conditions that led her son, Scott, to commit suicide; House Select Committee on Children, Youth, and Families, *Teenagers in Crisis: Issues and Programs*, 98th Cong., 1st sess., 1983, 48–51. On the Democratic position of poverty as an "environmental pressure" in terms of "inad-equate housing or small housing . . . [creating] the tensions of many people living together under the same roof . . . and the isolation of poor (urban) families," without opportunities to diffuse family tensions, see George Miller (D-CA) and witness testimony, House Select Com-mittee on Children, Youth, and Families, *Children and Families in Poverty*, 37.

68. House Select Committee on Children, Youth, and Families, *Alcohol Abuse and Its Implications for Families*, 99th Cong., 1st sess., 1985, 9.

69. See Dan Marriott (R-UT), House Select Committee on Children, Youth, and Fami-lies, *Violence and Abuse in American Families*, 98th Cong., 2nd sess., 1984, 3; Frank Wolf (R-VA), House Select Committee on Children, Youth, and Families, *Child Victims of Exploita-tion*, 99th Cong., 1st sess., 1985, 44, and also his remarks in contrast to Democratic-Hearth advocate, Elizabeth Holtzman (D-NY), in House Select Committee on Children, Youth, and Families, *Women, Violence and the Law*, 100th Cong., 1st sess., 1987, 105–106.

70. Mellow, *State of Disunion*, 137.

71. Cahn and Carbone, *Red v. Blue Families*, 119.

72. Ibid., 73.

73. House Select Committee on Children, Youth, and Families, *Children and Families in the South: Trends in Health Care, Family Services, and the Rural Economy*, 99th Cong., 1st sess., 1986, 84–89.

74. House Select Committee, *Children and Families in the South*, 80.

75. Senate Subcommittee on Family and Human Services of the Committee on Labor and Human Resources, *Forum for Families: Quality of American Family Life*, 98th Cong., 1st sess., 1983.

76. House Select Committee on Children, Youth, and Families, *Double Duty: Caring for Children and the Elderly*, 100th Cong., 2nd sess., 1988, 111–112.

77. House Select Committee on Children, Youth, and Families, *Native American Children, Youth, and Families, Part 1*, 99th Cong., 2nd sess., 1986, 54.

78. Fifty percent of the Republican family cases receiving welfare were from the South versus 26 percent of Democratic family cases on welfare. Many more Democratic families re-ceiving welfare were from the Northeast.

79. The chi-square statistic for income and party is 24.03, $p = .000$; chi-square for father's employment and party = 19.4, $p = .000$; and chi-square for mother's employment and party = 22.8, $p = .000$.

80. Coding of regions aggregates census divisions: where North = census divisions of New England, Middle Atlantic, and East North Central; South = whole of census region of South (i.e., divisions of South Atlantic, East, and West South Central); West = Mountain and West North Central divisions; and Pacific = Pacific division. See http://www.census.gov/geo/www /us_regdiv.pdf. For a similar aggregation also analyzing the significance of region to partisan development, albeit without the inclusion of District of Columbia, Hawaii, or Alaska, see Mellow, *State of Disunion*, 26–27. The Pearson's chi-square statistic of "family region" with "party" was 13.8, $p = .003$. Further significance tests reveal that a significantly larger proportion of Republican positive rather than negative case examples came from the Rocky Mountain western states, whereas for those Republican family cases from the North, a significantly larger proportion were used as negative rather than positive cases, illustrating pathologies for policy to correct rather than affirming virtues for policy to encourage. Interestingly, Democrats appear to use family cases from all regions more evenly as both positive and negative illustrations of policy concerns; no significant differences were found between positive and negative cases for Democrats, for family cases from any of the four regions.

81. For example, feminist scholars have long highlighted the gendered, racial, and cultural qualities of social policies instituted during the Progressive Era; see Gwendolyn Mink, *Wages of Motherhood: Inequality in the Welfare State, 1917–1942* (Ithaca, NY: Cornell University Press, 1995); also "The Lady and the Tramp: Gender, Race, and the Origins of the American Welfare State," in *Women, the State, and Welfare,* ed. Linda Gordon (Madison: University of Wisconsin Press, 1990); Mimi Abramovitz, *Regulating the Lives of Women: Social Welfare Policy from Colonial Times to the Present* (Boston: South End Press, 1988); Barbara Nelson, "The Gender, Race, and Class Origins of Early Welfare Policy and the Welfare State: A Comparison of Workmen's Compensation and Mother's Aid," in *Women, Politics, and Change,* ed. Louise A. Tilly and Patricia Gurin (New York: Russell Sage Foundation, 1990), 413–435.

Conclusion

1. Desmond S. King and Rogers M. Smith, "'Without Regard to Race': Critical Ideational Development in Modern American Politics," *Journal of Politics* 76, no. 4 (2014): 958–971; also see Joseph E. Lowndes, *From the New Deal to the New Right: Race and the Origins of Modern Conservatism* (New Haven, CT: Yale University Press, 2008), 157.

2. King and Smith, *Journal of Politics,* 967.

3. See, for example, Gwendoline Alphonso, "From Need to Hope: The American Family and Poverty in Partisan Discourse," *Journal of Policy History* 27, no. 4 (2015): 592–635, Fig. 7.

4. Alphonso, "From Need to Hope."

5. Holly Allen, *Forgotten Men and Fallen Women: The Cultural Politics of New Deal Narratives* (Ithaca, NY: Cornell University Press, 2015), 11–13.

Appendix

1. Majorie Randon Hershey, *Party Politics in America,* 15th ed. (Boston: Pearson, 2013), 202. Within their platforms, parties conventionally characterize their planks as sets of collective beliefs, such as "We, as Democrats believe . . ." or "Republicans pledge that. . . ." Thus, scholars of party platforms view the platform as "the only statement of policy made with

authority on behalf of the whole party," unlike, for instance, addresses and letters by individual party leaders that illustrate those members' personal policy position. Ian Budge and Dennis Farlie, *Voting and Party Competition* (London: Wiley, 1977); see also Adam Silver, "The Prevalence of Economic Issues Versus Cultural Issues in 19th Century American State and National Party Platforms," Paper presented at the Policy History Conference, St. Louis, MO, May 29-June 1, 2008.

2. Gerald M. Pomper, "Party Responsibility and the Future of American Democracy," in *American Political Parties: Decline or Resurgence?* ed. Jeffrey E. Cohen, Richard Fleisher, and Paul Kantor (Washington, DC: CQ Press, 2001), 170–172.

3. Republican Party Platform of 1988, Woolley and Peters, *American Presidency Project* (paragraph 30).

4. For the most part, each platform paragraph focuses on a central policy ideal or else invokes one policy ideal to bolster another. For other studies that code and analyze party platforms, see John Gerring, *Party Ideologies in America, 1828-1996* (New York: Cambridge University Press, 1998); Christina Wolbrecht, *The Politics of Women's Rights: Parties, Positions, and Change* (Princeton, NJ: Princeton University Press, 2001), chap. 1; and Edward G. Carmines and James A. Stimson, *Issue Evolution: Race and the Transformation of American Politics* (Princeton, NJ: Princeton University Press, 1989).

5. Bills merely designating special days (such as Mother's Day) or amending specific family legislation without mentioning a position in favor or against the policy were excluded. Thus, I included bills to "increase" or "limit" widows' pensions but excluded those that purported to "amend" such pension legislation without expressing a preference in favor or against.

6. Full title: Senate Subcommittee on Children and Families of the Committee on Health, Education, Labor, and Pensions, *Healthy Marriage: What Is It and Why Should We Promote It?* 108th Cong., 2nd sess., 2004.

7. Ibid., 3.

8. Statement of Winston Graham and Saundra Corley, Senate Subcommittee of the Committee on Appropriations, *Potential for Marriage Development Accounts in the District of Columbia*, 109th Cong., 1st sess., 2005, 66–67.

Index

146–47, 149–52, 157, 224n39; gender and, 54, 56, 65, 92–93, 107; New Right on, 143, 144, 172; parental responsibility for, 106–8, 115, 118, 151; partisan reversal, 30–31, 38, 44, 140; in party platforms, 30, 38, 40, 44, 121; positive-state approach and, 40, 122; race and, 45, 52, 60–61, 62, 70, 73, 170; regulation policy, 92–93, 211n61; religion and, 124, 143, 145–46, 149; sex and sexuality, 92–93, 107, 211n61; southern culture, 75, 145, 169; southern Democrats and, 70, 98, 100, 114, 115. *See also* New Right; secular-humanist values; Soul family ideal; traditional family values

moral values, family demographic transitions associated with declining, 155; family policy typology and, 66–67; industrialization and, 50, 156; New Right and, 143, 172; policy responses, 131–34; sex and sexuality, 60–64. *See also* economic deprivation, family demographic transition associated with; family demographic transitions

Morone, James, 18

Morris, John, 154–55

mothers and mother role, 4, 101, 205n79; in family cases, 107–8, 114–15, 117, 118, 152–53; fathers, 85, 105–6, 147–48, 214n98; during late twentieth-century period, 126; maternalist reform, 56–57, 214n102; responsibility of, 84–85, 106–8, 115, 117–18; widowed, 107, 117, 214n110. *See also* children; parental responsibility

Moyers, Bill, 148

Moynihan, Daniel Patrick, 216n4

nationalism, 30, 192n25

National Pro-Family Coalition, 122

national regulation. *See* regulation policy; welfare policy

national republicanism, 29, 191n12

National Review (magazine), 141

negative state support, 3, 40, 73, 138. *See also* positive state opposition; Soul family ideal

Negro Family, The: The Case for National Action (Moynihan Report, 1964), 216n4

neoliberal value, 3, 170, 193n36; in Democratic Party Platform, 42–43; individualism and, 33–35, 88, 93; New Right and, 144, 145–46; positive state opposition and, 58, 88, 95, 100, 123–24, 145–46; religion and, 145–46; in Republican Party Platforms, 32–34, 35, 37–38, 39–41, 43, 196n91; southernization and, 11, 145–46, 163; traditional values associated with, 37–38, 144. *See also* market-centered ideology; traditional family values

New Christian Right. *See* New Right

New Deal, 35, 88, 172; family prominence, 32, 102; Hearth ideals, 52–53; opposition, 16, 22, 27, 31, 90, 100; southern Democrats and, 16, 96. *See also* Progressive Era (1900–1932); welfare policy

New Left (New Politics Democrats), 19, 142, 151

New Right, 1, 16, 19, 141–49; emergence of, 141–42; evangelical language, 147; race and, 145, 147–49, 224n42. *See also* religion; southernization; traditional family values

non-nuclear family. *See* family demographic transitions

North, the, 11, 19; divorce rates, 76; family demographic transitions in, 74–75, 150, 156, 176; marriage rates, 76, 150; positive and negative family cases, 77–78; during Progressive Era, 70, 73–78; secular-humanist family values, 125. *See also* sectionalism; South

Norton, Eleanor, 148

nostalgia, 172

nuclear family, 40, 82, 84; "carrot-and-stick" policies to foster, 85–86; during late twentieth-century period, 126–27, 131; during post–World War II period, 85–86, 102, 114, 115, 117–20. *See also* family demographic transitions; family structure; marriage; traditional family values

Obama, Barack, 40, 173, 195n82

Obama, Michelle, 22–23

199n15; community-based welfare and, 86, 102–3, 108, 111, 122, 221n14; health care, 94–95; seen as effective, 108, 111, 122; seen as inadequate, 86, 91. *See also* welfare policy
Progressive Era (1900–1932), 2, 3, 4, 50–81, 191n10, 201n39, 204n68, 206n87; ascription policy, 13, 64–72, 135, 203n66; autonomy policy, 58, 66–73, 87, 135, 201n36, 203n66; bill (co)sponsorship, 44–48, 91, 197n101, 211n47; Democratic Party Platforms, 24–31, 48–49, 192nn20, 23, 24; egalitarian family structure, 51, 55–56, 65, 80, 203n65; family as state/local issue during, 21, 36, 52–53; family demographic transitions, 19, 50–51, 53, 54–55, 60–64, 66–67, 73–81; family policy typology, 58–59, 64–73, 87, 201n36, 203nn64, 66; gender and, 19, 167; income, 51, 57, 58–59, 79, 201n39; industrialization effects, 50–51; late twentieth-century period resemblance, 168–69; national republicanism, 29, 191n12; race, 19, 60–64, 68, 70, 76, 80, 116, 167, 171; regulation policy, 58, 64, 66–75, 203n66; Republican Party Platforms, 24–31, 48–49, 191n12, 191n15, 192n16, 192n25; sex and sexuality, 59–64; social progressive reform movement, 28–29, 31, 191n11; southern Democrats and, 16, 70, 73, 76, 169; woman suffrage, 19, 53–59. *See also* Democratic-Soul alignment; Hearth family ideal; late twentieth-century period to the present (1968–2012); post–World War II period (1945–55); Republican-Hearth alignment; sectionalism; Soul family ideal; welfare policy
prostitution, 92–93, 211n61
public/private spheres (separate-spheres ideology), 54–55, 56–57, 65, 128. *See also* gender
public school. *See* compulsory schooling
Purtell, William, 87

Rabaut, Louis, 105
race, 2, 166–68; black families, 122, 147–49; civil rights movement, 99, 100, 141, 147;

colorblind principles, 167, 168; in family cases, 59, 78, 80, 114–17, 118, 149; family demographics, 79–80, 114–15, 116–17, 148–49; Hearth ideal and, 63, 148, 171; during late twentieth-century period, 126, 145, 146, 149, 159; marriage and, 127, 148; moral values and, 45, 52, 60–61, 62, 70, 73, 170; New Right and, 145, 147–49, 224n42; during post–World War II period, 98–99, 100, 114–15, 116–18, 167; during Progressive Era, 19, 60–64, 68, 70, 76, 80, 116, 167, 171; religion and, 146; segregation, 98–99, 147; slavery, 59–60, 62, 203n57; Soul ideal and, 63, 70, 147, 149, 167–68, 170; southernization and, 126, 145, 146–49; traditional family values and, 30–31, 59, 60–61, 147–49; Trump campaign, 172–73; welfare and, 63–64, 87, 122, 149. *See also* ascription policy; miscegenation; South, race and; southern Democrats, race and; white supremacy
Reagan, Nancy, 146
Reagan, Ronald, 121, 143, 147, 210n41, 216n3, 222n19; New Right emergence and, 141–42
redistributionist values, 6, 42, 43, 57, 100. *See also* material/distribution benefits; welfare policy
Red v. Blue Families: Legal Polarization and the Creation of Culture (Cahn and Carbone), 130–31
reform, in Progressive Era, 199n15; by maternalists, 56–57, 214n102; social progressive reform movement, 28–29, 31, 52, 191n11, 199n17
regionalism. *See* sectionalism
regulation of family issues, national. *See* positive state opposition; welfare policy
regulation of family issues, state/local, 59, 90, 100; during Progressive Era, 21, 31, 36, 52–53; separate-spheres ideology, 54–55, 56–57, 65, 128, 151. *See also* autonomy policy; positive state support, by Soul advocates; Soul family ideal

regulation policy, 14, 170, 203n64; in committee hearings, 58, 64, 66–73, 135–36,
137, 203n66; defined, 66–67; electoral
consensus on expansion, 88–89; health
care, 91–92, 94–95; housing and, 94, 95,
212n68; during late twentieth-century
period, 121, 122–24, 134–38, 140, 168; morality legislation, 92–93, 211n61; parental
responsibility and, 105; during post–World
War II period, 82, 86, 90–95, 100–101,
134–35; during Progressive Era, 58, 64,
66–75, 203n66; for veterans' families,
92, 94, 212n68; wage legislation, 111–13;
welfare policy and, 102, 105. See also
ascription policy; autonomy policy; New
Deal; welfare policy
religion, 39, 109, 124, 223n36; evangelical
Protestantism, 143, 145–47, 223n32; in
family cases, 98, 110, 146–47, 149–50,
224n39; race and, 146; southernization
and, 145–47, 157, 224nn39, 40; teen pregnancies and, 130. See also New Right
reproductive rights, 21, 225n64; abortion, 30,
122, 143, 156
Republican-Hearth alignment, 31, 51–52,
53, 67–81; ascription policy, 72; autonomy
policy, 68, 72; family demographics, 73–80;
regulation policy, 67, 68, 69, 72; sectionalism and, 70, 72–73, 77–81; welfare policy,
67, 68, 69, 72. See also Democratic-Soul
alignment; Hearth family ideal; Progressive Era (1900–1932); Republican-Soul
alignment
Republican Party, 22, 98; New Right emergence, 141–42; post–World War II coalition composition, 89
Republican Party Platform, family prominence data, 18–19; Hearth values, 24–28,
31, 33, 36; late twentieth century to present, 24–28, 38–44, 48–49, 121, 144–45,
196n91; midcentury period, 22, 24–28,
31–35; 1960s, 24–28, 35–38, 194n56;
during Progressive Era, 24–31, 48–49,
191n12, 191n15, 192n16, 192n25; research
methods, 175–76; Soul values, 24–28, 37,

39–40, 43–44, 48. See also bill (co)sponsor-
ship; Democratic Party Platform, family
prominence data
Republican-Soul alignment: autonomy
policy, 93–94; core constituency, 89,
114, 116; founding of modern conservatism, 90, 210n41; framework outlined,
100–101; health care, 94–95; housing, 94,
95; late-century factional split, 123–24,
131, 140; during late twentieth-century
period, 10–11, 125–26, 133–34, 155, 167;
during post–World War II period, 83, 115,
118–20, 134–35, 167. See also Democratic-
Hearth alignment; Democratic-Soul alignment; Republican-Hearth alignment; Soul
family ideal; southernization
research methods, 175–83, 219n49; family
cases, 180–82, 203n66, 206nn87, 88,
220n51, 224n39, 227n80
Rhones, Rebecca, 153
Robertson, Pat, 143
Roddenberry, Seaborn, 62
roll call voting, 6, 45, 164, 196n93. See also
bill (co)sponsorship; committee hearings;
family cases
Roosevelt, Franklin Delano, 35–36, 88,
90–91, 172
Rosenthal, Howard, 6
rural families, 111

Santorum, Rick, 21, 139
school prayer, 143
schools, discipline in, 150–51. See also compulsory schooling
Schroeder, Patricia, 131–32
sectionalism, 51–52, 68–81, 155–63, 166, 169;
Democratic-Soul alignment, 53, 70, 71,
73, 75–81, 98; family cases and, during late
twentieth-century period, 149–50, 157–59,
161–63; partisan differential use, 69–70,
73, 76–77, 95, 115–18, 224n39; during
post–World War II period, 95, 115–18;
during Progressive Era, 68–73, 76–80,
204n68, 206n87; family demographic
transitions and, 173; during late twentieth-

tions and, 60–64, 66–67, 132–34, 140, 143, 155–56, 172; farm families and, 34, 35, 114, 170; gender roles, 153–54; learning and teaching, 134, 139, 150–51, 157; neoliberalism associated with, 37, 144; New Right and, 143–44; partisan reversal, 30–31, 38, 44, 140; in party platforms, 39–44; during post–World War II period, 101, 109–11, 113–14, 115; race and, 30–31, 59, 60–61, 147–49; regulation policy, 122–23, 170; respect and discipline, 150–51; self-sufficiency as, 131, 150, 157, 166, 170; southern family values, 10–11, 125–26, 144–45, 169, 223n31; wage legislation and, 112–13. *See also* community-based social relations; individualism value; localism value; market-centered ideology; marriage; moral values; neoliberal value; positive state opposition; secular-humanist values; self-sufficiency value; Soul family ideal
Truman, Harry S., 91, 99, 103
Trump, Donald, 172–73

unemployment, 31, 34, 154–55, 172. *See also* economic deprivation; employment; income
urban and suburban families, 111, 116

valuational concerns, 22, 190n5. *See also* moral values; secular-humanist values; Soul family ideal; traditional family values
Vann, Timothy, 146, 157
Van Sant, Thomas, 108
veterans' families, 29, 32, 45–46, 84, 85, 207n17; health care, 92; housing, 94, 212n68
Vietnam War, 142
voting: roll call, 6, 45, 164, 196n93; woman suffrage, 19, 53–59
Voting Rights Act (1965), 116
vulnerability scholarship, 23

wages. *See* income
Wallace, George C., 147

wealth, 136, 156, 170. *See also* economic deprivation; income
welfare opposition. *See* positive state opposition
welfare policy, 14, 26, 168, 169, 203n64; argument that curtailment causes deviance, 85, 90–92, 93, 102, 119; argument that expansion causes deviance, 85, 86–87, 107–8, 119; autonomy policy and, 135; child-centered, 25, 29, 30–31, 33; dependence on state objection, 86–87; emotional welfare, 103–4; health care, 91, 92; parental responsibility, 85, 86, 101, 105–9, 213n92, 214n98; in committee hearings, 28–29, 58–59, 64, 66–73, 135–36, 137, 158, 203n66; as community-based, 86, 102–3, 108, 111, 122, 221n14; defined, 66–67; Democratic-Hearth alignment, 13, 82–83; Democratic-Soul alignment, 68, 69, 70; eligibility requirements, 38, 86; emotional welfare services, 83, 86, 103–4, 117, 154; in family cases, 66–73, 96, 135, 158, 226n78; family-centered, 25, 58, 86; family demographic transitions and, 74; family structure and, 203n65; gender and, 153–54; Great Depression and, 31; hard work value, 43; health care, 63–64, 91–92, 94–95, 133; Hearth ideal: during late twentieth-century period, 134–35, 136; during post–World War II period, 13, 82–83, 86, 90–92, 94, 96, 105, 114, 120; housing, 94, 95, 212n68; juvenile delinquency, 37, 194n64; during late twentieth-century period, 121–22, 134–39, 153–54; as national priority, 88–89; nuclear family fostered by, 85, 102; parental responsibility and, 86, 101, 105–9, 138–39, 213n92, 214n98; in party platforms, 29–30, 34, 35–38, 194n51, 194n56, 196n91; during post–World War II period, 19, 82–83, 96–99, 102–5; during Progressive Era, 28–31, 52–53, 57–64, 65–73, 201n38, 203n66; race and, 63–64, 87, 122, 149; regulation policy and, 102, 105; Republican-Hearth alignment, 67, 68, 69, 72; Republicans acquiesce to, 89–90; sectionalism, during late

Acknowledgments

The book has been many years in the making, and along the way I have had the remarkable good fortune of encountering some of the most generous and talented people in the profession who have profoundly shaped its development. Any and all errors, of course, remain entirely mine.

I am grateful to Rick Valelly for his support and for including the book in the American Governance series at the University of Pennsylvania Press; to Suzanne Mettler for suggesting the connection; and to Peter Agree for his superb steering of the book from prospectus to publication. The book also benefited incalculably from the suggestions and comments of the anonymous reviewers.

I owe the greatest thanks to Julie Novkov, University of Albany, Priscilla Yamin, University of Oregon, Eileen McDonagh, Northeastern University, and Carol Nackenoff, Swarthmore College, who have gone above and beyond any professional or collegial norm to encourage and nurture the development of the book. I cannot imagine a set of scholars more willing or generous in providing feedback, constructive suggestions, and friendship, especially when it was needed the most.

At Cornell University, Richard Bensel's involvement was crucial and formative to the book's theoretical framing and methodological design. By reading the chapters in their entirety and offering brilliant insight at critical points, he helped the project find its footing. Ted Lowi inspired my decision to focus on classification of family ideals and their evolving policy configurations; his passion for asking big questions has indelibly marked my scholarship. Although deeply saddened by his passing, I take solace in the fact that scores of scholars like me continue to proudly carry his flame forward. Mary Katzenstein, Suzanne Mettler, Elizabeth Sanders, and Martin Shefter at Cornell's Department of Government, and Martha Fineman and Aziz Rana at the Cornell Law School also helped me consider the book's implications for multiple audiences and from diverse, interlocking perspectives across political science, family law, and race and gender studies. The book is so much richer for the constructive discussions I had with them.

At Fairfield University, Marcie Patton, Kris Sealey, Anna Lawrence, Jocelyn Boryczka, Emily Orlando, and Sonya Huber have been exemplars of friendship, professional support, and intellectual stimulation. I could not have asked for a more conducive personal network or professional space than what I have at Fairfield in terms of the extraordinary support I have received for developing my scholarship and teaching. I am also grateful to Janie Leatherman, Kevin Cassidy, Peter Bayers, Yohuru Williams, Joan Huvane, and Charlene Wallace for the diverse ways in which they have contributed to creating a space where I could flourish and bring this project to fruition. The undergraduate and graduate students in my "Battle over Family Values in American Politics" seminar helped me interrogate and clarify much of the book's argument. I am deeply thankful to them for their thoughtful readings, engaging discussions, and enduring enthusiasm. Thanks also to Richard Burke, Michael Durante, and Enxhi Myslymi for their excellent research assistance.

At the Miller Center of Public Affairs, University of Virginia, Sidney Milkis, Adam Sheingate, and Brian Balogh influenced the development of the core of my family-party thesis. The network of Miller Center scholars helped shape the trajectory of the book, including Emily Zackin, Maxine Eichner, Shamira Gelbman, Nicole Mellow, Christy Chapin, and Molly Michelmore. The book has also benefited from the financial or intellectual support from Martha Fineman's Feminism and Legal Theory Project, the Vulnerability and Human Condition Initiative at Emory University, the Jack Miller Center's Summer Institute (especially Peter Onuf and James Ceaser), the Institute for Humane Studies, and a semester of leave and a summer research fellowship from Fairfield University.

Previous versions of the chapters have been presented at the Policy History Conference and at the meetings of the American Political Science Association, Western Political Science Association, Midwest Political Science Association, and Northeastern Political Science Association. I am especially grateful for the comments and valuable discussions with Patricia Strach, Alison Gash, Ellen Andersen, Tom Ogorzalek, Stephen Engel, Megan Ming Francis, Zachary Callen, Daniel Sledge, Julia Azari, and Stephen Pimpare.

The book would not have been possible without the forbearance, kindness, and love of my family. My parents, Pius and June, made summers so much more joyful and productive and have always been unfailing in their warmth, love, and support. My sister, Lynn, and her family, Aaron and Joe, in all their encouragement and affection helped ground me through many of life's transitions. The Arnold family—Alison, Andy, Gil, Annelise, and Louie—have been a source of much laughter and togetherness and have made holidays so much more memorable. The colorful personal stories of my late father-in-law, Ed Arnold, of times during the Depression and World War II piqued my imagination and inspired my interest in those periods. He is sorely missed.

My dearest son, Nate, at second grade already the author of *Halloween*, has beaten his mom in the publication of his book. Through his humor, intelligence, and kindness, he brings joy to even the most mundane of days. Finally, my life and work would not have the purpose, happiness, and richness that it does without my husband, Ted Arnold. His unique wit, faith in my better nature, and ongoing companionship keeps me buoyant and looking forward to the next day. My interest in the family, and the relevance of policies to its possible success, is reinforced by my daily wonderment at just how meaningful our life together has been.